THE SUPREME DOCTRINE

Talks on the Kenopanishad

THE SUPREME DOCTRINE

Talks on the Kenopanishad

OSHO

JAICO PUBLISHING HOUSE

Ahmedabad Bangalore Chennai
Delhi Hyderabad Kolkata Mumbai

Published by Jaico Publishing House
A-2 Jash Chambers, 7-A Sir Phirozshah Mehta Road
Fort, Mumbai - 400 001
jaicopub@jaicobooks.com
www.jaicobooks.com

THE SUPREME DOCTRINE
ISBN 978-81-8495-352-7

First Jaico Impression: 2012
Fifth Jaico Impression: 2024

The material in this book is a transcript of a series of original OSHO Talks on the Kenopanishad, given to a live audience. All of Osho's talks have been published in full as books, and are also available as original audio recordings. Audio recordings and the complete text archive can be found via the online OSHO Library at www.osho.com/library

Page design and layout: Yogesh Typesetting, Pune

Printed by
Repro India Limited, Mumbai

These talks were given at a meditation intensive
in Rajasthan, India over an eight-day period.
Each talk was followed by a meditation
personally led by Osho,
often an active and "chaotic" meditation.
Osho explains the need for this form of meditation,
and the way it works, in detail as the days unfold.

CONTENTS

PREFACE

The Upanishads are not religious scriptures. They are poetic expressions of those who have known.

They are not Hindu, they are not Buddhist, they are not Jaina; they don't belong to any religion. They are the experiences of individuals sitting at the feet of their master – and when the experience overwhelmed them they danced, they sang, they uttered strange statements. And these were not made by their minds; it was almost as if they were just hollow bamboos. Existence has made them flutes; it was existence itself singing a song. That's why no Upanishad carries the name of its writer.

The Koran belongs to Mohammed, the New Testament belongs to Jesus Christ, the Gita belongs to Krishna, the Dhammapada belongs to Gautam Buddha; Ishavasya Upanishad belongs to no one.

Tremendously courageous people – they have not even signed their names. In fact it would have been ugly to sign because they were not the writers, they were not the composers, they were not the poets. The poetry was coming from above, from beyond. They were simply vehicles.

Because of this, you will be surprised also to know that the whole Koran consists of Hajrat Mohammed's statements, the Gita consists totally of Krishna's statements, but each Upanishad consists of many peoples' expressions – anybody who had reached to that beyond and allowed the beyond to descend through him.

The Upanishads have not bothered to collect the words of one person. Each Upanishad contains the words of many enlightened people, and without any signatures. Words have never been so golden. Words have never taken such high flights, and yet the people who allowed them to happen have remained anonymous. This is so beautiful, immensely beautiful, because they knew, "We have nothing to do. We have just been passages. Something has come through us."

One upanishadic rishi, one upanishadic seer – the name, of course, is unknown – is reported to have said, "If there is any mistake in my statement, that is mine. And if there is any truth, I cannot claim that it is mine. The truth belongs to the universe; the mistake belongs to me, I was not such a good vehicle." These were rare people, unique human beings, the very salt of the earth.

Osho

The Osho Upanishad

CHAPTER 1

TOWARD THE AWAKENING

Om, may brahman protect us both. May he nourish us both. May we both achieve energy. May this study make us both illumined. May we never hate each other.
Om, peace, peace, peace.
Om, may my limbs become strong. Also, let my speech, prana – vital air – sight, hearing, and all the sense organs, be vigorous. The entire existence is the brahman of the Upanishads. May I never deny brahman; may brahman not deny me. Let there be no denial at all. Let there be no denial at least on my part. Whatever virtues are in the Upanishads, may they abide in I who am devoted to the atman – self. May they abide in me.
Om, peace, peace, peace.

I don't know where to begin or where to end, because life itself is beginningless and endless. Like these hills around you or the clouds wandering above you, or like the sky, you are also beginningless and endless. Nothing ever begins or ends, and that which can have a beginning or an end is bound to be artificial. Nature remains, abides; it is always there.

So whenever the question arises of talking about the ultimate, the supreme, the innermost, the very ground of being, it becomes difficult to know where to begin and where to end because it is always there; it has always been so and it will always be so. There has never been a beginning to it and never will there be an end. So I will begin just in the middle because that is the only possible place to begin, and I will end just in the middle because there is no other way to end it.

The first thing I would like to say to you is that I have not chosen this Upanishad to comment upon it. There are already too many commentaries and they have not helped anyone. They may have harmed many, they may have become hindrances to many, but they have not helped anybody. Commentaries cannot help because commentaries are second rate. I am not going to comment on this Upanishad; rather, on the contrary, I am going to respond to it. I will just echo and re-echo.

Really, whatsoever I say will belong basically to me. The Upanishad is just an excuse. Through it I will explain myself – remember this. Whatsoever I have felt, whatsoever I have known and lived, I would like to talk about it. But I feel the same has been the case with the seers of the Upanishads. They have known, they have lived, they have experienced the same truth. Their ways of expression may be different. Their language is very ancient; it has to be decoded again so that it becomes available to you, to the contemporary mind. But whatsoever they have said, they have said the basic thing.

Whenever someone comes to be a void, whenever someone comes to be a nobody, this happens – that which has happened to the seers of the Upanishads. Whenever *you* are not, the divine becomes present; whenever *you* are, the divine is absent.

Your presence is the problem, your absence is the door. These *rishis* have become total nobodies. We don't even know their names; we don't know who wrote these Upanishads, who communicated them. They have not signed them. No photograph of these *rishis* exists, no knowledge about their lives. They have simply become absent. They have said whatsoever is true, but just as a vehicle. They have not been in any way involved in the expression. They have made themselves completely absent so the message becomes totally present.

These Upanishads are eternal. They don't belong to any country, they don't belong to any religion. They don't belong, they *cannot* belong, to anybody. They belong only to those who are ready to take a jump into nothingness.

I have chosen to talk about the Upanishads because to me they represent one of the purest expressions of the ultimate that is possible – if it is possible to express it at all. Really, it is difficult, in a sense impossible, to convey that which has been known beyond the mind through the mind. In a sense it is absolutely impossible to say something about that which is felt when you are in the deepest of silences. When words don't exist within you, when verbalization ceases completely, when intellect is no longer functioning, when the mind is not there at all to memorize – then it happens, then you experience. When the mind comes back, when the memory starts functioning, when the intellect takes possession of you again, the experience has already passed.

The experience that was there before is not there now: only echoes of it, only vibrations of it are left. They can only be captured, and they can be expressed only through the mind. That is why it has always been impossible – very, very difficult – for those who have known to say something. Those who don't know anything can say much. But for those who know, it becomes more and more difficult to say something because whatsoever they say appears false. They can compare the experience with its expressions because they have a living experience. Now they can feel what language is doing to it: it is falsifying it.

And when a lived experience comes into words, it looks dead, pale. A lived experience which is total, in which your whole being dances and celebrates, looks just dull, of no significance, when it is expressed through the intellect.

Those who don't know can talk much because they have nothing with which to compare. They have no original experience; they cannot know what they are doing. Once someone knows, he knows what a problem it is to express it.

Many have remained totally silent. Many have remained completely unknown because of that – because we can only know about someone who speaks. The moment someone speaks he enters society. When someone stops speaking he leaves society, he is no longer part of it. Language is the milieu in which society exists. It is just like blood: blood circulates in you and you exist. Language circulates within society and the society exists. Without language there is no society. So those who have remained silent, they have fallen out of it. We have forgotten them. Really, we have never known them.

Somewhere Vivekananda has said – and it is very, very true – that the Buddhas, Krishnas and Christs that we have known are really not the representatives. They are not really central, they are on the periphery. The most central happenings have been lost. Those who became so silent that they couldn't communicate with us are not known, *cannot* be known – there is no way to know them. In a way Vivekananda is right, but those who have become so silent that they have not uttered anything about their experience have not helped us. They have not been really compassionate enough. In a sense they have been totally selfish.

It is true that to say anything about truth is difficult, but even then it has to be tried. It must be tried because even a diluted truth will be helpful for those who live in total illusion. Even something which carries a very, very far echo will help them to change.

It is not that Buddha is very happy with what he says. Whatsoever he says, he feels it is not true. He feels the same way as Lao Tzu felt. Lao Tzu says, "That which can be said cannot be true. The moment it is said it is falsified." But still, those who live in worlds of many, many illusions, those who are deeply asleep, fast asleep, for them even a false alarm may be helpful. If they can come out of their sleep, if they can be brought to a new consciousness, to a new being, even a false alarm is good. Of course, when they themselves awaken they will know that it was false – but it will have helped.

In a sense, wherever we are and whatsoever we are, we are so false that, really, absolutely pure truth is not needed at all. It cannot penetrate you. It will not have any contact; you will not be able to understand it. Only a very diluted truth, modified – in a sense, falsified – can have any appeal for you, because then you can understand the language; it has been translated for you.

These Upanishads are very simple; they speak in a very heart-to-heart way. They are not philosophical; they are religious. They are not concerned with concepts, with theories, with doctrines. They are concerned with a lived truth – what it is and how it can be lived. You cannot think about it, you cannot philosophize about it. You can only move into it and allow it to move into you. You can only be pregnant with it, you can only be totally absorbed in it. You can melt in it.

We will talk about the Upanishads, and I will bring my own experience as a response to them. But that is only a stepping-stone. Unless you move into the same dimension, it will not be of much use. Unless you move and take a jump into the unknown, it will not help you. Or, it may even be harmful to you because your mind is already too much burdened, too heavy. It need not be burdened any more. I am here to unburden it.

I am not going to teach you some new knowledge. I am going to teach you only a pure type of ignorance. When I say a pure ignorance, I mean innocence. I mean a mind which is totally vacant, open. A mind that knows is never open: it is closed. The very feeling that "I know" closes you. When you feel that "I don't know" you are open: you are ready to move, ready to learn, ready to travel.

I will teach you ignorance, unlearning, not knowledge. Only unlearning can help you. The moment you unlearn, the moment you again become ignorant, you become childlike, you become innocent. Jesus says, "Only those who are like small children will be able to enter into my God's kingdom." I will try to make you like small children.

A very courageous effort will be needed for it. It is the greatest challenge that can be given to you, and unless you accept the challenge you will not be able to understand the Upanishads – or me.

For this challenge a few things are to be understood as basic requirements. The first: put aside all your knowledge. For these eight days, kindly be ignorant. You will not lose that knowledge. If you feel that it is good after eight days, you can start carrying it again. But for these eight days, please put down all the burdens that are on your mind. Whatsoever you know, don't allow it to interfere here because if you allow it to interfere, I will not be able to create the communion for which I have called you.

It is going to be a great experiment. If you put aside your knowledge... And you can, just a decision is needed: "For these eight days I will not carry my knowledge; I will not say 'I know'; I will just feel that I don't know anything." If you can feel this, you are ready to enter into the unknown – because the unknown can be entered only when there is no knowledge. Knowledge can lead you only to the known; only ignorance can lead you to the unknown. Ignorance is just wonderful if you can understand the meaning of it.

Put aside whatsoever you know. What do you know really? You simply go on pretending that you know. You go on talking about God and about the soul and about heaven and hell, and you don't know anything at all. But this pretension costs too much because, by and by, you yourself are deceived by it.

For these eight days the first thing to be remembered is to be ignorant. Don't discuss, don't argue, don't question, don't answer anybody. If you are ignorant, how can you discuss and how can you argue? If you are ignorant, how can you question? Really, if you are ignorant how can you even question? What can you question? Your questions also arise out of your so-called knowledge. What is there to answer? If you can feel that you are ignorant you will become silent, because what is there to think about?

Your knowledge goes on revolving around and around, it moves in circles in your mind. Put it aside! – and not in parts, because no one can put it aside in parts. Wholesale! – put it aside completely. Decide that for eight days you will be as ignorant as you were when you were born: just a child, a new baby who knows nothing, asks nothing, discusses nothing, argues nothing. If you can be a little baby, much is possible. Even that which looks impossible is possible.

If you are ignorant, only then can I work. Only in your ignorance can I transform you. Your knowledge is the barrier. If you feel that your knowledge is so significant and so important that you cannot put it aside, then go away. Don't remain here because then it is futile. I am not going to increase your knowledge. I am not interested at all in what you know, I am interested in you – what you are. That being that you are can explode only when these barriers of so-called knowledge are thrown away.

Be ready for the unknown, and you can be ready only if you are ready to be ignorant. I say that this is very courageous: to feel ignorant is the greatest daring possible to man. Why? – because knowledge gives you ego, knowledge gives you a feeling that you are somebody, that you know this and that. When you feel that you are ignorant, there is no food for your ego to feed upon. If you are ignorant ego disappears.

People come to me and they go on asking how to dissolve the ego, and I say, don't try. You cannot dissolve it. Rather, put aside your knowledge and the ego will disappear. It will disappear just like when the sun arises in the morning dewdrops disappear from the grass. The ego is a dewdrop. When you are really not knowing, that's what I mean by ignorance. When you are not knowing and you say, "I don't know anything, I am standing in darkness," where can your ego stand? Can it have a foothold? With the knowledge disappears the ego. The first thing: be ignorant.

The second thing: the human mind has been totally perverted by serious people. Those who have taken upon themselves the great work of making men serious have destroyed all that is beautiful in you. Puritans, moralists, religious teachers, churches have destroyed all that is beautiful in you because the beauty is related to the nonserious.

Ugliness is related to the serious, and religion has become ugly because it has become too much attached to seriousness. Don't be serious. For these eight days be playful, childlike; playful, nonserious – enjoying. Enjoy yourself enjoying others, enjoying the whole world around you. The hills are beautiful, and there will be rains and there will be clouds. This night is beautiful, the silence is beautiful. But if you are serious your doors are closed; then you are not open to the silence of the night – because except for man nothing is serious in existence.

Be playful. It will be difficult, because you are so structured. You have an armor around you and it is so difficult to loosen it, to relax it. You cannot dance, you cannot sing, you cannot just jump, you cannot just scream and laugh and smile. Even if you want to laugh you first want something there to be laughed at. You cannot simply laugh. There must be some cause: only then can you laugh. There must be some cause: only then can you cry and weep.

You are serious. You look at life like a business or like mathematics. It is not! Life is poetic, illogical. It is not like work, it is like play. Look at the trees and the animals and the birds; look at the sky: the whole existence is playful. You are very serious, so no wonder you have become separate from existence. You are uprooted from it, and then you feel alienated, then you feel like a stranger, then you feel that this existence is not your own. No one else is responsible for it except you and your seriousness.

Put aside knowledge, put aside seriousness; be absolutely playful for eight days. You have nothing to lose. If you don't gain anything, you will not lose anything. What can you lose in being playful? But I say to you, you will never be the same again. If you can really be playful, you will have a new perspective, a new way to look, a new way to be. When you go back you will not be the same man. Your whole life will change its meaning for you because the meaning is given by you. Now life looks boring, life looks meaningless. *You* have made it so because of your seriousness. Life is playful, beautiful, but it can be beautiful only if your eyes are open to beauty.

People go on asking, "Where is God?" You cannot find him because he is a player and you are serious. Hindus have been saying for centuries that this existence is God's play, and you are so work-oriented, so serious, that you cannot meet him. Of course! Obviously! There is no possibility of your meeting him. You move in different dimensions. He moves in play. The whole existence is just a play. It is not a work; it is not serious.

Put aside your seriousness, and for eight days become godlike, playful. It will be difficult because you feel you are very mature. You are not. You have not gained maturity. Of course you have lost your childhood, but just losing childhood is not synonymous with being mature. You can lose childhood without becoming mature. Maturity is not old age; maturity is not concerned with age at all. Maturity is a growth, and the growth must be through childhood, not against it, remember.

Your maturity is false because it has been against the child. The child was born; maturity has been created. The child was natural; you are artificial, cultivated. You will have to go back to the child to regain the source from where growth is possible.

My insistence on being playful is because of this: I want you to go back to the very point from where you stopped growing. There was a point in your childhood when you stopped growing and when you started being false. You may have been angry, a small child in a tantrum, angry, and your father or your mother said, "Don't be angry. This is not good." You were natural, but a division was created and a choice was there for you. If you wanted to be natural then you would not get the love of your parents.

Of course, you wanted the love; that was the only security for you, you could not have existed without it. So you opted, you surrendered. You pushed your nature aside. You started laughing and smiling; you became a good boy or a good girl. The day you became a good boy or a good girl was the day of catastrophe. From that moment you have never been natural. From that moment you have been serious, never playful. From that moment you have been dying, not alive. From that moment you have been aging, not maturing.

In these eight days I want you to go back to the point where you started being "good" as against being natural. Be playful so your childhood is regained. It will be difficult because you will have to put aside your masks, your faces; you will have to put aside your personality. But remember, the essence can assert itself only when your personality is not there, because your personality has become an imprisonment. Put it aside. It will be painful, but it is worth it because you are going to be reborn out of it. No birth is without pain. If you are really determined to be reborn, then take the risk.

For these eight days be small children again. Don't criticize anybody, don't condemn anybody. That type of nonsense belongs to so-called mature people, not to children. What children do, do. They enjoy, and they enjoy such simple things that for us so-called mature people it looks absurd. The whole world is filled with beauty, truth, love, but you cannot enjoy anything.

When we are meditating, from tomorrow morning, enjoy it. Remember this: regain your childhood. Everyone longs for it, but no one is doing anything to regain it. Everyone longs for it. People go on saying that childhood was paradise and poets go on writing poetry about the beauty of childhood. Who is preventing you? Regain it! I give you this opportunity to regain it.

Poetry will not help, and just remembering that it was paradise is not of much use. Why not move into it again? Why not be a child again? I say to you that if you can be a child again you will start growing in a new way. For the first time you will be really alive again, and the moment you have the eyes of a child, the senses of a child – young, vibrating with life – the whole life vibrates with you.

Remember, it is your vibration that needs transformation. The world is already always vibrating in ecstasy; only you are not tuned. The problem is not with the world, it is with you: you are not tuned to it. The world is dancing, always celebrating, every moment it is in a festivity. The festival goes on from eternity to eternity, only you are not tuned to it. You have fallen apart from it, and you are very serious, very knowing, very mature. You are closed. Throw away this enclosure! Move again into the current of life.

When the storm comes, the trees will be dancing; you also dance. When the night comes and everything is dark, you also be dark. When the morning sun rises, let it rise in you also. Be child-like, enjoying, not thinking of the past. A child never thinks of the past. Really, he has no past to think about. A child is not worried about the future; he has no time consciousness. He lives totally unworried. He moves in the moment; he never carries any hangover. If he is angry then he is angry, and in his anger he will say to his mother, "I hate you." And this is not just words, this is a reality. Really, in that moment he is in total hate.

The next moment he will come out of it and he will be laughing and he will give a kiss to his mother and he will say, "I love you." There is no contradiction. These are two different moments. He was total hate and now he is total love. He moves just like a river goes on moving, zigzag. But wherever he is – wherever the river is – he is total, flowing.

For these eight days be like children – total. If you hate, hate; if you love, love; if you are angry, then be angry; and if you are festive, then be festive and dance. Don't carry anything over from the past. Remain true to the moment; don't hanker for the future. For these eight days drop out of time. That's why I say don't be serious: because the more serious you are, the more time conscious you are. A child lives in eternity; there is no time for him. He is not even aware of it. These eight days will be real meditation if you drop out of time. Live the moment and be true to it.

So, put aside knowledge, put aside seriousness, and thirdly, put aside the division of mind and body. Divided, you cannot meet the oneness of existence. Divided you cannot come to the nondual reality. If you are dual, reality will be dual. You have to be one; only then does the reality begin to be one. It is you who ultimately decide what reality is. If you are mad, the whole existence is mad. If you are silent, the whole existence is silent. If you are in love, you feel that the whole existence is loving.

It is you who decide the quality of the existence around you – and you are divided. You think your body and your mind are two things; not only two, but contrary, opposed, fighting: enemies. No, they are not. They are two extremes of one rhythm; they are two poles of one existence. The outer is the body, the inner is the soul, but between the outer and the inner you exist. You are neither the inner nor the outer. The outer is your part and the inner is also your part. You exist in between.

Become a unity. At least for eight days, don't divide yourself. Become one. If you can become one, you will release a tremendous energy. Only that energy can lead you into meditation; otherwise there is no way.

Go into a church: they talk and they talk and they talk; they preach. Go to a religious meeting: words, word, words – as if God is only a cerebral question that has to be solved through mind.

No, this will not be of much help. Mentation alone won't do; the body has to be brought in. That's why, in my meditation techniques, I don't take you as divided – you are one. If your mind is feeling angry, allow your body to be angry. If your mind is feeling happy, allow your body to dance. Don't create a division. Let yourself come deep down into the body, and allow the body to flow to your innermost core. Become a flow.

You are frozen. I would like to melt you and create a flow again. That's why I insist on active meditation. By *active* I only mean that your body must be involved in it. If you simply sit in a buddha posture, you can go on thinking and thinking and thinking; the body is not involved in it and the body is the world. Through the body you are related to the existence, through the body you exist. Your meditation must in some way be deeply rooted in the body; otherwise it will become just a dream floating in the mind, just like clouds without any roots in the earth. I want to push you back to the earth.

For these eight days don't create any division. Be both body and soul simultaneously. The feeling, just the feeling that you are one, will dissolve the many anguishes, many tensions, which you have created by an artificial division. The whole society, the modern society, is paranoid because of this division, schizophrenic because of this division, this split. Standing against yourself, fighting with yourself – nonsense, but everyone is doing it.

In this camp be one with your body, have a nondual flow. Be alive in the body. In the meditations use your body as much as possible. Only then will you have a real depth in meditation. So don't create division. These three things you have to remember.

And now, a few more points and then I will take the sutra – a few more points for these eight days. One, give more and more emphasis to exhalation. Really, don't inhale, only exhale. Don't be disturbed when I say don't inhale. I mean allow the body to inhale. Exhale and allow the body to inhale; don't inhale. Whenever you remember, exhale deeply and then relax and leave the body to inhale.

This will give you very deep relaxation – because exhalation is death; inhalation is life. The first thing a child has to do is to inhale and the last thing an old man has to do is to exhale. Death begins with exhalation, life begins with inhalation. And remember that death is total relaxation. Life is tension, death is relaxation.

Meditation is more like death than like life, but death is not against life. Death is the very source of all life. Life comes out of death and moves again into death. Death is like the ocean and life is like a river: it comes and falls into the ocean. Then again clouds arise and again it rains and again a river is created, and it moves again to the ocean.

Death is like the ocean, life is like a river. Death is total relaxation. That's why we are unconsciously afraid of exhalation. We inhale, but we never exhale. Only the body exhales as a necessity. Change it completely! For these eight days, exhale and allow the body to inhale. That will relax you – your body, your mind, your whole nervous system. When I say exhale deeply, I don't mean for you to create any strain. Don't create any strain. Simply exhale deeply – enjoy it, as if you are dying in it. Your life is moving into the ocean of death. Relax and surrender, and exhale deeply and enjoy it.

And then wait. I don't say prevent inhalation – no. Simply wait. Don't do anything for inhalation, for or against. The body will take the inhalation by itself and if you have deeply exhaled, a deep inhalation will occur. But first your emphasis should be on exhalation.

Secondly: we will be meeting here three times a day, but there will be time in between. What are you going to do in that time? Remember one thing: don't do what you have always been doing. Don't continue it – the same talk the same way. Don't continue it, put it aside. Be new, be original. Don't do whatsoever you have been doing. Change it, because it has become a habit and if you continue that pattern new things cannot evolve. Put it aside, throw it away.

For these eight days don't move in your old patterns of habit. Don't say things which you have always been saying. The moment you remember, stop. You know you have said this so many times; you have been saying this to your wife for years, and you know what she will answer. Everything has become a routine, a mechanical repetition.

Don't say it. Say something new. Or if you cannot find something new to say, if it is very difficult to find, remain silent: that will be something new. Or, and this will look foolish, but I want you to be foolish for these eight days – don't use words, use gestures. If you want to say something to your friend or to someone in the room or to your wife or anyone, use gestures, don't use language. Just be as if deaf and dumb: use gestures, say something through gestures. Or, if you cannot express through gestures, then use sounds – but don't use words. A deep exultation will happen to you, a deep benediction will come to you.

Use sounds or gestures. Don't use words, because words are

the mind. Use sounds like birds and animals do, or gestures. You will have a new feeling in yourself, you will feel a new being within yourself, because the old pattern of the personality will not be functioning. You can also do this alone and it will be worth it. Anytime during the day, sit alone – go to a tree, sit alone near it and start making sounds. Don't use words; just as small babies do, go on uttering any sound, repeating and enjoying it: baby talk without any meaning. Just utter any sounds and enjoy the very utterance.

What I mean is: here, don't be a victim of the usual pattern. Don't be concerned with anyone else. You are always concerned. Be concerned with yourself. Be totally selfish; be concerned with your own self. Enjoy your being, enjoy the surroundings, meditate with the group and alone, and be totally centered in yourself. Don't think about what others are doing. Allow others to do whatsoever they want to do. Don't interfere with anybody. Even the idea that you can allow others to do whatsoever they want will free you because you are unnecessarily burdened by others. Be totally selfish.

It does not look very religious when I say be totally selfish. To me it is the only religion because only when you are really selfish can you do something for others. Because unless you have something, what can you do? How can you help? How can you love? How can there be compassion? You are nothing within and you go on serving others and thinking about others. That is only an escape to forget yourself. In this meditation camp don't do that. Remember yourself and forget others.

And the last thing: in the meditations, don't do them partially, don't do them half-heartedly. Nothing will come out of it. Meditation is not mathematical. Don't think, "If I do fifty percent, then at least fifty percent will be the outcome." No, zero will be the outcome. Only a one-hundred percent effort can bring you any results; less will not do.

It is just like heating water. At a particular degree, a hundred degrees, it evaporates. Don't think that at fifty degrees half will evaporate. It will not evaporate at all; it will just become lukewarm. I don't want you to become lukewarm here. Be either hot or cold. If you are cold, then leave. No need to make any effort unnecessarily. Why tire yourself? If you are a hundred percent hot, be here and you will evaporate. I guarantee that; that's absolutely certain.

If you make a hundred percent effort, if you don't withhold yourself, if you melt in the process completely and forget yourself, abandon yourself completely in it, the thing for which you have been hankering for lives together can happen. It can happen in a single moment – only a totality of abandonment is needed.

And we will be doing these three meditations a day in a group. That too is for a specific reason: because you are individuals only on the top. Deep down you are not individuals. We belong to each other; we are rooted in one consciousness. So a group meditation can be a tremendous experience. You are not alone here. If you can abandon yourself, if you can surrender, if you can melt completely, then the group soul takes you over, you are not there. Then the group dances and you dance as part of it. Then the group feels blissful and you feel blissful as part of it. Then the group moves, sways, dances, and you are part of it. Abandon yourself totally, and then the group takes you over. It becomes a fast, strong current and you are simply taken over.

These three group meditations are not individual meditations. You start as an individual, but sooner or later you are not there and the group soul has started functioning. When the group soul starts functioning, you have entered the divine. So don't remain individuals; that is false, egoistic. Melt into others, and things will start happening to you.

Many things are possible, and I hope they will happen to you. If you are really ready, if you have been dreaming about them, hoping about them, and you have come here not as a casual visitor but as a seeker – to stake something, to accept the challenge and to move into the greatest adventure that is possible to human consciousness – then everything can happen to you.

Now I will talk about the sutra:

> *Om, may brahman protect us both. May he nourish us both. May we both achieve energy. May this study make us both illumined. May we never hate each other.*
> *Om, peace, peace, peace.*

It is beautiful. The teacher and the taught both are praying to the ultimate – the disciple and the master both are praying to the ultimate.

> *Om, may brahman protect us both.*

Because as a master or as a disciple, you are not real. Because the master is a division, the disciple is a division. The master is a fragment and the disciple is also a fragment. Both are praying that the ultimate should take care, should take control. The master will lose himself as the master and the disciple will lose himself as the disciple. They will become one; in a deeper reality, they will melt into one. *...may brahman protect us both.*

Now forget the Upanishad. We are here and let this prayer be yours: *...may brahman protect us both.*

I should not function here as an individual, you should not function here as an individual. Rather, we should become one. I am ready; if you are also ready to meet me there is no difficulty. Then it is not that I am leading you toward something, not that you are led by me, but we both are moving toward something together. I am not the leader and you are not the led. I am not the teacher and you are not the taught. We both are moving toward a deeper reality together. No one is the teacher and no one is the taught. This is the feeling of the sutra.

...may brahman protect us both. May he nourish us both. May we both achieve energy. May this study make us both illumined. May we never hate each other. Om, peace, peace, peace. There is every possibility that the disciple may start hating the master

because if you love, the possibility of hate is always there. If you love the master, then the other part of that love is hate. When you love, hate can erupt any moment. Hate is part of it. Really, love and hate are not two things, but two aspects. Hate is not against love; it is the counterpart of it – the other side of the coin. So when a disciple loves the master, every moment there is the possibility that he may hate. The possibility will grow more when the master tries to transform him – because then he seems dangerous, then he seems destructive.

If I say, "Throw away your knowledge," you will feel that I am like an enemy to you because your knowledge is your treasure. If I say, "Don't be serious; be like children," your ego will feel hurt. You will feel, "This man is leading me toward something which will be stupid, foolish." You can start hating me any moment. If I am really bent upon transforming you, mutating you, then the possibility is always more and more that you will start hating me.

That's why the master says: *May this study make us both illumined. May we never hate each other.* This sentence is really something – something exceptional, extraordinary: *May this study make us both illumined.* The master is already illumined; otherwise he is not the master. The disciple is not illumined; otherwise there is no need to be a disciple. But the master says, *May this study* illumine us both – *make us both illumined.* This is really subtle. The master is awakened, but this awakening is his own experience, not the disciple's. The disciple only believes that the master is awakened; he cannot know it. When the master and disciple move as a couple, as a pair, not different and separate – together – then when the awakening comes, the disciple will come to know that both have become awakened, both have become buddhas.

This is one meaning; another meaning is also there. You can be illumined alone; that is one experience. But when you move with someone else and the illumination happens to both, it is something else again; it is not the same.

Buddha is illumined, enlightened, under the *bodhi* tree. This is individual illumination; he has come to an individual awakening. But the whole world around him, millions and millions of souls around him, are walking in sleep. Buddha moves among these sleepwalkers and tries to awaken them. Whenever someone is awakened, again Buddha's own illumination is increased.

Remember, whereas before one lamp was burning in the darkness, now two lamps are burning. Then a third one awakens and three lamps are burning, and a fourth one awakens and the light goes on growing. The light goes on growing and now Buddha is no longer an individual.

So whenever, wherever, enlightenment happens, it is his enlightenment also. This is deep and subtle, but worth remembering always – that a buddha's enlightenment also goes on growing. Whenever a disciple awakens, Buddha's light grows.

Buddha is already awakened; there is no problem about it. It is just like I burn a lamp in a room and the room is lit: there is no darkness. Then I bring another lamp, and the light increases. Then I bring a third lamp, and the light increases more. The whole world goes on being filled with more and more light whenever a master is capable of helping a disciple to be enlightened.

This seer says a wonderful thing. No one has said it anywhere: *May this study make us both illumined.*

> *Om, may my limbs become strong. Also, let my speech, prana – vital air – sight, hearing, and all the sense organs be vigorous.*

That's what I am saying to you. Allow your body to be relived by you. Don't separate it; be joined together with it; move into it deeply. When you move deeply into it, everything becomes strong, alive, new.

> *Also let my speech, my prana – vital air – sight, hearing, and all the sense organs be vigorous. All existence is the brahman of the Upanishads. May I never deny brahman...*

This is one of the most revolutionary things ever uttered.

> *May I never deny brahman; may brahman not deny me. Let there be no denial at all. Let there be no denial at least on my part.*

Don't deny, because everything is *brahman*, everything is that absolute. So whenever you deny, you deny existence. Whenever you condemn – and you may condemn whomsoever you like – whatsoever you condemn, you condemn *brahman*. If you condemn a thief, if you condemn a murderer, he is condemned because only it – *brahman* – is there. That is why I say this is one of the most revolutionary sayings.

All existence is the *brahman*. *May I never deny brahman...* in any way – conscious, unconscious, open or hidden. *May I never deny brahman. Let there be no denial at all.*

The negative mind, the denying mind, is the irreligious mind. The mind which goes on saying no, which does not have the capacity and courage to say yes, is the irreligious mind. The religious mind is a yea-saying mind. Even if there is something which looks wrong to you and your whole mind feels like condemning it, a religious mind will say, "It appears to me that way, but who knows? It is my judgment that it is wrong; it may not be so – because what is the value of my judgment?"

Some people brought a woman to Jesus and they said, "She has committed adultery and she has to be killed. And this has been the law – kill her with stones, by throwing stones at her."

And Jesus said, "The law is true, but only those persons can throw stones at her who have not committed adultery ever – not even in the mind. So come forward! – only those persons who have not committed adultery, actually or in imagination."

The crowd had stones; they were standing ready to kill her. But now people started dispersing because there was no one who had not committed adultery in the mind.

Finally, Jesus and the woman were left. The crowd had dispersed, and the woman said, "I have done wrong. I am guilty, punish me."

Jesus said, "Who am I to punish you? Who am I to punish you or condemn you? It is between you and your God."

This is the attitude of the religious man: no condemnation. Who are you to condemn? – self-appointed, unnecessarily creating problems for yourself and others. Don't deny. Denial goes deep: you deny your body, you deny your senses, you deny everything. You have become a great denier. Then, when you become suffocated, you cry and you say, "Why this anguish? Why this misery?" This misery is created by you. A person who goes on denying everything will become more and more shrunken, frozen inside. He cannot do anything: everything is wrong. He cannot eat this, he cannot love in this way, he cannot move in this way, he cannot do this or that. Only *cannots* and *cannots* all around him – denials and denials. Then life becomes suffocated. Then you feel miserable.

This is one of the most revolutionary sayings ever uttered – that there should be no denial at all: *Let there be no denial at least on my part.* This goes even deeper. Look at the beauty of it. Because there is every possibility that if I say to you, "Don't deny," and someone denies, you will deny him. Why are you denying? If I say, "Don't condemn" and someone condemns, you will condemn him. The mind goes on playing tricks. In new shapes it brings back all the old diseases again and again.

I was talking to a woman who has a great condemning mind. She goes on condemning everyone. Whenever she comes to me she goes on condemning this and that. Then I told her, "This is not good. I don't say that whatsoever you say is not true. It may be; that is not the point. Your condemning is wrong."

So she said, "If you say that, then I will not condemn anybody."

The next day she came again and she said, "Another of your disciples is condemning. He is not good." Now the definition of what is good and what is bad has changed, but the condemnation continues. Now *he* is not good.

The rishi says:

> *Let there be no denial at all. Let there be no denial at least on my part. Whatever virtues are in the Upanishads, may they abide in I who am devoted to the atman. May they abide in me.*
> *Om, peace, peace, peace.*

A master is really the home, the abode of all the virtues. Whatsoever the Upanishads teach, whatsoever virtues are there are nothing compared to the heart of the master. But the deepest virtue is in his humility, humbleness. He still goes on praying that all the virtues which the Upanishads sing about "should abide in me, they should not leave me, they should remain in my heart."

A real humbleness goes on praying: that is the point. It is never non-prayerful. Even when everything has been achieved, the prayer continues – because prayerfulness is humbleness, and because prayerfulness is simplicity, and because prayerfulness is innocence. Even if the ultimate is achieved, the prayerfulness goes on continuing.

I have heard about one Sufi mystic, Bayazid. He became enlightened, but still he was praying, just as ever. So one of his disciples became disturbed and he said, "Master, you need not pray. You are already enlightened. Why are you praying?"

Bayazid is reported to have said, "Before, I prayed for enlightenment, now also I pray for enlightenment."

The disciple couldn't understand and said, "What do you mean?"

The master said, "I prayed so that enlightenment may happen to me. Now it has happened, and I pray in thankfulness, in gratitude that it has happened." But prayerfulness continues – the same prayerfulness.

Prayerfulness is an attitude. The master is the abode of all the virtues. Of course, the Upanishads are created by the masters, not vice versa. No Upanishad can create a master, and a single master can create all the Upanishads. But the master says: *Whatever virtues are in the Upanishads, may they abide in I who am devoted to the atman. May they abide in me. Om, peace, peace, peace.*

...

CHAPTER 2

TRANSCENDING THE BASIC DUALITY OF SEX

> *At whose desire and by whom impelled does the mind alight on its objects? By whom impelled does the chief prana – vital force – proceed to its function? By whom impelled do men utter this speech? What deva or god directs the eyes and the ears?*
>
> *It – the atman – is the ear of the ear, the mind of the mind, the speech of the speech, the prana of the prana, and the eye of the eye. Wise men separating the atman from these – sense functions – rise out of sense life and attain to immortality.*

Life is not there at its maximum when you are born; it is at its minimum. And if you remain at that level, you will have a life which is just near death – just a borderline life. Only an opportunity is given by birth, only an opening is made.

Life has to be achieved. Birth is just a beginning, not the end. But we normally stay at the point of birth. That's why death happens. If you stay at the point of birth you will die. If you can grow beyond birth you can grow beyond death. Remember this very deeply: death is not against life; death is against birth. Life is something else. In death only birth ends and in birth only death begins. Life is something totally different. You have to attain it, achieve it, actualize it. It is given to you as a seed, just as a potentiality – something which can be, but which is not already there.

You also have every chance of missing it. You can be alive because you are born, but that is not synonymous with really being in life. Life is your effort to actualize the potentiality. Hence the meaning of religion; otherwise there is no meaning in religion. If life begins with birth and ends in death, then there is no meaning for religion. Religion is futile, nonsense. But if life doesn't begin with birth, then religion has some meaning. Then it becomes the science of how to evolve life out of birth. And the more you move away from birth in life, the more you also move away from death because death and birth are parallel, similar, the same – two ends of one process. If you move away from one, simultaneously you are moving away from the other.

Religion is a science to achieve life. Life is beyond death. Birth dies; life, never. To achieve this life you have to do something. Birth is given to you. Your parents have done something: they have loved each other, they have melted into each other, and out of their life force, melting into each other, a new phenomenon, a new seed – you – was born. But you have not done anything for it: it is a gift. Remember, birth is a gift. That's why all the cultures pay so much respect to parents – birth is a gift, and you cannot repay it. The debt cannot be repaid. What can you do to repay it? Life has been given to you, but you have not done anything for it.

Religion can give you a new birth, a rebirth. You can be reborn, but this birth will happen through some alchemical change within you. Just as the first birth happened through two life forces meeting outside you – they created an opportunity for you to enter, to be born: a deep alchemy – now a similar thing has to be done within you. Your parents, your mother and your father, met. Two forces, feminine and masculine, were meeting to create an opportunity for some new entity to be born. Two opposite forces were meeting, two polarities were meeting. And whenever two polarities meet, something new is born, a new synthesis is achieved. A similar thing has to happen within you.

You also have two polarities within you, the feminine and the masculine. Let me explain it a little in detail. Your body is born out of two polarities: cells from your mother and cells from your father – they create your body. You have both types of cells – those which came from your mother and those which came from your father. Your body consists of two polarities, feminine and masculine. You are both, everyone is both. Whether you are man or woman makes no difference. If you are a man you have a woman within you: your mother is there. If you are a woman you have a man within you: your father is there. They can again meet within you. And the whole of Yoga, the whole of Tantra, the alchemy, the whole process of religion, is how to create an orgasm, a deep intercourse between polarities within you. When they meet within you, a new type of being is born, a new life becomes alive.

If you are a man, then your conscious is masculine and your unconscious is feminine. If you are a woman, your conscious is feminine, your unconscious is masculine. Your conscious and unconscious must meet so that a new birth becomes possible. What can you do for their meeting to happen? Bring them nearer. You have created a separation, you have created all types of barriers. You don't allow them to meet. You try to exist with the conscious and you go on suppressing the unconscious. You don't allow it.

If a man starts weeping and crying, someone is bound to say immediately, "What are you doing? You are doing something womanish, feminine." The man stops immediately. The masculine is not expected to weep and cry. But you have the possibility – the unconscious is there. You have moments of feminineness, you have moments of masculineness; everyone does.

A woman can become ferocious, male, in some moods, in some moments. But then she will suppress. She will say, "This is not good, this is not womanly." We go on creating a separation, a distance. That distance has to be thrown away; your conscious, your unconscious must come nearer. Only then can they meet, only then can they have a deep intercourse. An orgasm can happen within you. That orgasm is known as spiritual bliss.

One type of orgasm is possible between your body and the body of the polar-opposite sex; it can happen only for a single moment because you meet only on the periphery. The peripheries meet and then they separate. Another type, a deeper type of orgasm, can happen within. But then you meet at the center and there is no need to separate again. Sexual ecstasy can only be momentary; spiritual ecstasy can be eternal. Once attained, you need not lose it. Really, once attained, it is difficult to lose it, impossible to lose it. It becomes such an integration the fragments disappear completely.

That's why when someone asked Buddha, "Who are you? A *deva*, a heavenly being?" he said, "No." And the questioner went on asking if he was this or that. Then the questioner became desperate, because Buddha went on saying no. Then finally he asked, "At least you must say that you are male. You must say yes." Buddha said, "No." "Then are you a female?" the man asked desperately. Buddha said, "No." – because a new unity had come into being which was neither male nor female.

When your inner man and inner woman meet, you are neither: you transcend sex. That's the meaning of the oldest Indian image of Shiva as Ardhanarishwar – half man, half woman. That is the symbol of the inner meeting. Shiva is neither: half man, half woman – both and neither. He transcends sex.

Remember, unless you transcend sex, you cannot transcend duality. This is a deep psychological problem – and not only psychological, but ontological also. If you remain a man or a woman, how can you conceive the oneness of existence? You cannot. Being a man, you cannot conceive yourself as one with the woman. Being a woman, you cannot conceive yourself as one with the man. A duality persists.

Sex is the basic duality. And we have been arguing and discussing for centuries how to attain the nondual. But we go on discussing it as if it is some intellectual matter: "How to attain the nondual?" It is not an intellectual matter; it is ontological, existential. You can attain the nondual only when the duality within you disappears. It is not a question of meditating on the nondual and thinking, "I am *brahman*." Nothing will come out of it; you are simply deluding yourself unless the basic duality of sex disappears within you, unless you come to the moment where you cannot say who you are – man or woman.

This happens only when your inner man and woman melt so much that they dissolve into each other and all the boundaries are lost, all the distinctions are lost, and they are one. When your inner orgasm, the spiritual ecstasy happens, you are neither. Only when you are neither is life born.

In a single moment of meeting between your parents – your mother and father – you were born: in a single moment of meeting. Remember, life is always out of meeting, never out of separation. Life comes only in a deep meeting, in a deep communion. For a single moment your father and mother were one, they were not two. They were functioning as one being. In that oneness you were born.

Life always comes out of oneness. And the life I am talking about, or Jesus talks about and Buddha talks about, is the life which will happen when inside you – within you – again a communion, a melting, happens, and the two sexualities within you dissolve.

Remember, I say again and again that sex is the basic duality, and unless you transcend sex, *brahman* cannot be achieved. And all other dualities are just reflections and reflections of this basic duality. Birth and death – again a duality. They will disappear when you are neither male nor female. When you have a consciousness which goes beyond both, birth and death disappear, matter and mind disappear, this world and that world disappear, heaven and hell disappear. All dualities disappear when the basic duality within you disappears, because all dualities are simply echoing and re-echoing the basic division within you.

That's why the old, ancient Indian seers put *brahman* in the third category. He's not male or female. They call him *napunsak* – impotent. They call him the third sex, the ultimate reality of the third sex. The word *brahman* belongs to *napunsakling:* it is neither or it is both. But one thing is certain: it transcends the duality. That's why other conceptions about God look immature, childish. Christians call him father. This is childish, because then where is the mother? And how is this son Jesus born? They say Jesus is the only son, but where is the mother? The father alone giving birth? If the father alone gives birth to Jesus, then he is both – mother and father. Then don't call him father. Then the duality comes in.

Or, some religions have called the ultimate being the mother. Then where is the father? These are just anthropomorphic feelings. Man cannot even think about the ultimate in any other form than human, so he calls it father or mother. But those who have known and those who have transcended the anthropocentric attitude, the man-oriented attitude – say he is neither. He transcends both; he is a meeting of both.

In the ultimate, mother and father both are merged. Or, if you allow me the expression, I would like to say: the *brahman* is mother and father in eternal orgasm – one in the eternal ecstasy of meeting. And out of that meeting comes the whole creation, out of that meeting comes the whole play, out of that meeting all that exists is born.

Here we will be trying to bring your unconscious and conscious nearer, your feminine, your masculine nearer. You will have to help me, to cooperate with me. In the meditation techniques you have to destroy all the barriers between your conscious mind and the unconscious. You have to be as free, as totally free as possible because suppression has created the barriers.

So don't suppress. If you feel like screaming, scream. The very scream will bring your conscious and unconscious nearer. If you feel like dancing, dance. The very dance will bring your conscious and unconscious nearer. Really, dance can be very helpful, because in dance your body and your mind are in a deep meeting.

It is not only the body which is moving; within the body your consciousness is also moving. A dance becomes a dance only when your body is filled with the grace of your spirit, when your spirit is flowing out of your body, when your spirit has taken a rhythm with the body.

All the old religions were dancing religions. They were more authentic. Our new modes of religion are just false. You go into a temple or into a church or into a *gurudwara* and you just verbalize. Someone preaches and you listen. It has become cerebral. Or, you pray and you talk with God. Even with God you use language. You cannot be silent with him; you cannot believe that he can understand you without your talking. You have no faith. You don't trust him; you want to explain everything to him.

I have heard…

A mother overheard her small child praying in the night to God, and he was saying, "Dear God, beloved God, stop Tommy from throwing things at me – and by the way, I have told you this before."

But this is what we all are doing: praying to God to "Stop Tommy from throwing things at me." Even if you go to the Vedic *rishis* they are doing the same: "Do this; don't do that." You cannot allow him to do whatsoever is his will. You give your own program. And if he follows you, you are a believer, and if he doesn't follow you, you will say that he doesn't exist. He can exist only if he exists as your follower.

But existence cannot follow you. Existence is greater than you; existence is the whole. You are just a fragment, and a fragment cannot be followed. The fragment has to follow the whole. This is what a religious mind is: the fragment following the whole, the fragment surrendering to the whole, the fragment not struggling, the fragment in a let-go.

Religion has become verbal, linguistic. Here we will try to bring the authentic religion. The secretmost core of it is that you must come to it totally – with your mind, your body, your emotions, everything. Nothing is denied. Cry and weep and laugh and dance, and then sit in silence. Do all the things that your inner being happens to do; don't force it to do anything. Don't say, "This is not good; I should not do it." Allow a spontaneous flow. Then the unconscious will come nearer and nearer to the conscious.

We have created the gap through suppression: "Don't do this, don't do that," and we go on suppressing. Then the unconscious is suppressed. It becomes dark. It becomes a part in our own house where we never enter. Then we are divided. And, remember, then there are perversions.

If you allow your unconscious to come nearer to your conscious, much sex-obsession will disappear. If you are a man and you deny your unconscious, you are denying your inner woman; then you will be attracted to outer women too much. It will become a perversion because now it is a substitute. The inner feminine has been denied; now the outer feminine will become obsessive to you. You will think and think about it: now your whole mind will become sexual. If you are a woman and you have denied the man, then "man" will take possession of you. Then whatsoever you do or think, the basic color will remain sexual.

There is so much fantasy about sex because you have denied your inner other. So now this is a compensation. Now you are compensating for something which you have denied to yourself. Look at the absurdity: the more you get obsessed with the other sex the more you feel afraid; the more you deny the inner the more you suppress it; and the more you suppress it the more you become obsessed.

Your so-called *brahmacharis* are totally obsessed with sex for twenty-four hours a day; they are bound to be. It is natural: nature takes revenge. To me, *brahmacharya* – celibacy – means you have come very near to your own feminine or your own masculine, then it has come so near there is no substitution for it. You are not obsessed with it; you don't think about it. It disappears.

When your own unconscious is nearer to you, you need not

substitute it with someone else outside. Then a miracle happens. If your unconscious is very near, then whenever you love someone, a woman or a man, that love is not pathological. If your unconscious is so near, that love is not pathological. It is not possessive, it is not mad. It is very silent, tranquil, calm, cool. Then the other is not a substitute and you are not dependent on the other. Rather, the other becomes just a mirror.

Remember the difference: the other is now not a substitute, something which you have denied. The other becomes a mirror of your inner part, of your unconscious. Your wife, your beloved, becomes just a mirror. In that mirror you see your unconscious. Your lover, your friend, your husband becomes a mirror. And in that mirror you can see your unconscious clearly mirrored, projected outside. Then wife and husband can help each other to bring their unconscious nearer and nearer.

A moment comes – and it must come if life has really been a successful effort – when wife and husband are no longer wife and husband: they have become companions on the eternal journey. They help each other; they have become mirrors to each other. They reveal the unconscious of the other and they help each other to know themselves. Now there is no pathology, no dependence.

Remember one more thing: if you deny your unconscious, if you hate your unconscious, if you suppress your woman or man within, then you can go on saying that you love the woman outside. But deep down you will hate her also. If you deny your own woman, you will hate the woman you love. If you deny your own man, you will hate the man you love. Your love will be just on the surface. Deep down it will be hatred. It is bound to be so, it has to be so, because you will not allow the other to become the mirror of your unconscious. And you will be afraid also. Man is afraid of woman. Go and ask your so-called saints. They are so afraid of women. Why? They are afraid of their unconscious, and the woman becomes a mirror. Whatsoever they have hidden, she reveals.

If you have suppressed something, then the other polar opposite can reveal it immediately. If you have been suppressing sex and you are sitting in meditation in a lonely place and a beautiful woman passes by, suddenly your unconscious will assert itself. That which has been hidden will be revealed in a woman passing and you will be against that woman. You are foolish – because that woman is not doing anything at all, she is just passing. She may not even know that you are there; she is not doing anything to you. She is a mirror, but the mirror is passing and in that mirror your unconscious is reflected.

The whole so-called spirituality is based on fear. What is the fear? The fear is that the other can reveal the unconscious, and you don't want to know anything about it. But not knowing will not help, suppression will not help. It will remain there. It will become a cancer; by and by it will assert itself more and more, and ultimately you will come to feel that you have been a failure and that whatsoever you have suppressed has become victorious and you are defeated.

My whole effort is to bring your unconscious nearer to your conscious. It should become so much acquainted with you so that it is not unknown. You become friendly to it, then the fear disappears – the fear of the polar opposite. And then the hatred also disappears because then the other is just a mirror, helpful. You feel gratitude. Lovers will be grateful to each other if their unconscious is not suppressed and they will be hateful to each other if their unconscious is suppressed.

Allow your whole being to come into function. Your emotions are imprisoned, encapsulated. Your body movements are imprisoned. Your body, your heart, has become just as if it is not part of you. You simply carry it along like a burden. Allow your emotions full play. In the meditations we will be doing, allow your emotions full play and enjoy the play, because many new things will be revealed to you.

You have not screamed; you cannot remember when you last screamed. When the scream comes to you and takes possession of you, you will become afraid. What is happening? – you are losing control. But lose control! Your control is the poison. Lose control completely. Allow your emotions to erupt like a volcano. You will be surprised at what is hidden in you. You may not even be able to recognize that it is your face.

And allow your body to have full play also, so every cell of the body becomes vibrant, alive. Just as a bird alights on a branch and the branch starts wavering – vibrant, alive – let your being alight on your body and allow your body to be vibrant, alive, alive with the inner force. Suddenly you will enter a new unknown door. You will open a new dimension of your own existence and that dimension will lead you to the ultimate, to the divine.

Now the sutra:

> *At whose desire and by whom impelled does the mind alight on its objects? By whom impelled does the chief prana – vital force – proceed to its function? By whom impelled do men utter this speech? What deva or god directs the eyes and the ears?*

The master is asking what the original source in you is – of all your life, of all your movements, of all your expressions. What force creates desire? What force impels you to be alive? What force gives you the lust for life? There must be a hidden force, and in a way inexhaustible: it goes on and on; it never tires.

> *At whose desire and by whom impelled does the mind alight on its objects?*

When you look at a beautiful woman or a beautiful flower or a beautiful sunset, who impels you? Who throws you outward? Who is the inner source of all your activity?

The Upanishads say that whatsoever you do, the doer is always the *brahman* – whatsoever you do, you are not the doer.

The doer is always the *brahman*. If you run filled with lust after a woman, the Upanishads say it is also *brahman*. Because of this, Christian missionaries could never understand what type of religion Hinduism is. Even lust is spiritual because the original source is always the *brahman*. Whatsoever you do with your energy, *brahman* is moving in it.

There is a story…

The god Brahma created the world and he fell in love with it. Christian theologians cannot understand it. And naturally, it is difficult to understand. Brahma goes on creating other beings and he goes on falling in love. He creates a cow then he falls in love and becomes the bull – and on and on: the whole creation is created. He creates the cow and he becomes the bull. He goes on dividing himself into two polar opposites.

The story is just beautiful, if you can understand it. He goes on dividing into two polar opposites. And remember, the reverse is the process to reach him again. Go on nondividing; go on meeting with the polar opposite. He creates the world through polar opposites. He creates the cow; he is the cow because he has created the cow out of himself. And then he becomes the bull, he is the bull. He is both the feminine and the masculine.

And then he follows the cow, and then the cow tries to escape the bull. The cow tries to hide and through her hiding she invites the bull. This is like hide-and-seek. That's why Hindus say the whole creation is just a play – a play of the same being dividing itself into polar opposites and then playing hide-and-seek.

You are a *brahman*. Your husband is a *brahman*; your wife is a *brahman*. And the *brahman* is playing hide-and-seek. The whole idea is simply superb. The reverse is the process to reach the ultimate again: don't play hide-and-seek. Allow the divided parts to mingle into each other. Let them merge, and the *brahman* arises again – the one.

This master asks:

At whose desire and by whom impelled does the mind alight on its objects? By whom impelled does the chief prana – vital force – proceed to its function?

Who breathes in you?

By whom impelled do men utter this speech?

Who speaks in you?

What deva or god directs the eyes and the ears?

Who is directing your senses?

The Upanishads are not against the senses. They are spiritually sensuous; they don't deny. Denial is not their slogan at all, denial is not their attitude. They accept and they say that even in the senses the divine is moving because there is nothing else to move. They make everything sacred, they make everything holy. They don't condemn, they don't say, "This is sin." Sin is unknown to the Upanishads, absolutely unknown. They say there is no sin – it is a play. Even in sin, even in the sinner, the same energy is moving.

Everything becomes holy. And if you can say with your full heart that everything is holy, you will become holy immediately because the very feeling that everything is holy and sacred makes the sin disappear. Sin is created by condemnation and the more you condemn, the more sinners you create.

The whole world has become a great crowd of sinners because everything has been condemned – everything. There is not a single thing which you can do which has not been condemned by someone or other. With everything condemned, you become a sinner. Then guilt arises – and when there is guilt you can pray, but the prayer is poisonous; it comes out of your guilt. When you are guilty you can pray, but that prayer is based on fear. That prayer is not love, cannot be. Through guilt love is impossible.

Feeling yourself condemned, a sinner, how can you love?

The Upanishads say everything is holy because he is the source of all. Whether or not the river looks dirty to you is irrelevant. He is the source of all – the dirty river and the sacred Ganges, to both he gives the energy. To the sinner and to the saint, he gives the energy. Really, there is no story like this, but I would like a story like this: that he created the sinner, then he became the saint, just like the cow and the bull, and then the hide-and-seek. He created the saint and then he became the sinner and then the hide-and-seek...

Total acceptance of whatsoever exists: just by being in existence, it is holy.

It – the atman,

or the *brahman*

– is the ear of the ear, the mind of the mind, the speech of the speech, the prana of the prana, and the eye of the eye. Wise men separating the atman from these – sense functions – rise out of sense life and attain to immortality.

Whatsoever you do are the functions of him, of the total. The total functions in you. When you breathe, what do you do? You do nothing. The breathing comes in and goes out. Rather, he breathes in you; you cannot do anything. If the breath leaves you, what will you do? If it doesn't come back, what will you do? If it has left then it has left and if it does not come back you cannot do anything. Really, when it is not coming you are no more. Who is there to do anything? He breathes, not you. The emphasis is on the total, and not on the individual.

This has to be constantly remembered, because we go on forgetting this. Our emphasis is on the individual, the I: "I am breathing, I am alive, I am seeing you." No. The master says he – the *brahman* – is seeing through the eyes, he is the eye of the eye.

When I speak, I am not speaking: he speaks. And when you listen, you are not listening: he listens. He becomes the cow, he becomes the bull; he becomes the speaker, he becomes the listener. It is a mysterious hide-and-seek, a great play, a great drama; beautiful, if you can understand. He is everywhere – in the listener, in the speaker, he is everywhere. When you are silent, he is silent within you. When you speak, he is speaking in you.

This emphasis is not only metaphysical, not only a doctrine. As a doctrine it is superb, but it is to help you toward a new realization. While speaking, if you can feel he is speaking, all the fever in it will be lost. While fighting, if you can remember he is fighting through you, the fight will become a drama. While being silent, if you can feel, he is silent within you. And if the silence is disturbed and thoughts start moving, you know that he is disturbed, not you. And he has become the thoughts and now he is moving like clouds in your inner sky. He is both, so why be worried? He is both.

When you are healthy he is healthy in you and when you are ill he is ill in you. You are totally unworried; you need not come in. Your whole burden has been thrown upon him. That's why I say this is not only metaphysical. It is deeper – one of the deepest techniques to transform your total being.

If he is doing everything, then why go on carrying yourself unnecessarily? He breathes and he is born and he dies. When you die, he will die – not you. Then why be afraid of death? You become unconcerned. This unconcern relieves you of all burden. And this is the actual fact; this is not make-believe. This is the actual fact: whatsoever is happening is happening to the total. The individual is just an illusion.

I have never been as an ego and I am not as an ego, and I cannot be; only he is. And when I say he, I mean the total. Don't try to conceive of him as a person. He is not a person; he is the total – the whole. That which breathes in you breathes in the trees and that which sings in you sings in the birds and that which dances in you dances in the rivers, in the brooks, in the springs, and that which speaks in you speaks in the breeze passing through the trees. The total.

Just change the gestalt, just change the pattern. Don't emphasize the individual; move to the total. And then what is the problem? Then there is no problem. Every type of problem enters with *you*; anguish and anxiety enters with you. Without any burden on you, you are liberated. You can become a *mukta*, you can become a *siddh*, a liberated one, this very moment. Just realizing, feeling, "I am not; he is," the past disappears, the future is no more because the future is created out of your worries, imagination, projections. Then he will take care. Then whatsoever happens will happen and whatsoever happens will be good because it is out of him.

This is what trust is – not that you believe in a God sitting upon some throne in heaven and guiding everyone from there, a great controller or engineer or something like that – no! He is not the managing director. He is not. There is neither any throne nor somebody sitting on it. And faith doesn't mean that you believe in a concept, in a philosophy. Faith means trust – trusting the whole. Then everything is blissful. Because how can anything else be? How can anything other than bliss be? You create misery because you come in. Go out just as if a lamp has been put out. Go out – and then he is.

> *It is the ear of the ear, the mind of the mind, the speech of the speech, the prana of the prana, and the eye of the eye.*

Whatsoever appears on the surface, whatsoever it is, makes no difference. Always, hidden, he is there. Look at me with full remembrance, with mindfulness that he is looking through you, and immediately the quality of consciousness changes. Just now look at me: he is looking, he is the eye of the eye, and immediately you are not there and a tremendous silence happens. The very quality of your being is different when you look at me as if he is looking, not you.

You are listening to me: forget that I am here; he is here – the total. The total has taken possession of me, the total has become active in me, the total has changed me into his instrument. Look at me as if he is speaking, listen to me as if he is speaking, and then everything is different. You are no longer there – a sudden flash and everything changes. It is not a question of time. You are not to practice it, you can see it this very moment.

Look at me. You are not there; the total, the whole, has become eyes, the whole has become eyes in you. You are just an expression of the will of the whole, of the desire of the whole. The whole has become words through me, he is manipulating me, he is using me. And then, in this room, only he is. Then the totality becomes one. Then the parts are lost and fragments are no more. Then there is a deep orgasm between the speaker and the listener. Then you will feel the presence, but the presence can come only if you forget yourself.

Remembering God is not really a remembering of his name. Remembering God is not going on chanting "Rama, Rama, Krishna, Krishna" – useless, futile. Remembering him means forgetfulness of yourself. If you are not – forgotten, completely forgetful of yourself, abandoned – he is. When you are not, suddenly he is – and this can happen in a single moment.

I am reminded of an incident that happened after the Second World War. Before the war, in a small village in England, there had been a statue of Jesus just on the crossroads – a beautiful statue with raised hands. And on the statue there had been a plaque, and on that plaque had been written: "Come unto me."

The statue was destroyed in the Second World War; a bomb fell upon it. And when there was restoration work and the village was again coming to be alive after the war, they remembered the statue, so they tried to find fragments of it. In the ruins the fragments were found and the statue was restored again. But the hands could not be found. They were missing.

So the village council decided to ask the artist to make new hands. But an old man in the village who was always seen sitting near the statue – both when it was there and when it was not – said, "No. Let Jesus be without hands."

The council asked, "Then what will we do about the plate underneath? It is written, 'Come unto me,' and it had raised hands."

The old man said, "Change the plate and write there, 'Come unto me. I have no other hands than your own.'"

And now the statue stands there without the hands, and written underneath is: "Come unto me. I have no other hands than yours."

In your hands he is moving, in your eyes he is moving, in your heart he is beating – the total. And he has no other hands, remember. He has no other eyes, he has no other heart to beat. He is beating all over, he is alive all over. This is the message.

> *It is the ear of the ear, the mind of the mind, the speech of the speech, the prana of the prana, and the eye of the eye. Wise men separating the atman from these – sense functions – rise out of sense life and attain to immortality.*

All these senses are the functions and he is the functionary within. Knowing this, you are not against the senses. Knowing this, you simply change the emphasis. Then you are not obsessed with the senses; you are always looking for the inner core. And the *rishis* say that by knowing this transcendence you attain immortality. Remember, only you can die; life never dies. Because you are born, you will die; that is the natural end to every birth. Life goes on – life goes on eternally moving; life never dies. Waves in it are born and die, and the riverlike life moves and moves and moves.

Once you come to feel the river within your wave, you are immortal. If you can realize him seeing through you, breathing through you, you are immortal. Only this shell, this vehicle of the body, will disappear. You will never disappear. You cannot disappear – you have always been.

Sometimes you were a tree because the tree was the vehicle –

because he willed to be a tree through you. Sometimes you were a cow because he willed himself to be a cow through you. Sometimes you were a butterfly, sometimes a flower, sometimes a rock – but you have always been here. You have always been here. You are not a new visitor. No one is a new visitor; no one is a stranger. You have always been here and now, but with different vehicles. Sometimes a rock was the vehicle; now you are a man or a woman: now this is a vehicle.

If you can understand and know that the vehicle is just the vehicle, the vehicle can be changed. It will have to be changed. But the inner one who goes on changing faces remains the same. That one is immortal, life is immortal. You are mortal. And why are you mortal? – because you get identified with the vehicle. Moving in a cart you become the cart. Riding on a train you become the train. Flying in an aircraft you become the aircraft. You go on forgetting that the aircraft, the cart, the train, the car are vehicles.

You are not the vehicles; you are the total, and the total goes on changing its vehicles. So then you are immortal. Remember, *you* cannot be immortal – *you* identified with the body. You are immortal knowing, transcending the body. The consciousness is immortal, the very aliveness is immortal.

The sutra says:

> *Wise men, transcending these – sense functions – rise out of sense life and attain to immortality.*

And the more you feel the inner, the essential, the eternal, the immortal, the less and less you are obsessed with the sense life. You can play it, but you are not obsessed.

Krishna playing on his flute is not obsessed with the flute; or Krishna dancing with his girlfriends, *gopis,* is not obsessed. It is just a play. Life becomes a play, not an obsession, when you know the immortal.

Now get ready for the meditation.

...

CHAPTER 3

THE "I" CANNOT BELONG TO YOU

The first question:

> **Osho,**
> **You said that when the master is in an absent-like presence and the disciple is also absent-like, then the divine work begins. If both are to be absent-like, then please explain the role of the master in the spiritual endeavor.**

There is no role as such. The role is possible only if the master exists as a person. If he exists as somebody, then he can play a role. Really, our personality consists of nothing but roles. Your personality is the many roles you go on playing: those roles are your faces. In the morning you have one face, a role to play; in the office you have a different face; back home again you change your face. You go on changing the whole day, moment to moment. Whenever you have to play a role, you create a face, you become an actor.

The master is one who has stopped playing roles. He is not playing anything, he is not doing anything; he has come to understand that the doer is the total. The individual is in illusion if he thinks that he is doing something. The master cannot think that he is helping the disciple or that he is endeavoring for his transformation. All this happens of course: the transformation happens, the disciple changes, is reborn, but this is not something done on the part of the master.

The master has become nobody. He exists not as a presence, but as an absence. Within him there is no mind, within him there is no ego, within him there is no center. The center has been given back to the divine; the ego has been surrendered. He has become a vehicle, he has become a passage – just a flute. Now the divine sings through it. Now no song belongs to the master – nothing. How can he play a role? How can he endeavor? How can he do something?

All these words – *do, role, endeavor, help* – are egocentric. They mean that the master is doing something. No, the master cannot do anything. He is not, but things happen around him. I am not saying that the disciple will not be transformed; he will be transformed, but he can only be transformed through a master who is not doing anything. If the master is doing something, the disciple cannot be transformed. The very effort on the part of the master shows that the master is not there yet.

There is no question of effort. The master exists as an absence, as a nobody, and this very fact becomes a tremendous force. This very fact, this existence of a void, creates mysterious happenings around it. But the master is not doing them. Remember, the river is flowing toward the sea, but the river is not really flowing, not doing anything. This flow is just nature. It is natural for the river to flow. There is no effort on the river's part. The tree is growing; the tree is not doing anything – there is no effort, no center, no ego to do. It is happening.

Life is a happening, and a man becomes a master when he has come to realize this: that the total is doing, and we are unnecessarily bothered and we unnecessarily interfere and we unnecessarily bring in our own centers – illusory, because no individual can have any center.

One of the greatest Christian mystics, Meister Eckhart, said that only God can say "I." No individual can really say "I" because the I belongs to the total. My hand cannot say "I," because the I belongs to me. My leg cannot say "I" because the leg belongs to me and the I belongs to me. My leg, my hand, my eyes cannot assert "I" because they are fragments, part of a greater unity. You are a similar phenomenon: you are not an entity in yourself, you are just part of a great organic whole. You are just a fragment, an atomic cell in it – you cannot say "I."

That is why all the religions say the I is the only barrier, because the I is the most fallacious thing possible. It cannot belong to you. You don't know why you are born, you don't know the forces that control your life. No one has asked about your choice. You simply find one day you are alive. Then who goes on breathing within you? You don't know.

Then suddenly one day you will be no more. No one will ask you. It is not your decision to be born and to die. But something happens and goes on happening. Something happens and you are born, and something happens – you are no more, you disappear again. How can you say "I"? No decision of yours has been used. No decision: the I can belong only to the divine.

Then a problem arises and the problem is this: if the master cannot help, if the master cannot do, how can a master promise? Someone has shown me the wall hanging [*Osho indicates the blue banner suspended behind him on the podium*] "I have come not to teach, but to awaken. Surrender and I will transform you. This is my promise."

Then how can I promise you? Then how can I say that I will transform you? Really, this is a trick. I am not going to transform you – *I* am no longer there. But if you surrender, you will be transformed. If you surrender you *will* be transformed – not that I will transform you. The very surrender brings you to the point where transformation happens, and when it has happened, then you will know and you will laugh because it has been a great joke.

I cannot do anything. The very concept of doing is irrelevant: I am no longer there. But you will not understand that language. You can understand only the language of the I; hence, I have said, "I will transform you," and it is true you will be transformed. It is true that once you surrender there is no barrier for your transformation. You will be reborn. I am not doing anything and I cannot do anything. Nothing is needed to transform you. You are enough.

But you have lost confidence and this trick is just to give you your confidence back. You have forgotten your own possibility. You have forgotten who exists within you, what tremendous energy is hidden within you. You have forgotten. Someone else is needed to tell you. You have the treasure, but you have forgotten it. I cannot give you the treasure – you are the treasure. But I can simply show it to you, just give you an indication.

When Jesus says, "I will deliver you," when Jesus says, "I will liberate you," or Buddha says, "I am your path, your way," when Krishna says to Arjuna, "Surrender to me and I will do everything for you," these are all tricks to help those who have forgotten themselves. But the promise is true because it happens. Not that someone helps you. Your own energy comes into being, your own energy becomes vital, your own sources are tapped, your own being becomes active.

You cannot understand the language of not-I. Hence, I have spoken in terms of I: "I have come not to teach, but to awaken." No one has come, no one can come. We have always been here, you and I. I cannot come, I cannot go. There is nowhere to go and nowhere to come from. We have been in existence, we have existed always. And who am I to teach you or awaken you? But you have forgotten your own potentiality, your own possibility, and some trick is needed to throw you back to yourself.

Remember, I am not doing this because I have a lot of compassion for you. No, nothing of the sort. I have no compassion at all for you. You don't need it. You are not slaves, you are not poor, you are not beggars. You are divine in your own right; you are as divine as any Krishna, any Buddha. Nothing is lacking there; everything is present but you are fast asleep. And when I say or when I teach or when I appear to do something, it is not that I feel compassion for you – no. This is just how it happens within me to play this.

For me, this is just a play. I enjoy doing it; you need not be grateful toward me. I enjoy it. You need not be at all in any debt toward me, because I have enjoyed it, I love it. It is just as if a flower flowers and you pass nearby and the flower gives you a gift of its perfume. Just like that something has flowered within me and you pass near me and I present a gift to you. If you take it, I am grateful toward you; if you refuse it, you are your master.

Really, if this attitude can penetrate deep within you, then there is no master and no disciple. Then relationship disappears. It must disappear. The divine starts functioning only when there is no master and no disciple and the relationship disappears.

When I am the master and you are the disciple, a duality exists. And there are so-called masters who go on telling you that you are the disciple and they are the masters, they are higher and you are lower. They create a hierarchy; really, they create a politics around it. That type of master will not be of much help. They may be harmful, because they are not giving you that which already belongs to you. They are again creating an illusion.

What I am doing here is not creating a relationship. But rather, on the contrary, dissolving the relationship. If we can be here without thinking in terms of being master and disciple – if we can just be here, present, alert, alive – the thing will happen. Wife and husband is a relationship. Father and son is a relationship. Master and disciple? – it is not a relationship at all; it only appears so. It is not a relationship because the whole effort is to dissolve duality, and relationship exists in duality.

A master is really trying not to be a master, and a master is trying for you not to be a disciple. The whole effort is to bring you to a point where relationship disappears, where there are not two, but a simple presence. And when there is no relationship, but you are alert and I am alert – remember, if you are alert and I am alert, I am not and you are not – in that alertness

"I" is dissolved and the flames of two lamps become one. Only in that oneness does the divine start working.

The divine works only in oneness; that is his mode of function. The more divided you are, the less he can function; the more divided, the farther you move away from the divine. That's what I have meant.

So two things about this question: one, the master is not doing anything, not playing any role. He is not making any endeavor. It is not in any way an effort on his part. He has become alert, awakened, and now something goes on flowing through him. This flow is riverlike. Wherever this river moves it will make people more alert. Not that there is any effort on its part: this is its nature. So a master is by nature a master, not by any effort. Wheresoever he moves he will be a master.

I remember one story about an Egyptian mystic, Junnun. Junnun always travelled hidden in the garb of a beggar, and he even had emperors as his disciples. One disciple, one very rich disciple, asked him, "Why do you dress as a beggar? Why do you mix with the common masses and crowds? This is not good, because you are a great master."

Junnun is reported to have said, "A master is by his nature a master, so wherever he moves he is a master – wherever; it makes no difference. If he is standing in a crowd, there also he is a master. He is the master and he is functioning and the crowd is being transformed by his presence, just by his presence."

Mohammed says in the Koran that no master should go to a rich man's house. If the rich man wants to meet him, he should come to the master. Then one Sufi mystic, Bayazid, was asked – because he was going to rich men's houses, to the palace of the emperor to teach there – "Why are you going against the prophet? Mohammed says no master should go to a rich man's house. There is no need. If the rich man desires, he should come to the master's feet. But you are moving even to the palace, so what is the matter? Are you against the prophet, or you don't believe in the saying?"

Bayazid said, "You don't know the reality. Mohammed is right, and I follow his teachings and his saying. But whether a master goes to the emperor's house or an emperor comes to the master's hut, it is always the master who changes the other. It makes no difference."

Basically, it is always the master to whom you come. Whether the master goes to the palace or the emperor comes to the master's hut, it makes no difference. It is always the emperor who is coming to the master because he is to be changed. He will be changed.

Bayazid says it is the nature of the master to change others; it is not an effort. Nothing is being done by the master, simply his presence – and if he appears to do something, that appearance is just a trick because you cannot understand the language of non-doing. You can only understand the language of effort. So he creates a language for you. Even if you cannot understand his language, he can understand your language very well. So he gives you whatsoever you can understand and by and by your understanding grows. And one day when you really come to the point when you can understand a master, you will start laughing – because he has not done anything. But you will feel grateful in that moment, because without doing anything he has totally transformed you.

Really, if something is to be done it is a violence. If in transforming you, changing you, I do something, it is going to be aggressive, it is going to be violent. Every effort is violent. But just by my presence, just by your being around me, something starts happening in you even though I am not doing anything. Only then is it love, is it not violence.

Then a very peculiar phenomenon happens: if someone tries to change you, you will resist him – because instinctively you become aware of the violence, instinctively you start defending yourself. If someone tries to change you and make you good, religious, moral, and all that nonsense, you will resist. Your ego will be hurt, and you will start defying him, and will start doing things which you never meant to do, just to defy him.

Good fathers are the cause of bad generations. So-called saints and sages are the cause of the degeneration, of the immorality that exists all over the world – because they go on forcing. And whenever someone forces you, even if he is forcing you toward heaven, you will refuse. And it is good to refuse, because he is killing you, your spirit. If you are forced into heaven you will be a dead man there. It is better to go to hell, but by one's own choice. You will at least be free. You will at least be a soul.

A real master never forces anything upon you, not in the least, not even indirectly – no. Because if a master cannot know the working of the mind, then who can know? If he cannot understand this working of the human mind and consciousness – that it becomes rebellious, resistant if you force something upon it – then who can know? A master knows; that's why he never does anything. He simply allows you to be near him. He may create tricks so that you can be near him. For example, I say to you, "Meditate." You are meditating, but the basic thing is you are just near me. And while you are meditating, without doing anything, something is happening.

I am talking to you: that is a trick. There is no need to talk. If you can understand, you can simply sit here near me. There is no need to say anything. But then you will get bored. You will ask, "What am I doing here – sitting and sitting?" Your mind needs some toys to play with, so I give you toys and your mind goes on playing with the toys. But all the while something is happening which is the basic thing. You are not aware of it, but one day you will become aware.

And then you will see what the trick was, what the technique was. The technique is to engage your mind somewhere else so that you are available to me and to my presence. And I can meet you without any interference from the mind.

The second question:

> **Osho,**
> **This morning you talked about the inner intercourse and orgasm which happens between the outer male body and the inner female unconscious, and vice versa. Please explain how this happens in the active meditation we are practicing here.**

It happens in the active meditation you are doing here because all that is hidden and suppressed is brought out by it. It is a catharsis, an expression. It is just the reverse process of suppression. So you will have to understand the process of suppression.

Someone has died: you feel very sad, but you think in your mind that it is not manly to weep and to cry. It will look like a weakness, and you have always maintained a strong image of yourself. Everyone knows that you are a very strong-willed man. How can you weep? – this is womanish. So you suppress the tears. They want to come out, they want to be released and relieved, but you suppress them. Those tears will become poison, because the system was throwing them out and you suppressed them. You go on smiling. Your heart is weeping and crying, and you go on smiling.

You are trying to maintain an image. You cannot be natural; you cannot allow your heart, your body, your mind, to function naturally. You go on manipulating them. You choose: something has to be expressed and something has to be repressed. That repressed part becomes the unconscious.

Really, there exists no unconscious. You repress something and you repress it very deeply because you yourself don't want to be aware of it, you don't want to be conscious of it. Otherwise it will be a heavy burden on the mind. So you go on forgetting it. You go on being unconscious about it, that it exists there. You forget its existence, and you yourself create an unconsciousness within.

This is the way you become divided, you become two. The

rejected part becomes the unconscious and the accepted part becomes the conscious. If you are a man, then you are rejecting the woman, because no culture has yet existed on earth which accepts bisexuality. All the cultures that have existed up to now were not really aware of the fact that to be a man or to be a woman is not something absolute. It is relative, it is a question of degrees.

If you are a man, it doesn't mean you are a hundred percent man. Nobody can be, because to be a hundred percent man you will have to be born out of your father with the mother not contributing anything. That's impossible. Or to be a hundred percent woman, the father would have not to be there at all. Only the mother would be involved because if the father contributes something the male element has entered; if the mother contributes something the female element has entered. This is a new fact brought out by depth psychology – a new fact for the West, but Tantra in the East has always been aware of it.

Man is only in relative terms a man: he may be sixty percent man and forty percent woman; or a woman may be sixty percent woman and forty percent man. That's why many things happen. Sometimes the degrees are so near that someone may be fifty-one percent man and forty-nine percent woman, so you cannot decide really whether he is a man or a woman. He will walk, he will talk, he will move, in a feminine way – forty-nine percent. And this difference is of hormones. New hormones can be injected. And this is a borderline case – forty-nine percent woman, fifty-one percent man. You can inject a few more feminine hormones, and the balance will change and the man will become a woman.

There have been many accidents when suddenly a boy becomes a girl or a girl becomes a boy. Then scientists became aware about this phenomenon. Then they came to understand that there are borderline cases. Now there are hormones available, and I think that the time is not very far off, it will happen, even before this century ends, that the alternatives will be available to everyone: you can change your sex.

And it is a good idea – because if a man has remained for thirty years a man, it will be a good change. Really, to be a woman is to move into another world, and this is a greater change than going to the moon. There is nothing much there; it is just like the earth. But a man moving to be a woman or a woman becoming a man is moving to a completely opposite pole.

Really, whenever the alternative becomes possible, only foolish people will not use it. Those who are wise will use it, because then you can become aware and you can live in two totally different worlds. And that will give a new light to the human mind, because man has never understood what woman is, neither women are capable of understanding men, because their psychologies differ so absolutely, they exist on such extreme poles.

Freud has said, "I have been working for forty years with human psychology, but still I cannot say what a woman desires, what a woman wants, what her mind is." It is difficult, because a man cannot understand a woman. Whatsoever he understands will be a point of view because he is standing at the other pole. He will be looking at a woman as a man, and that changes everything. A woman cannot understand man because she is always looking from the standpoint of being a woman. And we cannot change places. If biology helps us, then the old controversy between man and woman will disappear.

I am saying that you are a man only relatively, or a woman only relatively. And if you are a man, then you will have to suppress the other part – which is a woman, which your mother contributed to you. Why? What is the need to suppress it? We suppress it because we have been trying to live according to logic. That is the greatest fallacy man has committed. We have been trying to live according to logic, and life is illogical.

Life is both man and woman together, and logic is always either feminine or masculine. Your logic says you are a man, so cut all those qualities which don't belong to a man. That suppressed part becomes your unconscious. You are a woman, so everyone says that you must be kind, loving, sympathetic. You must not be cruel, you must not hate, you must not be aggressive, because that is not how a woman is conceived to be.

This is nonsense. Really, if a woman becomes aggressive, she is incomparable. No man can compete with her, because your aggression is exhausted already – you have used it too much. And she has not used her man – that man is still fresh and young. If she becomes aggressive, then no man can compete with her. If she is angry and violent, you will look just pale before her.

And similar is the case with man. They say a man must be aggressive, violent, powerful – must have willpower, must not be weak, must not show sympathy, love; these things are womanish. But if a man can really love, no woman can compete with him – because his "woman" has remained always virgin and fresh, unexhausted, unused. What I am saying is this: that your other is illogical, so you deny it in order to have a clear-cut image, a logical image.

I have heard…

Once it happened that a very great Zen mystic and master died. His disciple, Rinzai, was very well known, more known than his master. His master was known because of Rinzai. Rinzai was a great man, famous all over Japan. And when the master died, thousands and thousands of people gathered to pay their respects. They were surprised because Rinzai was weeping and crying, and tears were rolling down his cheeks.

Many friends said, "What are you doing? These people who have gathered are talking about you, and they say, 'We cannot conceive of Rinzai weeping. We thought he is a man who is totally unattached; we thought he is a man who has renounced all attachments, and now he is weeping. And this man Rinzai has been teaching us that the soul is immortal – only the body dies, and the body is nothing: dust returns unto dust. So why is he weeping now?'"

They demanded an answer. They were logical, because if a man says that the soul is immortal, then death should have no meaning. "Then why are you weeping?" they asked. "And when you say that no attachment is the key, why are you attached to your master? Only the body has died, and you have always been teaching that the body is just dead matter. So why be worried about it? A dead thing has become dead."

They demanded an answer, and they were logical. But what did Rinzai say? Rinzai said, "Your question is logical, but what can I do? The tears are coming down. I am weeping. I find myself weeping. Not only are you surprised: I am surprised. What can I do? This is how life is happening in me, and life is illogical."

Rinzai said, "It is good that my master has died, as he has made me aware of my total life. Without him I was thinking I was unattached. If he had not died, I could never have stumbled upon the fact that I have a heart and that I have tears and that I can weep.

"So, you are not the only ones who are surprised. Rinzai himself is surprised. But I will not suppress life. I have been accepting life totally, and I still say the soul is immortal and only the body has died. Only the body is dead, but the body was also so beautiful. I am weeping for the body. Dust unto dust: really, I still say that dust has gone back to dust, but that dust had taken such a beautiful form that I am weeping for it."

It is recorded in Zen chronicles that Rinzai proved to be real to life, not to logic.

Be real to life, not to logic, and then whatsoever you have suppressed will come up, will explode. This is what the active meditation is doing: bringing the suppressed up to be expressed; bringing your tears back to life, bringing your anger, your laughter, your sadness, back to life; throwing everything out of your system so that your system becomes purified, so that your system becomes innocent again. With this innocent system you can contact the divine. This poisoned system cannot have any contact.

Active meditation is catharsis. It is to purify you. And when you are purified and the unconscious has been acted out, the barrier between the conscious and the unconscious falls – because the barrier is created by suppression. When you are not suppressing, the barrier disappears and then there is no boundary between the conscious and the unconscious.

Then you are both: you are bisexual – man and woman both. And when you are both, you will have a new feeling of being, a new unity within you. You will not feel disrupted, divided. You will become organic, one. This oneness can lead you to the ultimate oneness; this oneness is the first step.

The third question and the last:

> **Osho,**
> **You said be a total yea-sayer, be totally with the body. But it is our common experience that then there is every possibility of the senses being permissive and indulgent. Please explain the wisdom behind the above saying.**

So let them be permissive and indulgent. Why be afraid? What is wrong in it? The fear comes from a long tradition of suppression. Why be afraid of your senses being permissive? Why not permit them? Who are you not to permit them? And what has happened to you? – do you think that you have enslaved your senses? Quite the contrary is the case: your senses have enslaved you, and you cannot be free unless your senses are free. Unless your total being is free, you cannot be free. This is one of the deepest problems for the human mind. You will have to understand it.

First you say something is wrong, then you become afraid of it. Then you try to suppress, not to do it. And the more you suppress it, the more your mind is filled with it.

For example, if you suppress sex then your mind will become sexual. Really, no animal is sexual except human beings. Sex exists for animals, but they are not sexual. For animals sex exists, but they are not sexual because they never think about it. They don't go on brooding about it, they don't create nude films, they don't publish nude magazines. They don't do anything about sex. Whenever the desire arises they move; whenever the desire is not you cannot move them. They simply follow their nature.

But man creates a sexual mind by suppressing sex. And the more he suppresses, the more he becomes sexual, because whatsoever you suppress goes into your blood, into your bones. It becomes part of your being. When I say be a yea-sayer, you become afraid. Why? It is not because what I am saying is dangerous, but because the moment you think of yea-saying you become aware of all the poisons you have suppressed: "If I say yes, all this poison will be released."

You think that if you say yes to sex you will become mad after it – you will commit adultery, you will become a maniac. The situation is just like this: if a man fasts for thirty days, then even a hint about food makes him mad. It's not that a hint about food can make anybody mad – the food is not the cause. The cause is his own suppression. He has been suppressing his hunger, his desire to eat. Any hint, however indirect, and he will become mad. And he will say, "Don't say such things."

A word can break his whole suppression, can explode his whole being. He will become afraid; he will not look at food. He will pass through the streets and he will not look at the signboards of the restaurants, he will just look down. But whatsoever he is doing, even looking down at the road, he will see food.

Really, everything will finally become an indirect invitation to food. If he looks at the moon he will think about bread – white bread floating in the sky. He cannot see his beloved's face there: impossible. He will see bread.

You will project whatsoever you are starved of. Really, if your beloved is not with you, only then can you see her face in the moon. If your beloved is with you, what you see? You will see simply the moon. And when you see the moon simply as the moon, you are healthy. When you see your beloved's face, you are unhealthy. Or when you see bread floating you are unhealthy, you are perverted.

A moon is a moon. Nothing else should be seen in it. Anything else that you see is a projection. Something suppressed goes out and creates an illusion; it is a hallucination. Whatsoever you suppress becomes hallucinatory. Then you are living in it, moving in it, and of course you become more and more afraid and scared. So the more you get scared, the more you suppress it.

You are in a suicidal effort; that's why such questions arise: "If I say yes, the first thing that comes to the mind is whatever I have said no to." That thing will assert itself immediately. If you have been starving your body, fasting, dieting, and I say, "Say yes," the first thing that comes to your mind will be to go and eat. And then you will become afraid, because you have been dieting and now the whole thing will go to the dogs if you say yes.

If a man who has been suppressing sex thinks about saying yes to the whole of life, he will be afraid of sex. Whatsoever you have suppressed, whatsoever you have said no to, will demand. It will be the first thing that will come to your mind to say yes to, and this will create trembling. But this trembling is coming not because of yea-saying – it is coming because you have said no. This is the point to be understood: it is coming because you have said no. The questions come: "What if the society becomes permissive? What if everyone indulges?" It is because the society has been repressive. It is because everyone has said no to life energies.

Try saying yes. In the beginning it may happen that you will become permissive. In the beginning it may happen that you will become indulgent, because whenever a suppressed force is released it moves to the other pole forcibly. But wait and be a witness. Sooner or later the suppressed force will be lost, and for the first time in your life you will become healthy. And then the pendulum will come and stand in the middle.

When the pendulum comes in the middle you are healthy – but you have been keeping it to the left, pulling it to the left. And now you are afraid that if you leave it, it will go to the very right. Of course it will go, but it is going to the right not because you are leaving it; it is going to the right because you have been clinging to it and pulling it to the left. Leave it – the sooner the better. It *will* go to the right. Allow it to go, and don't pull it to the left. Allow it to go. By and by, it will move from right to left, from left to right. The momentum that you have given it by suppressing has to be released, so it will have to move. But don't give it a new momentum; just become a witness.

By and by, the pendulum will become static in the middle. When the pendulum is in the middle of your mind and you are not afraid of indulgence or permissiveness, you have become free. Now you are healthy and natural.

My whole emphasis is to be natural. The more natural, the nearer to the divine. Nature is not against the divine; nature is the expression of the divine. But you have been taught again and again that nature is against the divine: "Kill nature so that you can reach godliness."

You will never reach in this way because nature is not against the divine. If it is against, it cannot exist. How can it exist? How can anything exist which is against the divine? It is part of the total, part of the game. Don't be against it. And how can you be? You are part of nature. You can go on deceiving yourself, that's all.

Allow it to flow in a natural way, allow it a natural rhythm, and by and by it settles. And when it settles, you will suddenly find you are standing in the divine. When there is no fight with nature, just an acceptance, you have moved beyond nature. But this "beyond nature" is not against nature. It is really a growth through it. You will come to *brahmacharya* – to a beautiful celibacy – but not through fighting sex. No one has come that way ever, no one can ever come that way.

When you are growing through sex, becoming more and more alert through sex, sex will be transformed. This is the way: if you suppress sex it becomes sexuality; if you express sex it becomes love. Through sexuality you cannot reach the divine. It is a perversion. Through love you can reach – it is a natural growth.

The more you accept natural instincts totally, without any

condemnation at all, by and by they subside and the fever is lost. And when they subside you have tremendous energy left with you. That energy can become the arrow toward the divine. It becomes! There is a celibacy which comes through growth and there is a celibacy which comes simply through negation, denial. The celibacy that comes through denial is perverted: your mind will be filled with sexuality. The celibacy that happens gracefully, through alertness, through acceptance, becomes grace. It has a beauty of its own, and by and by it goes beyond itself. Then it is love. Then it is prayer. And the love that was flowing toward the opposite sex starts flowing toward the divine – the same love, the same energy.

So keep it in your mind: I am not against anything. I am for transcendence, but not against anything. Godliness is not against the world: it is a transcendence. It has to be achieved through the world; that is why you have been thrown into the world. But you feel, and you go on thinking, that you are wiser than God himself. He has thrown you into the world to grow, to experience, to be enriched through it. And you are so wise...

Be a little foolish; don't be so wise. And allow the divine to have its own way through you; experience life with a yea-saying heart. And when you say yes, the very life becomes divine.

Now get ready for the meditation. A few things before you get into it: for fifteen minutes you have to stand and stare at me with your hands raised above as if a divine force is to come to you, and you are receptive and welcoming. While standing, you have to stare at me without blinking the eyes. Even if tears start flowing, do not bother – allow them to flow. And you have to go on jumping so that your energy is dynamic, not static.

I will give you indirect suggestions by my hands. I will raise my hands slowly upwards, and when I raise my hands upwards you have to bring your total energy up to jump, to dance. Be totally active when I raise my hands upwards. When I feel that now you have become a storm, that now the group soul has taken place, that now the individuals are thrown, that they have melted down and here only a group soul exists, whenever I feel this I will put my palms down this way. That means that now God can descend upon you. In that moment go completely mad so that you are totally open and something can happen within you.

For fifteen minutes, this first step. Then for fifteen minutes there will be total silence. You have to close your eyes. The light will be put off, and there will be total darkness and silence for fifteen minutes. And at the end, for ten minutes, you can celebrate; you can dance and sing and be grateful.

Now get ready for the meditation.

...

CHAPTER 4

THE UNKNOWABLE SELF

> *The eyes cannot approach it, neither can speech nor mind. We don't, therefore, know it, nor do we know how to teach it. It is different from what is known and it is different from what is unknown. Thus have we heard from our predecessors who instructed us about it.*
> *What speech cannot reveal but what reveals speech – know thou that alone as brahman and not this – anything objective – that people worship here.*
> *What mind does not comprehend but what comprehends the mind – know thou that alone as brahman and not this that people worship here.*

The deepest mystery of existence is the phenomenon of knowledge. You can know everything except your own self. The knower cannot be known because to know something means to reduce it to an object. The very process of knowledge depends on duality. I can know you because I am here, inside, and you are there, outside. You become an object. But I cannot know my self because I cannot make my self an object. I cannot encounter my self in any objective way. I cannot put my self in front of me. And if I could put my self in front of me then that which is put in front of me would not be my self. How can that which can be put in front of me be my self? Really, the inner one which will look at it will remain my self.

Self is subjective, and this subjectivity cannot be made objective. Hence, the paradox: that which knows all cannot know itself; that which is the source of all knowledge remains unknowable. If you can understand this, then this sutra will reveal much. This is one of the most profound sutras. It goes deeper than all that the mystics have said. It says self-knowledge is impossible. You have heard, it has been preached, it has been told everywhere, "Know thyself." But how can you know yourself? You can know everything other than you. One point will always remain unknown, unknowable. That point is you.

The word *self-knowledge* is not good at all. Knowledge of the self is not possible. But this may create a deep pessimism in you. If knowledge of the self is not possible, then the whole of religion becomes absurd because this is what religion is meant to do – to give you self-knowledge. Then there must be some other meaning to the word *self-knowledge*. Then there must be something, a hidden dimension, through which you can know the self and still not make it an object. Knowledge must be possible in an altogether different sense.

In the world, whatsoever we know is objective and the subject remains unknowable, the knower remains unknowable. But can this knower be known? This is the basic question, the basic problem. If there is only one way of knowing – that of objective knowledge – then it cannot be known. Hence, all the scientific thinkers will deny that the self exists. Their denial is meaningful. All those who are trained to think in terms of object, of objectivity, will say there is no self.

Their saying this means that they cannot conceive of another type of knowing. They think that there is only one type of knowing and that is objective. The self cannot be made objective; hence, it cannot be known. And that which cannot be known cannot be said to exist. How can you say that it exists? The moment you say it exists you have said that you have known it. You cannot assert its existence. If it is not known, not only not known but also unknowable, then how can you say that it exists?

Scientists go on saying that there is no self, that man is a mechanism and that what appears to be consciousness is just an epiphenomenon, a by-product. They say that there is no self, there is no center – that consciousness comes into existence just through chemical phenomena and when the body withers away, consciousness disappears.

So for science, death is total death; nothing remains after it. Consciousness is not substantial; it is a by-product. It cannot exist without the body. It is part of the body, just a combination of many material things. It comes into being; it is not elementary. It is a compound, a combination, a synthesis, something which depends on other things. There is no self. Science says there is no self because the self cannot be known.

The very word *science* means knowledge. And if something is unknowable, science will not approve of it, science will not agree to it. Science means that which can be known. Only then is science not mystical. It cannot fall into absurdities. For science, the very word *self-knowledge* is absurd. But still, religion is meaningful because there is another dimension to knowing.

Try to understand that dimension of knowing where the known is not reduced to an object. For instance, if a lamp is burning in a dark room, everything in the room is lit, is known through the light of the lamp. But the lamp is also known by its own light. Everything else – chairs, furniture, the walls, paintings on the walls – they are known through the light. But through what is the light itself known?

The light is self-enlightening: just by its presence it reveals others and it reveals itself also. But these two revelations are different. When the chair is known through the light, the chair is an object. The light falls on it and if the light disappears the chair cannot be known. The knowledge of the chair depends on the light, but the knowledge of the light itself doesn't depend on the chair. If you remove everything the light will still be light. There will be nothing to reveal, but it will go on revealing itself. The revelation of the light is self-revelation.

Similar is the case with the inner phenomenon, the inner self. Everything is known through it, but it itself is known not by anything else – it is a self-revealing phenomenon. It reveals itself. Self-knowledge doesn't mean that the self is known by something else, because then the something else will be the self. So whatsoever is known in an objective way cannot be the self. Always the knower will be the self. But how can this self be known? The self is a self-evident, self-revealing phenomenon; nothing else is needed to know it. You need not reduce it to an object.

Really, when all objects are removed from the mind, when all furniture is removed from the mind, suddenly the self reveals itself. It is self-revealing. That is the difference between matter and consciousness: matter is not self-revealing and consciousness is self-revealing; matter has to be known by something else and consciousness knows itself. That is the basic difference between matter and consciousness. There are trees, but if there is no conscious being they cannot be revealed; they need someone's consciousness so that they can be revealed.

There are rocks, beautiful rocks, but if there is no consciousness they will not be beautiful because then no one will become aware that they are there. Their existence will be mute. Even the rocks themselves will not be able to know that they exist. Existence will be there, but there will be no revelation of it.

A small child comes playing near a rock: suddenly the rock is revealed. Now it is not a mute existence. Through the child the rock has become assertive. Now the tree is revealed. Now everything around the child becomes alive in a new meaning. The child has become a source of revelation. Everything around him becomes alive. Hence, the deeper your consciousness, the deeper you reveal existence.

When a buddha is born the whole existence celebrates in him because of such a deep consciousness. All that is hidden in matter becomes manifest. It was never known before. Just by the presence of an enlightened person, the whole existence around him is enlightened. Everything becomes alive, feels through him.

Consciousness reveals others, but there is no need to reveal it for another consciousness. It is self-revelatory.

Take it from another angle: everything needs proof because everything can be doubted. But you cannot doubt the self; therefore the self never needs any proof. Can you doubt the self? One of the great Western thinkers, Descartes, used doubt as a method to know. He started his journey of knowledge through doubt – very penetrating doubt. He decided that he would doubt everything until he stumbled upon a fact which could not be doubted. And unless there is a basic fact which cannot be doubted, you cannot build a palace of knowledge because there is no foundation stone to make it. If everything can be doubted and has to be proved, then the whole edifice is just logical. Something deep down must be indubitable, something which does not need any proof.

God is not indubitable. Remember this: God is not indubitable. He can be doubted – not only doubted, he can be disproved. And really, when someone doubts God, you cannot prove his existence. You can only convince those who are already convinced, but you cannot convert a new man; that is impossible. Not a single atheist can be converted because he needs proof and you cannot prove God.

God is not indubitable. He can be doubted, rejected. The whole hypothesis can be said to be false. There is no proof that can help. So Descartes goes on discussing, inquiring, and he says that unless he comes to a point, to something in existence that is indubitable… Not that it can be proved – no. Rather, it cannot be doubted. And ultimately he comes to the self and says that the self is a greater reality than God. It is, because the self cannot be doubted. Can you doubt it? Even to doubt it you will have to have it.

For example, if you are in the house and someone comes and asks whether you are in the house or not and you say, "I am not," the very fact that you say "I am not" will prove that you are there. You cannot deny yourself. The very fact that you say, "I am not" shows that you are there. The denial becomes the proof.

There is no need to affirm it; even denial becomes the proof. When even denial is a proof, the fact is indubitable. How can you doubt it?

You cannot say, "I don't know whether I am or not" – or can you? Even to be in such confusion, you need to be there. How can there be confusion without you? You cannot say, "I don't believe that I am," because even not to believe, someone is needed to be there. There is no way to deny that you exist, that the *I* exists.

This self is the only indubitable fact in the world; everything else has been doubted. There have been skeptics who have doubted everything, even ordinary things of which you cannot conceive how they can be doubted. You are here, but the English philosopher Berkeley says, "I cannot believe that you are there. You may be just a dream. And there is no way to prove that you are not a dream, because when I dream, I dream of people such as you." And this is one of the essential qualities of a dream: in a dream the dream appears real.

So if you are appearing real, Berkeley says that does not prove anything, because in every dream the dream appears real. Can you doubt while you are dreaming? You cannot; the dream appears real. Even a very absurd dream appears real. It is just illogical, irrelevant, but still it appears real while it is there. So Berkeley says that there is no way to prove whether you are real or not. You can be doubted – everything can be doubted.

One of the great Indian mystics, Nagarjuna, has doubted everything – everything! He says nothing is real because everything can be doubted. But there is only one point which he goes on avoiding: he never talks about the self because then his whole edifice, his whole philosophy, would fall down – because that cannot be doubted. It can be asked of Nagarjuna, "Okay. The whole world is illusory and everything can be doubted, but who is this doubter? Do you doubt it – this doubter who denies the whole world?" The self is indubitable because it is self-evident. No proof is needed, no argument is needed. It is self-evident.

Mahavira denied God: he said there is no God. But he

couldn't say there is no self. Then the very self became divine for him. He said, "Only the self is God." And that is true: in you, the self is the nearest thing to divine existence. That is why it cannot be doubted. It is self-evident, self-revealing, self-enlightening.

This is the second way of knowing. The scientific way is to know a thing as an object. The religious way is to know the subject as the subject. In the scientific way, knowledge has three parts: the knower, the known and the knowledge. The knowledge is just a bridge between the knower and the known. But religious knowing does not have three parts. The knower is the known and the knower is the knowledge. This knowing is not divided into three. It is one, it is undivided.

Now we will enter the sutra:

> *The eyes cannot approach it, neither can speech nor mind. We don't, therefore, know it, nor do we know how to teach it. It is different from what is known and it is different from what is unknown. Thus have we heard from our predecessors who instructed us about it.*

The eyes cannot approach it, neither can speech nor mind. The eyes can approach everything else because everything else is in front of the eyes and the self is not in the front. The self is behind the eyes, only the self is behind the eyes. Everything else is in front. You can encounter everything through the eyes, but you cannot encounter the self because it is not in front; that is one thing. So the eyes cannot be used to see it. Really, you will have to become blind to see it. Not actually, but the eyes must become so vacant, nonseeing, so closed, not functioning, only then will you know it. Eyes cannot approach it. You will have to come to it without eyes. You will have to come to it just like a blind man.

So really, a blind man and a man with eyes are not different as far as the self is concerned. As far as the world is concerned the blind man is at a great loss; he cannot know anything. But as far as the self is concerned he is not at any loss – not at all. And if he is a wise man, his blindness may be a help to him.

That's why we in India have called blind men *pragya chakshu* – wise eyes. It is not that every blind man is wise, but potentially he is nearer to the self than those who have eyes because those who have eyes have wandered through the eyes far away into the world. They have gone very, very far away. You can move through the eyes to the very end of the world. And science goes on creating more powerful eyes for you so that you can see minute parts, atomic phenomena, and so that you can see to distant stars.

Science goes on removing you from the self. So the more an age becomes scientific, the less it comes to religious knowledge. Now you have more powerful instruments with which to see, and you have gone far away from your self.

Senses have become powerful. Really, science is doing nothing but creating more powerful senses for man: your hand can now reach to the moon; your eyes can now reach to distant stars. Every sense has been magnified, and this goes on.

A blind man is closed inside himself; he cannot go out. But he can go in if he is not disturbed by the fact that he is blind, and if he is helped by the society to know that this is not a misfortune but a blessing in disguise.

That's what we mean when we call blind men *pragya chakshu*. We say, "Don't be worried about the ordinary eyes. You can gain inner eyes through which you can know yourself, so don't be worried about the outer eyes. Forget them completely. You are not losing anything because no one gains anything through the eyes. You can move within easily because the outer door is closed."

Eyes are your doors for going out. Through eyes you are moving, through eyes the desire, through eyes the illusion, through eyes the projection – through the eyes moves the whole world. But the innermost cannot be approached through the eyes. You will have to become blind. Not that you have to throw away your eyes, but that your eyes must become vacant, objectless, without dreams. Your eyes must become empty – empty of things, empty of pictures, empty of reflections.

If you can look into the eyes of an enlightened one, you will see they are totally different. A buddha looks at you and at the same time he is not looking at you. You don't become a part of his eyes. His look is vacant. Sometimes you may get scared because you will feel that he is indifferent to you. He is looking at you so vacantly, not paying any attention to you.

Really, he cannot pay any attention to you. The attention is lost now; he has only awareness. He cannot be attentive to anything exclusively because that exclusiveness is created by desire. He looks at you as if not looking. You never become a part of his eyes. If you could become a part of his eyes, then you would become a part of his mind – because eyes are just the door to the mind; they go on transmitting the outer world to the inner. Eyes must become blind. Only then can you see your self.

This sutra says that the eyes cannot approach it; it is unapproachable by the eyes. But we go on asking how to see God and we go on saying that unless we see God we cannot believe. You cannot see; seeing is of no help. You can see only the world. God cannot be seen. And if someone says that he has seen God, he is in illusion. He has seen a vision, a dream – a beautiful dream, a holy dream, but still a dream. So if you say that you have seen Krishna and you have seen Rama and you have seen Jesus, you are dreaming – good dreams, beautiful dreams, but still dreams. You cannot see God. Eyes are of no help there. Through the eyes he cannot be approached. You must become blind to see him.

When you lose your eyes – really, when there is no desire to see – your eyes become vacant. Suddenly it is revealed within. It doesn't need any eyes to see it; it is self-revelatory. Generally things are not self-revelatory; hence, eyes are needed. The self is self-revelatory. Really, in a deeper sense, when you see through the eyes he is seeing through the eyes, not the eyes themselves. That is another dimension to be known.

When I look at you are my eyes looking at you? Eyes are just windows. I am looking at you through the eyes. Eyes are just windows; I am standing behind them. If I stand in the window and look out to the hills, will you say that the window is looking at the hills? The window will not be mentioned at all. I am looking through the window. Eyes are just apertures, windows. The consciousness looks through them and there is no way for this consciousness to look at itself through the eyes. The eyes are for others. The eyes are devices to look at the other. For your self no eyes are needed.

For example, if I want to look at the hills I will look out of the windows, but if I want to look at my self there is no need for the window. I can close the window. There is no need for it because I am not outside the window, I am inside it. For everything else eyes are helpful. Everything can be approached through them; only the self cannot be approached through them.

The eyes cannot approach it... Remember this. Then the false question of, "How can I see God?" will drop. You will not create that question or create around that question a false search. You will not ask where you can see him, where he can be found. He is nowhere, and really, eyes are irrelevant for him. He is hidden behind, within. Close your eyes and he will be revealed.

But he cannot be revealed just by closing the physical eyes because just by closing the physical eyes you are not closing anything. The world you have gathered in goes on and you go on looking at it. I can close my eyes and still I can see it there. Then the eyes are not vacant. Then the eyes are still filled. When all the pictures disappear, all the impressions disappear, the eyes are vacant. Then, when the eyes are vacant, you can approach it, you can approach the inner.

...neither can speech nor mind. Verbalizing will not help, intellectual thinking will not help. Whatsoever you can think will not be it because thinking is also outgoing, thinking is also for objects. Science insists on thinking; religion insists on no-thinking. Science insists: "Make thinking more rational, then the nature of things will be revealed more accurately." And religion says: "Don't think, then the nature of the self will be revealed to you." They are diametrically opposite.

Religion says, "Stop thinking, drop thinking, drop thoughts. They are the barrier." And science says, "Make thinking more logical, accurate, keener, analytical, rational. Don't bring any type of faith into it; don't bring any type of emotion into it; don't get involved in it. Let it be impartial – logical to the very extreme. Only then will the nature of things be revealed." And both are right. As far as the world is concerned science is true and as far as the inner subject is concerned religion is true.

But you can fall into a fallacy, and that fallacy is worldwide, universal. A scientist, when he comes to feel that the keener the thinking the more he reaches to the innermost core of a thing, starts thinking that the same method should be used for the inner search also. The fallacy has started. That method cannot be of any help for the inner search. And really, if the scientist insists on using the same method as he uses in science, the same experimental, objective methodology, then he will come to conclude that there is no self. It is not that there is no self, but that the method of the scientist is to reveal things; it cannot reveal the self. He will just bypass it. Because of his method he will miss it.

That which is helpful in the world is a hindrance for the inner. The same fallacy has been committed at the opposite pole also. When a religious person reaches the inner self through nonthinking, he starts believing that through nonthinking the nature of the world can also be revealed.

The East committed that fallacy very deeply; that's why the East couldn't create any science. You cannot create science through nonthinking. The East has been absolutely nonscientific. There were great minds born here, but they couldn't create any science. They discussed and discussed; philosophically they were superb, but nothing happened in the outside world. Nothing can happen.

The West has now created a great edifice of science with persons like Einstein. But the inner search remains nil. Even when Albert Einstein was dying, he felt frustrated. He had penetrated into the mysteries of the universe, and he had come to reveal one of its deepest cores – the theory of relativity. But he came to realize that although he knew many things never known before, as far as his own self was concerned it still remained a mystery. He knew nothing about it. The methods are opposite because the directions are opposite.

To know a thing you have to move out, to know your self you have to move in. To move out you have to move in thought and thought is an outgoing process. To move in you have to stop thoughts, to cease thinking. Nonthinking is an in-moving process.

This sutra says: *...neither speech nor mind.* The mind will not be of much help. Only meditation can be of help. Meditation is to create a "no-mind" within you. Remember this: meditation is to create a no-mind within you; hence, my emphasis on going completely mad so that the mind is dropped. The mind always resists madness. The mind says, "What are you doing? Are you crazy?" The mind always wants clear-cut logical things. The mind always asks, "Why are you doing it?" And if you cannot answer why, the mind will say, "Stop."

But life answers no whys. If you fall in love, the mind says, "Why have you fallen in love?" And then you create some idea around it: because the face of the girl is so beautiful... This is not the case. Really, the face of the girl looks beautiful because you have fallen in love, not the vice versa. It is not that the face is beautiful and that is why you have fallen in love; otherwise everyone will fall in love with your girl. But no one is falling – the face may not be beautiful, but your love gives it beauty. Your love creates a beauty around it.

That's why you go on laughing about others' lovers. You think that a certain man is crazy, going mad, falling for that type of girl. You feel repulsed and he feels attracted. You think he is crazy. No, he is not crazy because love is not a logical phenomenon. You fall in love. We call it a falling because you fall from the head. It is not a rising in love, it is a falling because the head sees it as a fall. You have lost your reason, you have gone mad.

Love is a sort of madness. Really, life itself is a sort of

madness. If you go on asking why, you cannot live for a single moment. If you go on asking, "Why breathe? Why get out of bed today? Why?" there is no answer; "Why go to sleep?" – there is no answer; "Why go on eating every day? Why go on loving the same person every day?" – there is no answer. Life is answerless. You can raise the questions, but there is no one to answer them. Life is a sort of madness.

Reason is death, not life. The more you become rational, the more dead you will be because again and again you will ask why, and there is no answer. Then you will not do anything and then you will go on ceasing, shrinking. Life is a mad expansion and in meditation we are moving deeper and deeper into life – to the very depth, to the very central core.

The mind has to be left behind. That's why I say don't ask why – just move. And whatsoever comes to you spontaneously, allow it to happen. If you allow it, in the beginning the mind will say, "Don't do it. What will others think? What will they say? A man like you, so rational, dancing like a child? Crying and weeping and screaming like a madman? Don't do this." The mind will go on checking you and you will need courage not to listen to your mind because the mind cannot approach it: you have to put the mind aside.

The mind is a device to deal with the world. It is of no use to you. You existed before the mind, you exist deeper than the mind; the mind has come to happen to you. It is just on the periphery. We have different types of minds, but our being is not different. The mind is a gathering, an earning. A child is born; he is born without a mind. He is a simple being, then by and by the mind goes on being created around him. He will need a mind to move in society, to work, to survive – he will need a mind.

The mind is an instrument. That is why every society will create a different type of mind. If you are born in an aboriginal village, hidden in the hills, not knowing any technology of the modern world, oblivious of whatsoever is contemporary, your parents will give you a different type of mind because you have to move in a different world. If you are born in the East you have a different type of mind, if you are born in the West you have a different type of mind. If you are a Christian you will have one type of mind and if you are a Mohammedan you will have a different type of mind, even if you are born in the same village.

Mind is a creation, a cultivated thing. But a being without the mind is the same everywhere. If you penetrate deeply, then another thing will be revealed: if you are a human being you have one type of mind and the tree standing just outside the window also has a mind – a different type. As far as being is concerned, you and the tree have similar beings. Only the mind differs.

Because the tree has to exist among trees, she has to create a mind, an instrument, to exist among them. You don't need that type of mind. That's why you feel that trees don't speak – you don't know their language. You think animals don't speak, they don't have any language. Really, the case is that because you cannot understand them, you think they have no language. They have their own language. They have their own mind, which is suited to their milieu, suited to their atmosphere, suited to their society.

Mind is a device to survive in the outer world; it is not needed within. And if you carry it, you cannot move within. With the mind you will move out, you cannot move within. Drop the mind, put it aside. Say, "Now you are not needed. I am moving withinwards – you are not needed."

We don't, therefore, know it, nor do we know how to teach it.

That which can be known by the mind can be taught by the mind. But if it is impossible to know it by the mind, how to teach it? – because the teaching is going to be through the mind. So the *brahman*, the absolute, the self, cannot be taught; it is impossible to teach it. Then what am I doing? Or what is a Buddha or a Christ or a Krishna doing? What are they doing if it cannot be taught? And what is the seer of the Upanishad, Kena, doing if it cannot be taught? It cannot be taught, that is absolutely true, but still something can be done.

A situation can be created in which it becomes infectious. It cannot be taught, but the "infection" can be given to you. In a particular situation you can become infected by it. So the whole phenomenon of master and disciple is not a teaching phenomenon. The master is not really teaching anything. The master is just trying to pull you into a situation, to push you into a situation where it can happen to you.

All the devices of Yoga and Tantra are just to create a situation in which the thing can happen. I can lead you into a situation where you will become aware of a different sort of reality, but that reality cannot be taught. Can you teach a blind man what light is? You cannot. Whatsoever you do, you will not be able to teach it. But one thing can be done: you can treat his eyes; the eyes can be operated upon. And if the blind man comes to see, he will know what light is.

Light can be experienced, but cannot be taught to a blind man. And we are just like blind men as far as the inner reality is concerned. Your inner eyes can be opened to it, but you cannot be taught it.

That is why faith has been the cornerstone of all religious phenomena. The blind man must have faith, otherwise he will not allow you to operate on his eyes. He will say, "You may destroy my eyes." He has none, but he will become scared: What are you going to do? And if he thinks you are going to operate, that you are going to do surgery, he will say, "Don't touch my eyes. You may destroy them. And how am I supposed to know that when you have operated there will be light? And what is light? First tell me. First prove what light is and whether light exists at all. Unless you prove this I cannot allow you to operate on my eyes."

And there is no doctor who can prove that there is light. The doctor can only say, "Have faith in me." Nothing else is possible, no argumentation is possible. The doctor can only say, "Trust in me. Even if you are not going to gain anything, one thing is certain: you are not going to lose anything because you have no eyes to lose."

That's what Buddha, Krishna, and Jesus have been saying: "Have faith. And you have nothing to lose, so why get so worried? What can you lose believing in me? What have you got? If you have anything, then escape from me as fast as possible. But you have nothing - nothing to lose - but you are so worried." People come to me and they ask, "How can I believe?" I tell them it is not a question of how because the "how" needs answers. Faith means you have nothing to lose - so why not experiment? Why not try?

Karl Marx has said to the proletarians of the world, "You have nothing to lose except your chains." He may not be right about the proletarians, but I tell you that you have nothing to lose except your chains, nothing to lose except your bondage, nothing to lose except your blindness. And the whole phenomenon is possible only when you trust – because you are moving into an unknown territory, uncharted.

I say I have known it, but I cannot teach you. I can lead you to the point where you will become aware that it exists, but I cannot teach you. There is no language to teach it, no mind to teach it. There is no way to teach it, no symbols to teach it. Whatsoever you know, it cannot be translated into that knowledge. It is beyond it. I have known something; I can take you to that point where you will also become aware of it and you will say, "It is!"

The mind cannot know it; therefore, we don't know it because whatsoever we know, we know through the mind. Our whole knowledge consists of mind and mind and nothing else. So we cannot know it, nor do we know how to teach it.

> *It is different from what is known and it is different from what is unknown.*

That creates a deeper problem again. *It is different from the known*... obviously, because if it were not different from the known, then you would have known it already.

Whatsoever you know, it is not it. And the way you know, you cannot know it, otherwise you would have known it by now, because you have been in existence for millions and millions of lives. But you have been missing it again and again. And buddhas go on talking about it and you go on listening to them about it and nothing happens.

It is different from the known and it is different from what is unknown – because the unknown can be known. *Unknown* means just that which is not known yet. Use the same methods of knowledge and someday it will be known.

Science divides the world into two: the known and the unknown – there is nothing else. Science says the known and the unknown. The known is that which we have come to know and the unknown is that which will be known sooner or later. Religion brings a third category: the unknowable. Religion says there is something which is known, something which is unknown, and something which is unknowable. If there is something which is unknowable, only then is religion possible; otherwise science is enough. The unknown will go on being reduced to the known.

It is conceivable that one day science will come to the point when there is only one category: the known. By and by, the unknown will become known. At a point somewhere there will be nothing unknown. It can be conceived of through science. But religion says there is something which is neither like the known nor like the unknown: it is unknowable. Whatsoever you do you cannot know it. So when everything becomes known, still the unknowable will be there – the mystery, the mysterious, the mysterium, will remain.

Why insist that it is unknowable? Why not say it is unknown? – because the known is through the mind and the unknown will become known through the mind, but the unknowable is behind the mind. Whatsoever you do by the mind, you will never approach it. You will have to drop the mind. And with the mind the known drops and the unknown also, because those two are the dimensions of the functioning of the mind. The known and the unknown are the workings of the mind. When the mind drops, both have dropped and you have entered the third dimension. This third dimension is of the unknowable. You are there in that dimension; the self is there.

But the *rishi* says a very beautiful thing:

> *Thus have we heard it from our predecessors who instructed us about it.*

He says, "Thus have we heard from our own masters." He knows himself also; he can say, "I have known this. This is what I have known." There is no difficulty in saying it. But he says, "This is what we have heard. Our masters have said it."

This has a quality of its own – the Indian heritage, the Indian attitude of saying things, the Indian way of always being humble, not assertive. So Buddha says, "Whatsoever I am saying was known before me by other buddhas. This is nothing new." This is the emphasis. The emphasis is that this is nothing new, nothing original. And really, truth cannot be original; only untruth can be original. You can invent lies, but you cannot invent truth – or can you?

Truth cannot be invented. Truth is eternal, timeless. So it is absurd to say that I have discovered it. You only rediscover it; you never discover it. Rediscover – it has been discovered again and again, millions of times. It has been known again and again, millions of times. You always rediscover it; you never discover it.

To emphasize this fact the *rishis* say, "It has been said so by those who preceded us. It has always been known." He doesn't claim any originality. That claim belongs to the ego. That claim, "This is my discovery," belongs to the egoistic mind. Really, the ego always feels hurt if you say, "This is nothing original." If someone says something and you say it is nothing original, he will feel hurt. If someone writes a book and you say, "This is nothing original; it has been written so many times by so many people, so why have you unnecessarily labored on it?" he will feel hurt. Every author, every thinker, tries to prove somehow that whatsoever he is saying is original. This is a modern disease.

In the West, if you are not saying anything original then what is the use of saying it? Why are you saying it? Don't say it. In the East, quite the opposite has been the case. If you are saying something original, then the East will say: "Wait and ponder over it. Don't assert it, don't say it, because if it is original then something must be wrong with it; otherwise someone must have known it before. The truth is eternal. If it is original, then something must be wrong with it. Wait, don't tell anyone; otherwise you will be in difficulty because you will be proved to be a liar. Wait, ponder, meditate. The world has existed so eternally, beginningless, how can you conceive that you have come to know an original truth which was not known before? It is impossible."

But it happens because our span of knowledge is very little. It is just like this: in the season the trees will bloom, the flowers will come. These flowers cannot know about the flowers of the last season. They cannot know; they have never met them. They will think themselves so unique, so original: "We have never been on this earth; this earth has become so beautiful because of us. Because *we* bloom, the whole existence has bloomed."

They don't know that this has been going on eternally. Every year the season comes and the flowers bloom. But the flowers cannot meet with each other, so every flower thinks he has come for the first time. This gives him a flavor, an ego. He feels he is something, somebody.

The Eastern emphasis has always been that truth is eternal; you can only rediscover it. Many have known, many will know. You are just a part of a long procession. It is your season so you have bloomed – but other buddhas have bloomed. It is just like when you fall in love: you think this type of love has never been, that something new has entered into existence. No lover can believe that anyone ever could have loved in the way he loves his beloved.

And this is good as far as it goes. This is good. How can you believe otherwise when you are in love? You think others have loved, but not this way; others have loved, but it was not such a deep intense thing. It has never happened; it is original.

The same is with thoughts: when a thought appears in your mind, you think such a thought never happened before. But thoughts are just like clouds: they gather in the sky every year, then they disappear and then they gather again. The world moves in a repetitive circle.

So Indians, particularly wise Indians, have always been emphasizing that whatsoever they say is nothing new; it has all been said before. This is a very non-egoistical attitude, and there is a very deep wisdom hidden in it. How can truth wait for me to be discovered? How can it wait for me to discover it? It has been discovered again and again. But one discovers it and it gets lost again because it cannot be transferred.

If I have come to a truth, I cannot give it to you. It cannot be transferred because truth is not a thing. It is a happening in the being; it cannot be transferred. So the truth that I rediscover will be rediscovered again. And when you rediscover it you will feel something new has happened, something original. But if you know and if you can appreciate a non-egoistic way of life, then you will know that the *rishi* is right: it has been said before, known before.

> *What speech cannot reveal but what reveals speech – know thou that alone as brahman and not this – anything objective – that people worship here.*

What speech cannot reveal but what reveals speech... You cannot say it, you cannot speak it, but through speech it is being expressed. Really, without it you cannot speak, without it you cannot see, without it you cannot feel. It is your life. You cannot speak about it but he is the speaker; you cannot see it anywhere but he is the seer; you cannot think about it but he is the thinker; you cannot do anything without it because he is the doer. So whatsoever you do, he is revealed. You cannot reveal it, but whatsoever you do he is revealed because he alone is. *Brahman* means life: he alone is.

What speech cannot reveal but what reveals speech – know thou that alone as brahman and not this – anything objective – that people worship here.

People go on worshipping idols. We make God into an object because we cannot feel comfortable unless something is there in front of us. We feel uncomfortable, uneasy. A God unknown, unknowable, is difficult. We create an idol and then we put the idol in front of us and worship it.

This is stupid in a way because you created the idol and now you are worshipping it as if it was the creator. You worship the idol as if the idol created you. You created the idol; the real creator is hidden behind. Really, God is not in the worshipped object, it is in the worshipper. It is not in the object to which you pray, it is in the innermost source from where the prayer bubbles up, from where the prayer comes up. It is always within. But for us, something becomes significant only when it is without because we have become fixed in a mode where everything must be objective in order to be. That creates the problem, so we have created temples and churches and mosques just to objectify that which cannot be objectified. But human stupidity is such.

Mohammed preached that he cannot be objectified; you cannot make any idol of him. He was right. He was saying what the Upanishad is saying. But what have the Mohammedans done? They thought it was their duty to destroy idols, to destroy temples, to set them on fire. Because he cannot be objectified, so wherever he is objectified, "Destroy the object."

See the human stupidity: Mohammed was trying to say that you can forget the object and move within. But they did not forget the object, they became obsessed with the object again. "Move and destroy!" So someone is worshipping God in a stone and someone is destroying the stone, but both are attached to the stone in their own ways and both think that the stone is very significant – one to worship it and the other to destroy it. One feels if he does not worship this stone he will not be religious, and one feels if he does not destroy this stone he will not be religious. The stone is for both very significant. We go on moving to the object. Either we love or we hate, but the object remains there.

The emphasis of those who have known is to forget the object and remain with the subjectivity alone. Don't create any object, any image, any name, any form. Don't create anything. The creator is already there; you cannot improve upon it. Don't do anything. Just move within and know it.

> *What mind does not comprehend but what comprehends the mind – know thou that alone as brahman and not this that people worship here.*

Mind cannot comprehend him, but he can comprehend the mind. Mind is included in him – everything is included; even the stone is included in him. But the stone cannot include him: this is the point. Draw a big circle and then draw a small circle in it. The big circle includes the small circle; the small circle is part of the big circle, but the small circle cannot include the big circle.

Your mind is included in the divine, but your mind cannot include the divine. It is a part and the part cannot include the whole. The whole comprehends all, includes all. And when a part starts saying, "I include the whole," the part has gone mad, the part has gone neurotic.

You – whenever you try to comprehend *that*, the total, through the mind, you are doing something absurd. It is impossible. A drop of water cannot include the ocean, but the ocean includes it. And if the drop of water says, "I am the ocean," then the drop has gone crazy. But this drop of water can become the ocean. If this drop of water drops into the ocean, loses the boundaries, loses the finiteness, the limitations, then that drop has become the ocean.

The mind cannot say, "I know." The mind can drop into the oceanic totality and then it is included there.

Whatsoever we worship is just a game. It is good: if you feel good worshipping, then it is good. It is a good game and I never intend to destroy anybody's game. If you worship, if you feel good going to a church, it is good: go on doing it. But remember that you are missing the basic point: the ultimate is within the worshipper. So while you worship don't focus your eyes on the worshipped object. Focus yourself within, on the worshipper. There it will be revealed, there it is hidden.

...

CHAPTER 5

IT IS YOUR BEING

The first question:

Osho,
You have said that intellectual learning and knowledge have helped no one and that the Upanishad says that nothing is to be denied. If the intellect is there and we are not to deny it, what is the best way in which to use it?

The first thing to be understood about the intellect is this: that the intellect exists on denial. The very function of the intellect is to deny, to say no. The emphasis of the Upanishad on not denying is basically to relieve you of your intellectual effort.

Intellect always says no. So the more one becomes intellectual, the more and more one becomes incapable of saying yes. Yes-saying means faith, no means doubt, and intellect depends on doubt. If you doubt, intellect has a function. If you don't doubt, there is no function left for the intellect.

Intellect is denial. When the Upanishad says, "Don't deny anything," it means that the intellect will have no function at all. Think of your own mind: whenever you say no, it starts working; whenever you say yes, yes becomes the end – there is no further journey.

This age is one of the most intellectual ones, and this intellectual milieu is created by thoroughgoing doubt about everything. The greater the intellect, the more skeptical it will be. It can function very keenly if you say no. If you say yes, intellect is annihilated; hence, the emphasis of all religions on faith – because in faith intellect cannot move. There is no basis for it to move. There is no further goal; yes becomes the end. If you can say yes to the whole existence, thinking will stop. Thinking has the quality of denial. The master says, "Don't deny." In the *non*denial, intellect disappears.

And you ask me what to do about intellect. It will not be there. You will not have to do anything; you will not have to deny it. And you cannot deny intellect because denial is intellectual. If you deny intellect, the very denial gives more roots to your intellectual mind. You will become a victim. If you deny intellect, you will become a victim of a deeper intellectual effort. You cannot deny it. How can you deny it? – because denial starts thinking. You can find reasons why not to deny, but those reasons will be appeals to the intellect. You can find arguments why to deny, but those arguments will be intellectual.

Faith has no arguments for or against. So really, those who have given arguments for God's existence I call irreligious because arguments have nothing to do with religion. There have been many well-known thinkers all over the world, particularly in the West, who have tried to prove that God exists. I call them irreligious – because if you can prove God's existence, then the intellect becomes superior to God's existence. Then it is proved through the intellect, and whatsoever is proved through intellect can be disproved through the same intellect. So those who try to prove are really the persons who challenge others to disprove.

Atheists exist because there are argumentative theists. When you say, "Because of this God exists," then you are giving a challenge to someone, to someone's intellect, who can say, "This reasoning is false." And arguments can be given for and against, ad infinitum; they never reach to any conclusion. Really religious persons have not argued about God: they have lived. They have lived in the way in which one should live if God is. You cannot see God, but you can see a divine person. You can see a person who is living godliness. That is the only proof. But that proof is not for the intellect. That proof is not intellectual at all. That proof is absolutely beyond intellect – it reaches directly to your heart; you feel it.

Whenever you see a Ramakrishna or a Ramana, whenever you see a person like Jesus, it is not the intellect that comes to conclude that this man is divine. You feel it first. Your heart starts vibrating in a new dimension; you feel a new perfume of being. But this is feeling; you cannot prove it.

Intellect can prove or disprove, but it can never give you faith. Even when it proves, it proves only itself; nothing else is proved. If you can prove the existence of God, you have not proved the existence of God; you have simply proved that you are a very intellectual being, that's all. You have proved that you have a very keen intellect, you have proved your own ego, nothing else. And intellect is the subtlest food for the ego – you feel that you know, you feel that you can prove, you feel that you can disprove, you feel to be the center. Even God depends on you: if you prove him, then he is; if you say no, then he is no more. He is secondary. Remember, for intellect everything is secondary and intellect is primary. Everything else becomes number two; intellect remains number one.

Faith says that this supremacy of intellect should be thrown away. Only then can the total being assert itself. And then being is primary and intellect becomes secondary. Then existence is primary; then intellect is just a part. Intellect is dictatorial; faith is democratic because faith gives expression to your whole being. Intellect is only one part trying to be supreme.

When you do as the Upanishad says and you don't deny, then the intellect disappears. If you don't deny, you will not have the intellect there at all. The no is needed. That is the foothold. Without the no, the intellect cannot stand. So the question,

"What to do about intellect?" really doesn't arise. Don't deny anything and there will be no intellect to be worried about.

The second question:

Osho,
The first few days of active meditation tend to tighten muscles, causing pain everywhere. Is there any way to get over that?

Go on doing it! You will get over it – and the reasons are obvious. There are two reasons. First, it is a vigorous exercise and your body has to get attuned to it. So for three or four days you will feel that the whole body is aching. With any new exercise it will happen. But after four days you will get over it and your body will feel stronger than ever.

But this is not very basic. The basic thing goes deeper, and that basic thing is something modern psychologists have come to know. Your body is not simply physical. In your body, in your muscles, in the structure of your body, many other things have entered through suppression. If you suppress anger, the poison goes into the body. It goes into the muscles, it goes into the blood. If you suppress anything, it is not only a mental thing, it is also physical – because you are not really divided. You are not body and mind; you are bodymind – psychosomatic. You are both together. So whatsoever is done with your body reaches to the mind and whatsoever is done with the mind reaches to the body, as body and mind are two ends of the same entity.

For instance, what happens to the body if you get angry? Whenever you get angry certain poisons are released into the blood. Without those poisons you will not get mad enough to be angry. You have particular glands in the body, and those glands release certain chemicals. Now this is scientific, this is not just some philosophy. Your blood becomes poisoned.

That's why, when you are angry, you can do something which

you cannot do ordinarily – because you are mad. You can push a big rock; you cannot do it ordinarily. You cannot even believe afterwards that you could have pushed this rock or thrown it or lifted it. When you are back to normal again, you will not be capable of lifting it again because you are not the same. Particular chemicals were circulating in the blood. You were in an emergency condition; your total energy was brought to be active.

But when an animal gets angry, he gets angry. He has no morality about it, no teaching about it. He simply gets angry and the anger is released. But when you get angry, you get angry in a way similar to any animal. But then there is society, morality, etiquette, and thousands of things. You have to push the anger down. You have to show that you are not angry; you have to smile – a painted smile. But you have to create a smile, and you push the anger down. What is happening to the body? The body was ready to fight – either to fight or to fly, to escape from the danger; either to face it or escape from it. The body was ready to do something: anger is just a readiness to do something. The body was going to be violent, aggressive.

If you could be violent and aggressive, then the energy would be released. But you cannot be – it is not convenient, so you push it down. Then what will happen to all those muscles which were ready to be aggressive? They will become crippled. The energy will push them to be aggressive, and you will push them backwards not to be aggressive. There will be a conflict. In your muscles, in your blood, in your body tissues, there will be conflict. They are ready to express something and you are pushing them not to express. You are suppressing them. Then your body becomes crippled.

This happens with every emotion, and it goes on day after day for years. Then your body becomes crippled all over. All the nerves become crippled. They are not flowing, they are not liquid, they are not alive. They have become dead, they have become poisoned and have all become entangled. They are not natural.

Look at any animal and see the grace of the body. What happens to the human body? Why is it not so graceful? Why? Every animal is so graceful; why is the human body not so graceful? What has happened to it? You have done something with it: you have crushed it and the natural spontaneity of its flow has gone. It has become stagnant. In every part of your body there is poison. In every muscle of your body there is suppressed anger, suppressed sexuality, suppressed greed and everything. Suppressed jealousy, hatred – everything is suppressed there. Your body is really diseased.

So when you start meditating, all these poisons will be released. And wherever the body has become stagnant, it will have to melt, it will become liquid again. This is a great effort: after forty years of living in a wrong way, then suddenly meditating, the whole body is in an upheaval. You will feel aching all over the body. But this aching is good, and you have to welcome it. Allow the body to again become a flow. Again it will become graceful and childlike; again you will gain the aliveness. But before that aliveness comes to you the dead parts have to be straightened and this is going to be a little painful.

Psychologists say that we have created an armor around the body and that this armor is the problem. When you get angry, if you are allowed total expression, what will you do? When you get angry, you start crushing your teeth together; you want to do something with your nails and with your hands, because that's how your animal heritage will have it. You want to do something with your hands, to destroy something.

If you don't do anything your fingers will become crippled; they will lose the grace, the beauty. They will not be alive limbs. And the poison is there. So when you shake hands with someone, really there is no touch, no life, because your hands are dead.

You can feel this. Touch a small child's hand – a subtle difference is there. When the child really gives you his hand... If he is not giving, then it is alright – he will withdraw. He will not give you a dead hand, he will simply withdraw. But if he wants to give you his hand, then you will feel that his hand is as if it is melting into your hand. The warmth, the flow – as if the whole child has come to the hand. The very touch, and he expresses all the love that is possible to express.

But the same child when grown up will shake hands as if a hand is just a dead instrument. He will not come in it, he will not flow through it. This has happened because there are blocks. Anger is blocked; before your hand becomes alive again to express love, it will have to pass through agony, it will have to pass through a deep expression of anger. If the anger is not released, that anger is blocked and love cannot come out of it.

Your whole body has become blocked, not only your hands. So you can embrace someone, you can take someone near your chest, but that is not synonymous with taking someone near your heart. These are two different things. You can take someone near your chest: this is a physical phenomenon. But if you have armor around your heart, a blocking of emotions, then the person remains as distant as he ever was; no intimacy is possible. But if you really take a person near, and there is no armor, no wall between you and the person, then the heart will melt into the other. There will be a meeting, a communion.

Your body has to release many poisons. You have become toxic, and you will have pain – because those poisons have settled down. Now I am creating a chaos again. This meditation is to create chaos within you so that you can be rearranged – so that a new arrangement becomes possible. You must be destroyed as you are, only then can the new be born. As you are, you have gone totally wrong. You have to be destroyed and only then can something new be created. There will be pain, but this pain is worthwhile.

So go on doing the meditation and allow the body to have pain. Allow the body not to resist and allow the body to move into this agony. This agony comes from your past, but it will go. If you are ready it will go. And when it goes, for the first time you will have a body. Right now you have only an imprisonment, a capsule, dead. You are encapsulated; you don't have an agile, alive body. Even animals have more beautiful, more alive bodies than you.

By the way, that's why we have become so much obsessed with clothes – because the body is not worth showing. We have become so much obsessed with clothes. Whenever you stand naked you will see what you have done to your body. Clothes go on hiding your body from you.

This has been my experience through so many meditation camps: if some people become naked in the camps, really only those people are the ones who have beautiful bodies; thus, they are not afraid. Those who have ugly bodies come and they complain, and they say, "This is not good, people going nude." Their fear is natural. They are not really afraid of others going nude, they are afraid of themselves; they cannot face their own bodies.

This disease is a vicious circle, because if you don't have a live body you want to hide it, and when you hide it, it becomes more and more dead – because then there is no need to be alert about its being alive.

Through centuries of clothing we have lost touch with our own bodies. If your head is cut off and you encounter your own body without a head, I am sure you will not be able to recognize that this is your body – or will you be able to recognize it? You will not be able to recognize it because you are not even acquainted with your own body. You don't have any feeling about it; you are simply living in it without caring about it.

We have done much violence to our bodies. So in this chaotic meditation I am forcing your bodies to be alive again. Many blocks will be broken; many settled things will become unsettled again; many systems will become liquid again. There will be pain, but welcome it. It is a blessing and you will get over it. Continue! There is no need to think what to do. You simply continue the meditation. I have seen hundreds and hundreds of people passing through the same process. Within a few days the pain is gone. And when the pain is gone, you will have a subtle joy around your body.

You cannot have it right now because the pain is there. You may know it or you may not know it, but the pain is there all over your body. You have simply become unconscious about it because it has always been with you. Whatsoever is always there, you become unconscious about. Through meditation you will become conscious and then the mind will say, "Don't do this; the whole body is aching." Don't listen to the mind. Simply go on doing it.

Within a certain period the pain will be thrown out. And when the pain is thrown out, when your body has again become receptive and there is no block, no poisons around it, you will always have a subtle feeling of joy wrapped around you. Whatsoever you are doing or not doing, you will always feel a subtle vibration of joy all around your body.

Really, joy only means that your body is in a symphony, nothing else – that your body is in a musical rhythm, nothing else. Joy is not pleasure; pleasure has to be derived from something else. Joy is just to be yourself – alive, fully vibrant, vital. A feeling of a subtle music around your body and within your body, a symphony – that is joy. You can be joyful when your body is flowing, when it is a riverlike flow.

It will come, but you will have to pass through suffering, through pain, and that is part of your destiny because you have created it. But it goes. If you don't stop in the middle, it goes. If you stop in the middle, then the old settlement will be there again. Within four or five days you will feel okay – just the old, as you have always been. Be aware of that okayness.

The third question:

> **Osho,**
> **Will you please indicate something about the fifth stage in the active meditation.**

Nothing can be said about it; that's why I never talk about it. The fourth is the last – the fifth will happen, but nothing can be said about it. There is no need either. The fifth is not a stage, it is your being. The first four are states, steps, but the fifth is not a stage, it is not a step. It is your own being, it is your nature. But nothing can be said about it. If you come to the fourth the fifth will happen to you, that much is certain.

If you can come to a total silence in the fourth, then the fifth will happen. It is a growth of your silence. But nothing can be said about it – or whatsoever can be said will be misunderstood. For example, if I say it is absolute bliss – and it has been said that it is absolute bliss – you will misunderstand it because you don't know what bliss is. You know certain pleasures and you think that bliss must be something like pleasure. It is not. You can think only in terms of pleasure because that's what you are acquainted with. You can think it is infinite pleasure; it is not. It is not pleasure at all.

Or you can think negatively, that there will be no pain, no suffering as Buddha has said. Buddha said: in that ultimate state of being there will be no suffering. And when people used to ask to him, "This is not enough. Tell us something more. You are saying what will not be there. Please tell us something about what will be there. You are saying there will be no suffering, but what will be there?" Buddha refused to answer. He said, "I will not say anything. This much I can say: there will be no suffering."

But even that will be misunderstood – because you are left nowhere, hanging. If it is said that it will be pleasure-like, then it is wrong. If it is said that there will be no pain, it is better than the first, but still not exactly right because you may carry the impression that it is going to be of negativity when it is not. Buddha was misunderstood in this country. He was thought to be a nihilist, a negativist, who was saying that in nirvana there will be no suffering, that's all. But what about bliss, *sat-chit-anand* – existence, consciousness? Simply no-suffering?

But whatsoever is said will be misunderstood because we understand only that which we know. You know pleasure, you know pain, but in the fifth there will be neither. The duality will cease: there will be no pain, there will be no pleasure. Now it becomes inconceivable. What will it be like? If there is no pain and no pleasure, what will it be like? It becomes inconceivable; you cannot imagine it.

Bertrand Russell has said somewhere that if it is really so, that nirvana or the ultimate is beyond pain and pleasure, then it must be like a deep slumber, a deep sleep. That seems logical. If there is no pain and no pleasure, how can you be conscious? – because consciousness needs something there to be conscious about. If there is nothing – no pain, no pleasure – then there is no challenge for consciousness to be there, and you will fall into a deep coma.

Everything will be misunderstood; that's why I never talk about it. I simply lead you to the door of the temple and leave the temple for you to enter and know. I leave you at the door of the temple. These four steps help you reach to the door. Then you can enter. You are standing right in front of the door and the door is open. If the temple magnetizes you, calls you, challenges you, you will enter. No one has returned from the fifth step. No one can return because it is the ultimate ecstasy. Your whole being simply gravitates toward it.

The fifth is left out of discussion. It is your own being; it is not a stage. The first four are stages. In the first you are working with your vital energy, with your *prana* – with breathing. Breathing is life. In the first step, you are working with your life. You are destroying the pattern of your breathing. Through chaotic breathing, you are destroying the settled pattern. And if you can destroy the pattern of breathing, then all the patterns in all your bodies will be loosened – because breathing is the most subtle thing to work with.

You may not have observed, but whenever your mind changes, your breathing changes. Even a subtle change in mood and your breathing immediately changes. Or, to be more correct, even before the mood changes, the breathing has already changed. When you are happy you breathe differently; when you are angry you breathe differently; when you are tense you breathe differently;

when you are sad you breathe differently; when you are relaxed you breathe differently. The rhythm always goes on changing.

Observe it. Observe the moods of your breathing. You are not breathing the same way the whole day. In the morning you breathe differently, in the evening differently. Just by knowing about your breath, everything can be said about your mind, what is happening to your mind.

Sooner or later, when medical science and psychology can penetrate into this phenomenon of breathing more deeply, they will make a graph of it. Your breathing graph will show what types of moods you have been passing through during the day. When you are asleep you breathe differently; when you are alert you breathe differently, when you are sleepy you breathe differently. Breathing can be changed easily, and if you change the breathing you change the mind.

You can work from both ways. There are many schools of Yoga. Some schools, particularly the schools of Raja yoga, start with the mind. They say first change the mind, then the breathing will change by itself. And there are other schools, particularly of Hatha yoga, which say change the breathing and the mind will follow. Both are right because both are related.

Do one thing: while you are feeling relaxed – someday just sitting in your armchair, and the whole world seems to be happy and at ease and you feel at home – note your breathing. Just observe the rhythm: how are you inhaling and how are you exhaling and what is the proportion of time, how much gap is there between inhalation and exhalation? Note everything; then do one thing more. Sometime, when you feel angry, breathe the way you were breathing when you were relaxed – and it will be impossible to be angry. Then you cannot be angry. You *cannot* be angry! It will be impossible to be angry because anger needs a different type of breathing.

When you are in love, sitting with your friend or with your wife or with your beloved, note down how you are breathing and then try to breathe that way anywhere and suddenly you will feel love bubbling up. Note it down. While just lying on the bed with your beloved, note down how you are breathing. Then sit beside a tree and breathe the same way. Suddenly you will feel that the tree has become the beloved because now the love is flowing.

When you are unaware of this fact you unnecessarily create much misery for yourself. You go on breathing wrongly in wrong places and you create many riddles, many puzzles and confusion.

In the first step, we work with breathing to create a chaos, because unless a chaos is there you cannot be born. The first step is to break all the old patterns of breathing.

In the second step, we are working with emotions to bring out all the suppressed emotions. If you have really taken deep, chaotic breaths, the suppressed emotions will come out easily. They will start coming out by themselves: you will not need to do anything. The second step will follow automatically if the first has been done rightly. If you have not been resistant in the first, the second will follow easily. In the second we are working with the emotions to bring them out, to act them out, to throw them out.

When you are angry with someone and you throw your anger on him, you are creating a chain reaction. Now he too will be angry and this may continue for lives and you will go on being enemies. You can continue this for centuries. It is not going to end. Where will it end? There is only one possibility. You can end it only in meditation, nowhere else, because in meditation you are not angry with someone: you are simply angry.

Remember, this difference is basic. You are not angry with somebody; you are simply angry, and the anger is released into the cosmos. You are not hateful toward anyone. If hate comes, you are simply hateful and the hate is thrown out. In meditation, emotions are not addressed; they are unaddressed. They move into the cosmos, and the cosmos purifies everything.

Remember, it is just like a dirty river falling into the ocean: the ocean will purify it. Whenever your anger, your hate, your sexuality, moves into the cosmos, into the ocean, it becomes purified. But whenever a dirty river falls into another river, then the other river also becomes dirty. When you are angry with someone, you are throwing your dirt at him. Then he will also throw his at you and this will become a mutual dirtying process.

In meditation you are throwing yourself into the cosmos to be purified. All the energy that you throw is purified in the cosmos. The cosmos is so vast and so great an ocean you cannot make it dirty. In meditation we are not related with persons. In meditation we are related directly to the cosmos.

In the second step, we are throwing emotions out. It is a catharsis. In the third we are using a mantra: "*hoo*." It is a Sufi sound just like the Hindu sound om, but more useful for the modern man than om can be because om is a very delicate sound. When you say om, it never goes below the heart. It is not very violent; it is very nonviolent. Om is one of the most nonviolent sounds.

It was invented by and for a different type of people from you – for those who were very loving and nonviolent, for those who were simply natural, simple; for those who lived in nature, in villages; for those who were not educated, uneducated; for those who were simply human, not very cultivated and conditioned. They were animal-like – pure, simple, innocent. The om was invented for them. Even this much was enough to change them. Om is a very delicate hammer. It hits the heart very delicately. But it was enough for them because they had hearts. For you it will not do. You need a very violent hammer.

Sufis invented this second sound, *hoo*. This is part of *Allah-hoo*. Sufis repeat, "Allah! Allah!" and when you repeat it continuously, it becomes "*Allah-hoo! Allah-hoo! Allah-hoo! Allah-hoo!*" Then the beginning part is dropped, the Allah is dropped, and only *hoo* is retained. Then it becomes, "*Hoo! Hoo! Hoo!*" When you say *hoo* it goes directly to the sex center. It penetrates directly to the sex center; it hits the sex center.

This age is so sexual that you need a hammering on the sex energy. The heart is no longer there. If you are going to try om, you are knocking at a door which is vacant. No one lives there now. The center of gravity has shifted down to the sex center. Your center is not the heart. The heart can be the center when you are centered in love, but now you are centered in sex, not in love.

Psychologists say that love is nothing but the foreplay to sex. They are right – because they have no other specimen to study. They study you and then they come to conclude that love is nothing but foreplay – just creating a situation in which sex can happen, nothing else. So when sex has happened, love disappears. It is just like when you feel hungry you gravitate toward food and look at food with enchanted eyes. But when your hunger is satiated, you look away from the food. All the enchantment is lost.

So when you love your wife or your husband, the love is just the etiquette to enter into sex – because it will be too rude to start immediately. So it just acts like a lubricating agent. And when sex is satisfied, the husband moves to his own side of the bed and goes to sleep. Finished! – all the enchantment is gone. It will come again only when he feels that type of hunger. Psychologists say that love is nothing but foreplay – just a mannerism. And they are right, because they don't know any other type of man.

Om was invented, discovered, for a different type: for those who were in love. Not that they never had sex: they had it; otherwise you would not be here. They were having sex, but the basic difference in quality is this: they were centered in love and their sex was but an expression of it, nothing else. Love was basic and sex was just one of the many expressions of it – the deepest expression, but an expression of love anyway. They loved first and then sex happened. It was not cerebral, it was not planned.

If you want to use the contemporary jargon, then I can say that sex was nothing but afterplay. The psychologists say love is nothing but foreplay, but I say that then sex was nothing but afterplay – just to finish the game. It was the peak, but it was not the center. Love was the center. Then the heart functioned in a different way, vibrated in a different way. Then om was enough to work with. Om can help a person who is very loving and who has a heart; otherwise, it cannot help him.

Hoo is the sound for this age. It will hit you directly at the sex center. If you really hit loudly with "*Hoo! Hoo! Hoo!*" you will feel a subtle hammering inside. And sex energy can move in two ways: it can move outward and it can move inward.

When you feel attracted to a woman or to a man, the energy has started moving outward. Really, a woman or a man – a person of the opposite sex – is hitting you from without. And this is literally true. When you feel that some woman is attracting you, if you can become alert and observing you will feel a subtle hit at your sex center. The feminine energy, or if you are a woman, the masculine energy hits you on that center. The same hit will be felt when you shout *hoo*, but from within. And if you go on hammering the sex center from within, an opening is created and the energy starts to flow inward and upward.

Once you know how to make this energy flow upward and withinward, you will reach to higher orgasms, higher peaks of ecstasy, than you can ever reach with any woman or any man. An inner meeting will have started.

The first step is to change your *prana*, your breathing pattern. The second stage is to throw out your emotions, the suppressed part of your mind – a catharsis. And the third is to hit your life energy to move upward. And when the energy starts moving upward, then you are not to do anything, you are simply to lie down as if dead.

There is to be no diversion there. The energy simply moves upward and you are not to do anything. That's why I go on emphasizing not to move. After the third step when I say "Stop!" stop completely. Don't do anything at all because anything can become a diversion and you miss the point. Anything, just a cough or a sneeze, and you may miss the whole thing because the mind has become diverted and the flow will stop immediately because your attention has moved.

Don't do anything. You are not going to die. Even if the sneeze is coming and you don't sneeze for ten minutes, you will not die. If you feel like coughing, if you feel an irritation in the throat and you don't do anything, you are not going to die. Don't be afraid: no one has ever died. Remain dead as far as the body is concerned so that the energy can move in one flow.

When the energy moves upward you become more and more silent. Silence is the by-product of energy moving upward and tension is the by-product of energy moving downward. You will be more and more in anxiety when energy moves downward; you will be more and more silent, quiet, calm and cool as energy moves upwards and withinwards. And these words *downwards* and *outwards* are synonymous, and *inwards* and *upwards* are synonymous. And when you have become silent, that energy is moving like a flood, it is passing through all the centers, all the chakras. When it passes through the chakras it cleanses them, it purifies them, it makes them dynamic, alive, and the flood goes upward, upward to the last chakra.

Sex is the first chakra, the first center, the lowest – and we exist at the lowest. That's why we know life only at its minimum. When the energy flows upward and reaches to the last chakra, to the *sahasrar*, energy is at its maximum, life is at its maximum. Then you will feel as if the whole cosmos has become silent: not even a single sound is there. Everything becomes absolutely silent when the energy comes to the last chakra.

You know the first chakra; it will be easy to understand through that. When the energy comes to the sex center, you become absolutely tense. The whole body is feverish, your every cell is in a fever. Your temperature goes high, your blood pressure goes high, your breathing becomes mad. Your whole body is in a temporary delirium – at the lowest.

Quite the opposite is the case at the last chakra. Your whole body becomes so cool, so silent, as if it has disappeared. You cannot feel it. You have become bodiless. And when you are silent, the whole existence is silent because the existence is nothing but a mirror: it reflects you. In thousands and thousands of mirrors, it reflects you. When you are silent the whole existence has become silent.

This is the fourth step and I will not say anything about the fifth. This is the door – absolute silence. Then you can enter the temple and you can know it, but I cannot say it. And if you come to know it, you will also not be able to say anything about it. It is inexpressible.

The last question:

> **Osho,**
> **In the morning and afternoon meditations I start off with vigorous movements, but somewhere in the middle – especially as the music and the surrounding screaming increase – a strange silence envelops me and the movements gradually die down. This silence deepens as the tempo of the music mounts and I feel as if I am a center of silence in the surrounding tempest. It feels welcome. Is this a reaction and hence to be discouraged? Should I willfully continue the vigorous movement and remain silent only at the end? Even at the end, when we are to celebrate, I enjoy remaining silent – and the more the music and screaming, the deeper the silence tends to be.**

This is the silence I was talking about just now. When the energy floods upwards, this silence will happen to you. Don't discourage it. This is what we are endeavoring for. Welcome it. This is the guest for which we are waiting. Remember, start vigorously. But if you feel that the movement and the noise are dying down by themselves and a deeper silence is descending upon you, and the storm all around you and the noise and the screaming and the maddening milieu don't affect your silence – rather, they deepen it – then you can be certain that this is real and you are not deceiving yourself. Then remain silent. And at the end this will happen. If you have become really silent, silence will be your celebration.

But it may be different with different individuals; it depends.

It depends on the type of individual. Someone would like to express his joy by dancing, someone by singing, or someone will simply weep: tears will flow down – not in agony, but in bliss. Someone else may remain just silent: this is his celebration.

So don't get worried about how to celebrate. The way it happens to you is your celebration. And if this type of silence comes to you, then welcome it, enjoy it. Cooperate with it so it deepens more and more.

Now get ready for the meditation.

...

CHAPTER 6

THE DISTINCTION BETWEEN PRAYER AND MEDITATION

What sight fails to see, but what sees sight – know thou that alone as brahman, and not this that people worship here.

What hearing fails to hear, but what hears hearing – know thou that alone as brahman, and not this that people worship here.

What prana does not reveal, but what reveals prana – know thou that alone as brahman, and not this that people worship here.

This century started with a very strange declaration. The declaration was made by Friedrich Nietzsche. He said, "God is dead, and hence man is totally free from now on." The declaration looked very strange the moment it was made, but it proved prophetic. And, by and by, it became the base of the modern mind.

Really, for the modern man, God is dead. It is not that God *is* dead: if God can be dead then nothing can be alive because by God we mean the essential, eternal life, the very ground of existence. But for the modern man God is dead. Or, we can say in another way that modern man is dead to God. The relationship has broken; the bridge is no longer there. Whether you believe or disbelieve makes no difference. Your belief is superficial; it doesn't go very deep.

Your disbelief is also superficial. When belief itself is superficial, how can disbelief go very deep? When theists are very superficial, how can atheists be very deep? When the yes itself has lost meaning, how can the no carry any meaning? All the meaning that atheism can carry comes from the depth of theism. When there are people who can say with their total being yes to God, only then does the no become meaningful. It is secondary.

God is dead, and with God even disbelief is dead. Belief is dead and with it disbelief is also dead. This century and the modern mind are, in a way, in a very peculiar situation. It has never been so before. There have been persons who were theists who really believed God exists. There were persons who were really atheists and who believed with the same intensity that God doesn't exist. But the modern mind is indifferent: it doesn't care. Whether God exists or not is irrelevant. No one is interested in proving it one way or the other.

Really, this is the meaning of Nietzsche's declaration that God is dead. You don't care even to deny him. You don't care even to argue against him. The bridge is simply broken. We have no relationship for or against. Why has this happened? Why has this phenomenon become so prominent in the modern mind – this indifference? We will have to seek the causes.

The first cause is we were always thinking of God as a person, and to think about God as a person is false, untrue, and that idea had to die. The idea that God is a person – controlling, managing, creating, maintaining – is false. God is not a person. The idea became so significant because of our minds. Whenever we think about something, either we can think of it as a thing or as a person. Only two alternatives are open: if something exists, then it must either be a thing or a person.

We cannot think, we cannot imagine, that things and persons are both manifestations of something deeper – hidden. The force becomes a thing; the same force becomes a person.

But the force itself is neither. God, taken as a person, is dead. The concept is dead, and the concept had to die because God cannot be proved as a person. And taken as a person, he doesn't solve any problem. Rather, on the contrary, he creates more – because if God is a person then why is there evil in the world? He must be allowing evil, he must be cooperating with it. Then he becomes an evil person.

André Gide has said somewhere, "It is difficult for me to conceive that God exists as good. But I can conceive that God exists as evil, as Satan, because there is so much evil in the world, so much suffering, so much pain, so much anguish." He cannot imagine that God is managing this whole affair. There must be something like a Devil in charge of it, a supreme Devil. God should be good; otherwise what type of God is he? Basic goodness must be there. But as the world appears, it seems God is devilish, not good: he is playing with evil, and somehow it appears that he is enjoying this whole suffering – torturing and enjoying it.

If God is a person, then there are two alternatives: either he will become the Devil or we will have to deny that he exists. And the second is better. God as a person had to die because it became impossible to conceive of him as good. But the concept was wrong; it was anthropocentric. We conceived of God as a supreme man, as a superman. God was conceived as a magnified person like ourselves. We only magnified man.

In the Bible it is said that God created man in his own image, but this is said by man and the real thing is just the reverse: man created God in his own image. The image created by man had to disappear. And it is good that type of God is dead, because with that conception removed, we can start a fresh inquiry into what godliness is.

The Upanishads are totally different. They never say God is a person; that's why they have relevance for the modern mind. They don't say that God is a person. They say God is the very ground of being, not a person. God is existence, not existential. This distinction is subtle, but try to understand.

A thing exists, a man exists, a woman exists, a person exists, but they can go out of existence. Whatsoever exists can become nonexistent – it is implied. Whatsoever exists can go out of existence. But existence itself cannot go out of existence. So we can say the chair exists, we can say the house exists, because they can go out of existence. But we cannot say that God exists.

God is existence – it is not that God exists; God is simply synonymous with existence. Really, to say God is, is to repeat. God means *is*. It is bad language to say God is, because *is*, the very isness, is God. God means *is* – isness. "God exists" is wrong. God is existence. Or God is just another term for existence. Existence never dies, never goes out of existence. Forms come and go, forms change. Nothing is permanent in the world of forms. So the Upanishads say *nama* and *rupa* – name and form – are the world, and that which is beyond name and form is God. But what is beyond name and form? Existence itself is beyond name and form.

The Upanishads think of God not as a person but as existence itself – as the very ground of existence. *Nama-rupa-ateet* – beyond name, beyond form. What is beyond name and beyond form? There are trees around this house; they exist. There are hills beyond those trees; they exist. You are here; you exist. In the trees, in the hills, in you, what is in common? The forms are not common: you have a different form, trees have a different form and the hills have an altogether different form. The names are not in common, the forms are not in common. What is in common? That common denominator will be God. You exist, trees exist, hills exist. Existence is in common: everything else is just accidental. The essential is that you exist, the trees exist and the hills exist. Existence is in common. That existence is God.

But the Upanishads never became very popular. They cannot become popular because for you, if God is existence, it loses all meaning – because how can you relate to existence? If God is a person, a father, a mother, a brother, a beloved, you can relate, you can think of relationship. But how to relate with existence?

Existence is so pure, so abstract. How to pray to it? What to call it? How to cry and weep before it? There is no one there.

Because of this human weakness, the Upanishads never became very popular. They are so true they cannot become very popular. To make truth popular is almost impossible because the human mind will not take it as it is. The human mind can only think, "If God is a person, then we can relate." That is why there is so much influence of *bhakti* cults – of devotional cults. One needs to pray, to be in devotion, to surrender, and a person is there so it becomes easy. You can pray, you can talk, you can communicate. Of course there is no one there, but for you it becomes easy. If you can imagine someone is listening to your prayer, it becomes easy for you to pray.

No one is listening. There is just abstract existence which has no ears to listen to you, no eyes to see you, no hands to touch you. It will be difficult for you to pray. Because of this difficulty, man always thinks that God is a person. Then everything becomes easy, but everything becomes wrong. It becomes easy on the one hand, but it goes wrong on the other hand.

That God is dead, and there is no possibility to revive him, no possibility to give blood and a heartbeat to him again. He is really dead. That God cannot be introduced again in the world. We have passed that moment. The human mind has become more mature; the childish attitude toward God cannot be there again. But it has become a hangover. We still go on thinking in terms which are dead. We still go on picturing him although all name and form has dissolved.

The Upanishads have relevance now. Five thousand years ago they were before their time. When this Kenopanishad was written, it was before its time; now the time has come and the Kenopanishad can be understood. The Upanishads can be understood because God as a person is no longer there. Now God can exist only as an impersonal existence.

But there will be difficulties because then you will have to change everything; your whole religion will have to be changed because the center has disappeared. For the old religion the center has disappeared, and a new religion will arise with a new center, a new religious attitude.

Hence my insistence is on meditation, not on prayer. Why? – because prayer needs a person, meditation needs no person there. You can meditate without there being a person to listen to you, because meditation is not a prayer; it is not addressed to anyone. It is just something you are doing without someone else being there. It is not a relationship.

If God is dead, then prayer has become meaningless. Only meditation can be meaningful. When you pray, you pray to someone. When you meditate, you simply meditate. When you pray, prayer is dual – dualistic: you are there and someone else is there to whom the prayer is addressed. Meditation is nondualistic – *advaita;* there is no one else. It is not a relationship at all. You are alone. And the more you enter this aloneness, the more you enter meditation.

Meditation means the capacity to be alone – and not only to be alone, but to enjoy the very aloneness; to become so alone that the other disappears completely – the other is not there. It is to become so alone that you start falling within yourself and the abyss opens, and you go on falling within yourself. When you fall within yourself, sooner or later the form will be lost, the name will be lost, because they exist only on the surface. The deeper you drown the more you come nearer to God – God as existence, not as a person.

So this is the distinction. If you are praying, God is outside you. That God is dead: now that outside God is no more. You can go on thinking about him, that he is somewhere there in heaven, in the skies, but you yourself will feel this is childish. There is no one there. That God has been escaping from every abode.

Once, in the days of the Rig Veda, God lived in the Himalayas, because the Himalayas were unapproachable. He used to live on Mount Kailash. But then men entered there, so he had to fly from there to where he could not be found. He made his abode on the stars, on the moon. But now man has reached the moon, and now he is not there. Sooner or later, man will be everywhere and God will be nowhere, because where can he hide? Nothing is unapproachable now, or everything will become approachable sooner or later. He has no place to hide. This concept cannot exist anymore. God as a person is not to be found anywhere. And it is good because now you can turn from prayer to meditation.

Really, prayer is childish. In a way it is neurotic, because you create a God in your imagination and then you start praying to it. And you can become so hallucinatory that you will start answering your prayer from the side of God. Then you really have gone mad. Then you are not in your senses. You can do it; many people have done it and they are known as great saints. They were ill, because with godliness only silence is possible. When you become silent you cannot relate to the other; you fall within yourself. God has now come to be a force within. It is not a person without; it is now a force within.

There is one beautiful story in the old Indian literature. It is said it happened that God created the world, and then he used to live on earth. It was his own creation, so he enjoyed it and lived with men and animals and trees. But soon he was in great difficulty, because the whole day he was disturbed – even in the night he was not allowed to sleep, because people would go on complaining: "This is wrong, that is wrong; why have you done this, why not do it this way?" Everyone would come to advise him and give suggestions.

He got so fed up that he called a council of his wise deities, wise counselors, and he asked them, "Find a place for me to hide from my own creation, because they will kill me or I will commit suicide. Every single moment they come to advise me, and they keep saying, 'Do this, do that; this is wrong, and this must not be done,' and their opinions are so contradictory that if I follow them the whole thing will become a mess."

So someone suggested, "Go to the Himalayas. Hide there on Gourishankar, Everest."

"But," God said, "you cannot see further ahead. Some day Tensing and Hillary will come there, and it is only a question of a few hours." For God it is only a question of a few hours, so he said, "This will not do."

Then someone suggested, "Go to the moon."

"But," he said, "you don't know. Only a few minutes more and men will be there."

Then one old, wise counselor came to him and said in his ear, "It will be better that you hide in man himself. There he will never try to enter."

And it is said that God accepted the suggestion, and from that moment he has not been troubled at all.

Now the moment has come to trouble him there. And only through meditation can you enter there, not through prayer, because prayer goes on believing that he lives somewhere – on Everest or on the moon; prayer goes on trying to locate him outside. Meditation completely washes away the whole concept that he is outside, or that he can be prayed to, or that he can be talked to, or that you can relate to him. No, you can simply move within yourself. And the deeper you move, the deeper you are moving into him. But this meeting will be in silence because he is not the other. He is *you* – he has been hiding as you.

If you can follow me, if you can understand the distinction between prayer and meditation – God as a person and God as existence – then it will be easy to follow this sutra:

> *What sight fails to see, but what sees sight – know thou that alone as brahman, and not this that people worship here.*

What sight fails to see… because if he was without, you could see him. Then the sight couldn't fail to see. Then ways and means could be found, and you could see him if he is without.

But he is not there. That's why the sutra says: *What sight fails to see...* You cannot see him; there is no way to see. Whatsoever you do you cannot see him. But people *have* seen him, so what to say about them? What to think of them? They have seen!

There have been Christian mystics who say they have seen Jesus standing before them. There have been Hindu devotees who say they have seen Krishna playing on his flute. There are other types of devotees all over the world. Someone sees him as Rama, someone sees him as Krishna, someone sees him as Jesus, someone as Mary – and they go on seeing.

This Upanishad says, *What sight fails to see...* Then they must have been imagining. Beautiful imaginings, very deeply satisfying! When you see Jesus standing before you, you are filled with a deep contentment, with deep satisfaction. But it is still a dream – beautiful, but a dream: a vision that you have created, a vision that you have desired, a vision that you have longed to see. And whatsoever you long to see you are capable of seeing, because the human mind can create any imaginary thing and give it reality. That is the capacity of the human mind. You can create a dream and you can make it real.

Of course, it will be real only for you, no one else. When you see Jesus you cannot make him a vision for others also. If your friends ask you, "Allow us also to see your vision," you cannot help. You cannot do anything because a dream has a peculiar quality: it cannot be shared. You can dream your dream, I can dream my dream – but you cannot enter into my dream, I cannot enter into your dream. A dream is the most private thing in the world. Everything can be made public, but dreams cannot be made public.

Howsoever you love your friend, your wife, your husband, howsoever intimate you are, you cannot enter into each other's dreams. That remains private. And same is the case with visions such as your seeing Jesus. No one else can share this experience. You will walk with him on the street, and everyone will see you walking alone; that is a private dream of your own.

I have heard one anecdote…

It happened once that a girl, a young girl, dreamed that a very beautiful prince came riding on a horse. He picked her up, kissed her deeply, and then rode away with her. The horse was running fast and the girl asked the prince, "Where are you leading me? Where are you taking me away to?"

The prince said, "It is your dream – you tell me. It is your dream, and you will have to tell me where I am leading you. You tell me!"

When you are seeing a vision of Jesus or Krishna, really you have only divided your own mind into two parts: one which has become the devotee and the other which has become the God. And if you ask Krishna, "Where are you leading me?" he will say to you, "It is your dream. You tell me."

But when I say it is a dream I am not condemning it, I am simply stating a fact. It is beautiful. You can enjoy it. There is nothing wrong – what is wrong with enjoying a dream, a beautiful dream? You can enjoy it. The problem arises if you start thinking it is reality. Then you are moving on dangerous terrain; then be aware. The mind can project anything.

Go to any madhouse and see. There you will see everyone talking to someone who is not present; everyone is talking and answering also. Every man there has become split. They go on seeing visions, they go on seeing projections. And those projections appear so real to them that we have to put them in madhouses because now they cannot be relied upon. They have lost contact with reality and are now in contact only with the dream world.

That is what a madman means: he has lost contact with reality. There is now no contact with fact; there is contact only with his own fiction. He lives in his own private world. He is not living with you in the real world, he is not a part of it and you cannot convince a madman that he is wrong. That is impossible. He may confuse you, but you cannot confuse him. And if you live a long time with a madman you may go mad yourself.

I have heard it happened once that an emperor became mad. He had a passion for playing chess, so some psychologist suggested that if a great chess player went on playing chess with him, this might relax his mind. He was still interested in chess. The whole world had become nonexistent; only chess had remained as a link to the real world. So the greatest champion was called, and that champion played chess with the mad emperor.

For one year this continued – he was playing chess with the mad emperor. And in the end it happened that the emperor became okay, but the chess player became mad. The emperor had traveled back to reality and the poor man who was playing chess with him had become mad.

If you live with a madman for one year, it will be difficult for you not to become mad. He will confuse you, but you cannot confuse him. He is beyond that. You cannot touch him, because he lives in his own private world. You cannot enter that world. It is impossible to enter into his private world. And you cannot convince him that he is wrong. Wrong and right, true and false, are the distinctions of the real world. In the dream world nothing is wrong, nothing is right. Whatsoever is, is right by its own right; just by being there it is right.

There are religious madnesses, there are secular madnesses. People can go mad in two ways – a secular way and a religious way. When you go mad in a religious way, people will respect you because they think you have achieved something. So don't go mad secularly – remember! Whenever you want to go mad don't go secularly, always try the religious way. Then people will respect you – but only in the East. It is now no longer so in the West: whatsoever the type, they will call you mad.

Whenever you are projecting a reality through your own mind, you are creating an illusion around yourself and then you can see it. But the Upanishads are so realistic. They say you cannot see: *What sight fails to see, but what sees sight*... You cannot see him through the eyes, but he can see your eyes because he is hidden behind you. Your eyes are just in front of him. He is you; he can see your eyes. But you cannot see him through the eyes. He is hidden behind all your senses. He can see your senses.

If you go deep into meditation you can see the inner core of your body, the inner wall. This has been a strange happening, because in the West it has been only three hundred years since medical science came to know about the inner structure of the body – and that too by dissection. By cutting the body, analyzing the body, dissecting the body, Western medical science came to know about the inner structure of it.

But for the East it has been a strange phenomenon. *Yogis* and *tantrikas* have always known it, and they never dissected a single body. They know how many *nadis*, how many nerves there are. They have completely determined how the whole inner body functions – but they never dissected a body, they were not surgeons. How did they come to know about it? They came to know it through a totally different way. They became so meditatively silent within that in that silence they became detached from the body. They became just an awareness inside. Then they started to see what is inside.

You know your body only from the outside. This is peculiar because you live inside and yet you have not observed it from the inside. It is as if you live in a house, and you go around and around it never coming to know it from within – how it looks from within. Your body has two surfaces. There is the outer surface which we are aware of because we can see it through the eyes, touch it with the hands. Then there is the inner surface of the body for which the eyes and the hands cannot be used.

If you can simply become alert and silent, detached, you will come to know the inner surface. Then you can see your eyes, and then you can hear your ears, and then you can touch your hands, and then you can know your body. But your body cannot know you.

This is what the sutra says:

> *What sight fails to see, but what sees sight – know thou that alone as brahman, and not this that people worship here.*

Except for your body, there is no temple to enter and search in. There is no mosque and no church where God abides – he abides in you. If you can enter and fall back upon your center of consciousness, know that alone to be the *brahman* – to be the ultimate, to be the real, to be the existence, and don't fall a victim to all that which is worshipped by people here.

People go on worshipping their own imaginations, people go on worshipping their own creations. Then fashions change, and when fashions change, imagination changes. Then you have to create new idols, new images, new places of worship. Hence, so many religions on the earth; otherwise, it is absurd. How can there be so many religions? If truth is one, then how can there be so many religions? Science is one, but why is religion not one? Why is science not Christian science, Hindu science, Mohammedan science? It is not possible, because science deals with fact. And if you deal with fact, then there can be only one science because fact is not a private thing. If you come upon a fact, then everyone has to accept it; there is no other way. You cannot go on denying it. And if you deny science, it will be at your own loss. If physics comes to know a law, then you cannot say, "I am an Indian and I cannot believe a man who is discovering a law in England. How can I follow an Englishman or a Chinese? We are of different nations; our cultures are different." You cannot say that. A physical law is a physical law. It makes no difference who discovers it. Once discovered it is universal.

Science is one, but why is religion not one? If it is the ultimate law it must also be one – more one than science, because science deals only with outer facts and religion deals with the inner truth. Why should it be so that there are three hundred religions? – how is it possible?

These three hundred religions exist because of fictions, dreams, not because of truth. They can exist because they are your creations, not your realizations. You create your own mode of worship, you create your own temple. Your religions are artistic creations, not scientific realizations – artistic creations! You paint your own religion and you like your paintings and you cannot think that any other's painting is better than your own. You like it, so you go on fighting that your painting is supreme; no one else can paint such a thing. All else is secondary. If you are a good man you can tolerate others' paintings. You can tolerate others with a patronizing attitude thinking, "They are a little stupid, foolish. Just wait. They will come to the right thing."

Christians go on waiting for Hindus to come to their senses and become Christians. Hindus go on waiting for these foolish Christians thinking that some day or other they will be converted, they will become Hindus. How can they escape the truth? And Jainas go on thinking that all the followers of Krishna and Christ are following untrue masters. How can they follow a false master for so long? Some day or other they will come to the right master, Mahavira. They will follow him. Everyone goes on thinking inside that he is right and everyone else is wrong.

This happens because for the masses, religion is imagination. They have their own imaginations; they have painted their own world. It is artistic. Nothing is wrong with it. You decorate your house in your own way; it is good. Who is there to say that it is wrong? It is no one's right. You decorate your house in your own way, but you don't fight about decoration. You don't say, "My decoration is the ultimate truth." Everyone is allowed to decorate his house in his own way.

But you are doing the same thing with your mind. You decorate it with your own images, worship, prayer, your own Bibles, your own Gitas. You go on decorating your inner world and then you become part of it and you live in it. This is illusory.

The sutra says: That alone is *brahman* which you realize when you transcend the senses, when you go behind the senses, when you can see the eyes, when you can hear the ears, when you can touch the hand from within.

> *...that alone know as brahman, and not this that people worship here.*
>
> *What hearing fails to hear, but what hears hearing – know thou that alone as brahman, and not this that people worship here.*
>
> *What prana does not reveal, but what reveals prana – know thou that alone as brahman, and not this that people worship here.*

All temples are false, all mosques are false, all churches are false. I am not condemning them; I am simply stating a fact – because they are creations of the imagination. I don't say destroy them, I say enjoy them – but don't think that this enjoyment is leading you toward the ultimate. Enjoy the creations. It is a good game; nothing is wrong with it. People are going to the movies, people are going to dance halls. Why should they not be allowed to enjoy a religious fantasy? In their temples, in their mosques, in their *gurudwaras*, they should be allowed – they are free. And it is better to have a religious fantasy than not to have anything. But don't think that you are realizing the *brahman* there; you cannot. It is not there, so you cannot do anything. You can enjoy yourself. You can enjoy your fantasy, your dream world.

If this is understood, then temples can exist. They are beautiful, artistic creations, but don't be lost in them. Go there, but don't be lost there. Go on remembering that whatsoever is worshipped by the people is not the real *brahman*, because the real *brahman* is hidden in the worshipper. This is the emphasis. When I worship, I am there and the object of worship is there. Where is *brahman*? – in the object of worship or in the worshipper? The emphasis of the Upanishads is: it is in the worshipper, not in the object of worship. The object of worship is secondary, it is created by the worshipper. The value of what you feel there is projected by you; it is given by you. It is a gift to the object from you.

You can put a round rock in your house and you can worship it as Shiva – it is a *shivalinga.* And the rock was lying in the street or just on a riverbed for millions of years. No one worshipped it; no one knew that this is Shiva. The river never cared; the animals passed by it, they never looked at it. And suddenly you transform the rock. Suddenly the rock becomes an object of worship, sacred, and now no one can touch it. And people were walking over it. Their feet touched it for centuries. Now you create a pedestal. You put the rock there. You say that this is a *shivalinga*, that this is the symbol of the god Shiva, and then you worship and you feel very good.

Nothing is bad about it. The rock is beautiful and if you enjoy, then enjoy. But remember, the rock is simply a rock and Shiva is your creation. You have projected him; you have made that rock into Shiva. The god is created by you; the rock is not even aware. And if the rock could see you it would laugh: "This man has gone mad. What are you doing worshipping me?" The worshipper creates the worshipped, the devotee creates the god.

The Upanishads say that there you will not find the real, you will only find the imagined. Move, rather, into the worshipper; penetrate into the worshipper. Forget the objects of worship and just try to know who this worshipper is – who is this who is worshipping? Who is this who is praying? Who is this who is going to the temple? And if you can find out who this is who worships, you have found the *brahman*.

I have heard that once it happened that a Zen master, Huang Po, was delivering a sermon. Suddenly a man stood up. The man said, "I have been listening and listening for years, and everyone says 'Know thyself,' but I don't follow the meaning. What do you mean by knowing thyself? Please try to explain it to me in simple terms. I am not a very learned man; I don't know the jargon.

Simply state the thing. What do you mean by 'Know thyself'?"

Huang Po said, "If you cannot follow the jargon, then I will not use language." He said to the people who were listening, "Make way, so that I can reach that man." Huang Po came down from his rostrum and walked to the man. The man became a little afraid, uneasy, because he never thought there was any need to come so near. Is this man going to attack? And Huang Po looked very aggressive – he was a man like a lion. So the man became afraid, and others also became uneasy about what was going to happen. And they knew about Huang Po. Sometimes he had slapped, sometimes he had thrown inquirers out of the door, and sometimes he had beaten… So what is going to happen? There was silence, dead silence; no one was breathing.

Then Huang Po came near. He took the collar of that man in his hand, and he said, "Close your eyes." So the man, just out of fear, closed his eyes. There was total silence. The man closed his eyes, and then Huang Po said, "Now know who is there." So the man stood there, the whole hall silent, no one was breathing, and Huang Po just standing there.

The man closed his eyes. He must really have been a simple, innocent man. He closed his eyes and he tried to find out who he is. He searched and searched and searched, and time went on.

Then Huang Po asked him, "Now open your eyes and tell me who you are."

The man opened his eyes. His eyes were totally different; the quality had changed. The man began smiling, then he bowed down to touch the feet of Huang Po and he said, "I never thought you would throw me upon myself, but I was thrown. Now don't ask me because I cannot say. I am not a learned man. But now I will never ask who I am. I have known it."

The Upanishads are trying to throw you to yourself. Forget the object of worship – just move within. And how can you move within? It is easy to forget the object of worship, but it is difficult to move within because there are objects still in the mind which go on clinging around you. Whenever you close your eyes, there is a world of imagination around you: dreams go on floating, images come up, thoughts move in a procession. Again you are in a world. The world of things is no longer there, but the world of thoughts is there. Unless this world of thoughts also ceases, you cannot know the worshipper.

And how will it cease if you go on cooperating with it, go on creating it? You cannot destroy the world of things because you never created it. Remember, you cannot destroy the world of things. How can you destroy the hills, the earth, the moon, the stars? You cannot destroy them because you never created them. But you can destroy the world of thoughts because you are the sole creator there. No one else has helped you. You alone have done the whole work.

Thoughts exist because you cooperate with them. Don't cooperate – this is the only technique. Be indifferent. Just look at them without loving them, without hating them, without condemning them, without appreciating them, without saying they are good, without saying they are bad. Don't say anything; don't take any attitude. Just be indifferent, an onlooker.

The clouds are floating in the sky; sit under a tree and just look. The clouds are floating; you don't take any attitude. You don't say, "Why are these clouds floating? They should not," or "They should." You don't take any attitude. You are simply an observer looking at the clouds passing in the sky.

In the same way look at the thoughts passing in the inner sky. Don't take any attitude. The moment you take an attitude you have started cooperating. The clouds in the sky will not disappear if you don't take any attitude, but the clouds in the inner sky *will* disappear. They only exist because of you. If you are indifferent, they simply go. They are invitees.

You may or may not know it or you may not know it – they are guests you have invited before. It was very long ago, and you have forgotten that you invited them. It may have been in some other life that you invited them. But nothing happens to your inner world uninvited. Each thought has been invited, and now it comes and you still give energy to it. You can give energy in two ways: if you are for it, you will give energy and if you are against it you will also give energy. In both ways the thought will feed upon it.

There is only one way to be disconnected, and that is to be indifferent. Buddha has called it *upeksha.* He said if you are indifferent to the process of thoughts, they will disappear.

Insist on being indifferent. Don't take any attitude, don't choose. Just remain a witness, and thoughts will disappear. And when they disappear, suddenly the worshipper is revealed: suddenly you are revealed to yourself. That revelation alone is *brahman*, and *...not this that people worship here.*

Now get ready for the meditation.

...

CHAPTER 7

MEDITATION AND THE INNER EYE

The first question:

> **Osho,**
> **In the morning you said that the brahman is not to be found through the worshipped, but in the worshipper himself. But the satgurus – the spiritual masters – have always been worshipped by their disciples as God. Please explain the significance of this.**

The masters have been worshipped as God, but this is only the beginning, not the end. The master is really a master if he makes his disciples ultimately free from all worship. But in the beginning it will not be so because in the beginning the relationship between the master and disciple is a love relationship, it is passionate. And whenever you are in love, the other appears to be divine.

Even in ordinary love the beloved appears to be divine. And the relationship between a disciple and a master is a very deep love relationship: you fall in love with the master – and nothing is wrong in that. And when you fall in love with the master you start worshipping. But the master takes it only as a game. If he is also interested in it and takes it seriously or significantly, then he is not a master at all. To him it is just a game – but a good game, because it can help the disciple.

How will it help the disciple? The more the disciple worships the master, the nearer he will come to him, the more intimate he will become, the more he will be surrendered, receptive, passive. And the more he is passive, receptive, surrendered, the more he can understand what the master is trying to do. When the intimacy comes to the last point, when only an inch separates, when just a minute separation remains, when the intimacy has become so deep that now the master can lead the disciple towards himself, then finally the master can help the disciple to become free from him.

In the beginning it is impossible. You will not understand if the master starts trying to free you from himself – you will not be able to understand. In the beginning you need someone to lean upon, in the beginning you need someone to depend upon; in the beginning you need someone you can be totally a slave to. This is an inner need. You cannot be made a master from the very beginning; the beginning will be a sort of spiritual dependence.

But if the master *also* feels happy that you depend on him, then he is not a master. He is harmful, he is dangerous; he doesn't know anything at all. If he also feels gratified, then this dependence is mutual. You depend on him, he depends on you. And if the master depends on you in any way, he cannot be of any help. But if he rejects you from the very beginning there will be no intimacy. If there is no intimacy, the final step cannot be taken.

When you trust your master so much that if he says, "Leave me," you can leave him, only then will you be able to be freed. If you can trust your master so much that if the master says, "Kill me," and you can kill him, only then will you be able to be freed – not before that. And this has to be brought about by and by. It is a long process. Sometimes the master goes on working with the disciple his whole life, and sometimes many lives.

The disciple is not aware, he doesn't know; he moves in darkness. But the master is leading him toward the point where the disciple will not be a disciple, but will become a master in his own right. When this need to depend has completely disappeared and you can exist alone, when you can be alone and there is no pain, no suffering, no anguish, when you can be alone and in ecstasy – when you become a master, only then are you free.

Really, when a disciple happens to be near a master, the master appears to be a god. For the disciple this is a fact because such love flows from the master, such high vibrations flow through the master. He becomes a source and just in his presence, just by his presence, you are uplifted. Just by being in touch you are different. Just by being near him you vibrate in a different dimension altogether.

So if the master appears to be a god it is a fact for the disciple and nothing is wrong in it. The master is a god. It is only wrong when the disciple is not aware that he himself is also a god. He is not wrong about the master, he is wrong about himself. And if the master says, "I am no god," he is closing the very possibility of saying to the disciple someday, "You are also a god." The master will not say it in the beginning because this has to be revealed.

It is a great step when the disciple has come to feel that the master is a god. Now the second step will be the disciple comes to feel he himself is a god and when this happens the whole existence will become godly. Then there is no need to even say that the master is God. It is irrelevant because the whole existence is God, so what is the use of calling the master "God"? But in the beginning it is significant.

Remember, for the disciple, truth has to be revealed in many steps. It cannot be revealed totally because you will not be capable of bearing it – it will be too destructive. It has to be revealed slowly, part by part. Only that much can be revealed to you which you can absorb, which can become your blood, your bones, your heart, which will not prove destructive.

Hence, many things will be said later on. The master will go on saying things. The more you become capable, the more he will say. And when really you have become so capable that now you can be independent, the last thing the master will say is, "I am a bondage to you. Now leave this last fetter; now leave this last slavery."

When Zarathustra was going away from his disciples, moving

to the hills to disappear forever, he said to his disciples, "Now the last message, and the last message is this: Beware of me; I am dangerous. You may become dependent on me and my whole effort is to make you independent. You may take my word as truth and my whole effort is to tell you that no word can be truth. Now beware of me."

The last message of any real master will be, "Beware of me" – but this cannot be said in the beginning. So masters have allowed their disciples to worship them. They must have been laughing within: they know what game is going on. The disciple is very serious; he thinks he is doing something very significant. But the master is just playing. It is just like when you are playing with your children, with their toys, and you also pretend to be serious: the master is really amidst children. They live on such different levels that if the master is to do something to be of any meaning he has to speak the language of the children. By and by he will drag the children toward a different world of a different language. This is going to be a long process.

But the Upanishads are saying the last things; they are the essence of all religion. Really, they are not for the beginners, they are for those who have left the beginning far behind; they are for those who have been struggling for a long time – meditating, searching, inquiring. Only then can the Upanishads be helpful. I am speaking on the Upanishads because you are meditating. Through your meditation you may have a glimpse which will make the Upanishads easy to be understood. But if you are not meditating then the Upanishads will just pass over your head, they will not mean anything. Only with a meditative heart will you be able to make a contact with the message.

The message of the Upanishads is the simplest, but the most supreme, the highest. The language used is very simple, the simplest possible, but the content – that which is said through that language – is the last word. It cannot be improved upon. Nothing can be said which the Upanishads have not already said. If even one Upanishad can be saved and all other religious scriptures are burned, nothing will be lost because all the seeds are there. Sow these seeds and you can reap the whole human religiousness through them. But you will be able to understand the Upanishads only if you are meditating deeply, moving with them into the heart, the innermost center, and not simply making an intellectual effort to understand.

Someone has said that this Upanishad seems repetitive; it goes on saying the same thing about this sense and that sense – and again about eyes and about ears. Why does it go on repeating? Is there some significance in it? Yes, there is, because the master is speaking to children. Your memory cannot be depended upon. The truth has to be repeated constantly. Still it is only a hope that it may be understood.

Buddha goes on repeating the same thing again and again. The Upanishads go on repeating the same thing again and again. They are talking to children – to children who are not attentive. They may miss many times. It is hoped that sometimes their attention may be caught, so things have to be repeated. You are not alert, that is why; otherwise the ultimate can be expressed even in a single word. And that too is too much. It can be expressed through silence. Not even a single word is needed to express it. But then you will not understand silence.

Someone came to the Zen mystic, Rinzai, and asked, "Tell me only that which is the very essential, because I am in a hurry and I am a big official in the government and I have no time. I was just passing by your hermitage and I thought it would be good to go in and inquire. This has been on my mind for a long time. But tell me in essence: what do you think religion is? – basically, foundationally."

Rinzai remained silent. The great official felt uneasy. He said, "Have you heard me or not? You seem to be deaf. I am asking you to give me a key word about religion."

Rinzai said, "I have given it. Now you can go."

The official said, "But I have not heard."

Rinzai said, "That which can be heard will not be essential. I have given you the key; silence is the key. Now go. You are in a hurry."

But now the officer started being interested. This master looked interesting. He said, "Please elaborate a little more. It is too short, it is too condensed, it is too seedlike. A little elaboration will be helpful."

Rinzai said, "But that will be a repetition, because all that can be said I have said. Now you are forcing me to repeat."

The officer said, "Let it be a repetition, but elaborate a little."

So Rinzai said, "*Dhyana* – meditation." It is again the same because meditation means silence. What else can it mean? Now it is a word. Before it was simple silence – that was more real. Now it is a word – *meditation*.

The man said, "It is still difficult for me. I am a worldly man. Explain it to me; it is still a puzzle."

Rinzai said, "Now if I elaborate more, it will be false. The truth was given at first; now it is just a repetition in words. Already it has become half false, but now if I elaborate more it will be totally false. So don't force me to commit a sin. Now you can go. You are in a hurry."

The Upanishads go on repeating for you because your attention is not reliable. Buddha has a very tedious way: he will repeat every sentence thrice – but only because of compassion. You may not have heard once, you may not have heard twice. The hope is that you may hear it the third time.

Jesus goes on using parables. I myself go on using parables, anecdotes, stories. Not that they are essential – they are a sheer wastage of time – but I use them just for you because children can understand stories better than anything else. It is hoped that if nothing is understood, at least the stories will be carried in the mind, and just around the story some flavor of the real thing may also be carried unconsciously. But you might not forget the story, and if you can remember the story, then just by association something else may also be carried in remembrance. Jesus used so many parables because no other way is possible when talking to children. Buddha also goes on telling stories.

It is because of you that the Upanishads repeat. There is no significance other than that. It can be said in a single sentence that senses will not lead to the ultimate, but the Upanishads go on saying that sight will not lead to it, hearing will not lead to it, the hands will not lead to it.

A single thing has to be repeated because of you and still you don't understand. This is the mystery: you hear it – and not only do you hear it, you feel it is a repetition. But no understanding happens yet. Try to understand; don't try to analyze. Don't try to think about the mind of the *rishi* – why he is repeating. Think about your own mind – *why* is he repeating? And be alert so that *rishis* won't need to repeat.

I have heard, once it happened…

A Zen priest gave his first sermon, and the next week he again repeated the same sermon, and the third week also he repeated the same sermon, word for word. The congregation became uneasy; it was too much. Religious sermons are by themselves boring, but then he repeated the second time, he repeated the third time, exactly the same thing in exactly the same words. So the congregation thought something had to be done.

A spokesman was appointed. He went to the priest and said, "What is the matter? Do you have only one sermon to preach?"

The priest said, "No, I have quite a few."

Then the spokesman said, "Then why have you been repeating the same sermon three times? We are fed up with it."

The priest said, "But you have not done anything about it yet. Unless you do something about it, I cannot go to the second. I have got quite a few, but what have you done about the first? I have preached it three times – what have you done about it? You have not done anything. And unless you do something about the first, I cannot move to the second."

It is said that the congregation, by and by, stopped coming. And it is said that the priest went on preaching the same sermon. Even to the vacant temple, when there was no one, he would preach the same sermon. Then people stopped coming anywhere near the temple because sometimes, just passing by, they would hear the same sermon being taught. Then people started to be afraid, scared of the man. They would not greet him in the street or anywhere. If they saw him they would just avoid him because he would stop and ask, "Have you done anything about the sermon?" He became like a haunting phenomenon around the village.

That is why the Upanishads go on repeating – because you have not done anything about the first thing. You have not done anything about the first so they repeat a second time, a third time. There are one hundred and eight Upanishads and they don't say anything new; they go on repeating the same thing again and again. One Upanishad is repeated one hundred and eight times. But still, nothing has been done about it. You need more Upanishads.

Don't think about the mind of the master. Think about your own mind.

The second question:

> **Osho,**
> **You said that through chaotic breathing you want to destroy our old wrong patterns – to rebuild us in a new dimension. Please explain how this rebuilding in a new dimension happens after the old has been destroyed.**

You have misunderstood me. The chaotic method is to destroy the old patterns, not to create a new one. It is not to create a pattern at all. Just the old pattern has to be destroyed. The method, all meditative methods, just destroy your conditioning – without conditioning you in any way because that will be simply a change of fetters, a change of prisons. The new prison may look a little better, but it is still a prison.

The unconditioned mind is the end – a mind which has no pattern around it. The old pattern has to be destroyed, and the new is not to be created because the new will become the old again. Nothing has to be created in its place; you are to be left alone without a pattern. But you have lived so long in patterns that you cannot conceive how you can live without a pattern. How can you live without conditioning? How can you live without discipline? How can you live without fetters? You have lived so long in slavery, in conditioning, that you cannot conceive of what freedom is. But you *can* live in freedom. Really, only then will you live.

A conditioned mind is not alive. For instance, people come to me and they say, "You don't give us any discipline: what to eat, what not to eat, what to do, what not to do. You simply give us meditation and leave us in chaos. You don't give us something to live by. You just push us into chaos without any discipline."

I don't give you any discipline because only those who are enemies to you can give you disciplines. I give you awareness, not discipline. Your awareness will give you spontaneous light about what to do and what not to do. Who can decide beforehand? And what is the need to decide it beforehand? When the moment arises, when the situation is there, whatsoever happens to you, you will be alert enough in your awareness to do what needs to be done.

You don't need any discipline if you are aware. Only people who are fast asleep need discipline because they don't know what to do. They need a pattern to follow. Their whole life becomes a misery because no pattern can be helpful in a changing life. Every pattern will become a prison because life is constantly changing. This moment one act may be good, the next moment it may become bad because the situation has changed. And you go on following a dead pattern; you never fit anywhere.

Look at your own lives: everyone is a misfit for life. Everyone is a misfit; no one fits anywhere. And the reason? – the pattern, the discipline, the conditioning. You carry it everywhere. Whatsoever the situation, you have a constant pattern around you. You will never fit. Life is changing, life is a flux; it is riverlike, it is never the same again. Not for a single moment is life the same. It goes on changing and you have a fixed pattern which doesn't change. You are unfit for life.

Everywhere in the world, human beings have become misfits. And when you feel that you are a misfit, you feel discarded, rejected – as if life is against you. Quite the reverse is the case: your conditioning is against life. Only an unconditioned mind can respond to a changing life – because it has no pattern. Life creates a situation: a wise man is alert; he behaves in a way which happens in that moment. That type of man will never regret but you will always regret. That type of man will never repent; you will always repent – whatsoever you do.

You love a girl: now the alternatives are whether to marry her or not. Whatsoever you do, you will repent. If you marry her, then for the whole of your life you will think the other alternative would have been better. If you don't marry, the same will happen: you will think that the other alternative was better. This happens because you have not been alert. Only an alert person can respond totally.

You can respond only in parts, fragments, and when you are responding it is a fragmentary response – there are other parts within you which are against it. Sooner or later they will take revenge. They will say, "We were saying not to do this." What does repentance mean? Repentance means you are divided. You do a thing and at that very moment something in you is against it. That part is watching you and that part is saying, "Don't do it. This is wrong." And another part goes on saying, "This is right. Do it." And you do it.

You will not fit because you can fit only when you are fluxlike, changing. A fixed entity cannot fit in a riverlike existence. You must be fluid. Only when you are liquid, fluid, flowing, changing, alert, aware, will you not repent. You will never feel guilty; you will never feel that something was better than what you did. Nothing can be better because you responded totally. That was all that could have been. Nothing else was possible.

My meditation technique is not to give you a new pattern; it is simply to drop the old pattern, to destroy it and leave you completely free without any imprisonment around you – without any prison. Of course, you will feel a difficulty because the prison was also a shelter. Now there will be rains and there will be no shelter, and the wind will come and there will be no shelter, and the sun will be there, hot and burning, and there will be no shelter, and you would like to hide somewhere. Your eyes have become so accustomed to darkness that in the light you will feel uneasy. But this is what will make you free. You will have to get the feel of life under the open skies. Once you know the freedom and the beauty of it, once you have become aware, once you have come out of the prison, the old habit, you will not ask for any pattern or any discipline.

And this doesn't mean that your life will become a chaos – no. Your life will be the only ordered life possible. The life that you are leading is a chaos. It only seems to be ordered on the surface but behind it, underneath, there is disorder and turmoil. Only on the surface have you created the appearance of order. Look within yourself: there is disorder. A truly ordered life will be disordered; a disciplined life will be chaotic within. This looks paradoxical, but this is so, this is the truth. Only an alert life will have an order – not forced but spontaneous, alive. The order will go on changing with life. It must.

A spontaneous life is just like your eyes. Do you know that your eyes go on changing continuously? And when they stop changing, then you need some technical help. When I am looking at you and you are ten feet away from me, my eyes have one kind of focus. When I start looking at the hills, which are faraway, my eyes immediately change. The lenses of the eyes change immediately. Only then can I see the hills. When I look at the moon, my eyes change immediately.

You come into the house, it is dark; your eyes change. You go out of the house, it is light; your eyes change. And when your eyes become fixed, they are ill. They must be fluxlike; only then are you capable of seeing. The more fluxlike the eyes, the more liquid they are, without any pattern, just changing with the situation, the more alert your consciousness will be.

Meditation will give you an inner eye which will be constantly changing, constantly aware of the new situation, constantly responding. But the response will come from your total being, not from a pattern. The response will come from you, not from conditioning.

Now, whatsoever you do, howsoever you react, it comes from your conditioning. If you have been born in a Jaina family, then you feel revolted, you feel nausea just looking at nonvegetarian food. That nausea is not coming from you; that nausea is coming from the conditioning. It never comes to a Mohammedan; it never comes to a Christian – not that you are more nonviolent and others are violent: it is just a conditioning from the childhood, and that conditioning starts functioning the moment you see meat.

Even the word *meat* and you will feel a subtle nausea. Just a word and the nausea will be felt. Is it coming from you? If it is coming from you, then your whole life will be a life of love. But it is not. You are as cruel as anybody else. The Jaina is as cruel as the Mohammedan and sometimes even more. He has to be crueler because he cannot express his violence through food. It has to be expressed from somewhere else.

When you eat, you express your violence. If you eat meat, your violence moves through food – it is released. This is a common observation: people who are non-vegetarians are more loving than the vegetarians – more loving, kinder than the vegetarians. Why? This should not be so. Their violence is released through food.

In your body, your teeth are the most violent part. Violent people eat more food than nonviolent people. Just crushing the food with the teeth gives release to violence, anger and hate. Persons who are eating meat and other such things have a natural outlet for their violence. I am not saying go and eat meat, but if you don't eat meat simply by conditioning, if you don't eat nonvegetarian food, don't think that you have become loving and nonviolent. Your violence will find other ways, more subtle ways. Your relationships will become crueler, poisoned.

But it is totally different if you are really not behaving according to a pattern. If love has arisen in your heart; if by yourself you have become alert to the cruelty of eating animal food – not by any tradition, not by birth, not by any teaching, not by any scriptures, but by your own meditative experience – if you have become alert that eating meat is stupid, that to kill an animal for food is stupid, idiotic; if you have become alert of this fact by your own meditation, then your whole life will be nonviolent and loving. Then you will not be obsessed with food; it will be an alive phenomenon and you will not be mad after any fixed rules. There will be no fixed rules, really; there will be only a constantly alive awareness.

So I am not going to create a new pattern for you. I am a destroyer. I am not going to create anything, really. I am just going to destroy, because there is no need to create. You are already there behind the structure. If the structure is destroyed, you will be freed. If the structure which binds you is no longer there, *you* will be there. You are not to be created; you are already there. Only the walls of the prison have to be destroyed and you will be under the open sky.

You have misunderstood me. I told you this chaotic meditation is to destroy your conditioning, your slavery, your mind, your ego – in a deep sense, *you.* It has to destroy and then the new will be born. I am not saying I will create it. Nobody can create it. And there is no need: it is already the case. It is there. Only the shell has to be broken and it will come out.

All religion is destructive in this sense. The society is constructive, religion is destructive. Society constructs the conditioning. Society makes you a Hindu or a Christian or a Jaina. Society never allows you to be yourself. Because society is an organization, it gives you a pattern,. The society wants you to fit into that organization according to its own rules. The society doesn't want *you;* the society only wants your efficiency. You are not the point, you are not the target. You must behave like a mechanical thing. The more mechanical you are, the more society will appreciate you because you will be less dangerous.

No machine can be dangerous. It never goes out of the way: it never disobeys, it never rebels, it is not revolutionary. No machine is revolutionary; it cannot be. All machines are orthodox: they obey, they follow. Society tries to change you into a mechanical thing. Then you are more efficient, reliable, responsible – less dangerous. There is no fear, no danger; you can be relied upon.

The society creates a mechanical device around you: that is the conditioning. And it allows you only certain outlets and closes certain things completely. It chooses some fragments from you and approves them, then rejects all else. It says that only a part of you is good and the other parts are bad, so deny those bad parts. Society doesn't accept you as a whole, as a unity; it accepts only certain parts. Hence, the conditioning.

Religion is always destructive; in a way, religion is always antisocial. But society is very cunning. It tries to convert religion also into its managerial system. It wants to make religion also a part of it.

Jesus is rebellious, the church is not. Jesus is against society – has to be, because he is trying to destroy the mechanical part and he is trying to free your spontaneity. He is bound to be against the society; the society will crucify him. But you cannot destroy Jesus just by crucifying him. Really, if you want to destroy Jesus, crucifixion will be of no help. You will have to organize a church around Jesus; only then will he be destroyed.

It is said that once it happened that the Devil was very much disturbed because one man had achieved enlightenment on earth. He called his advisers and he asked them, "What to do now? One man has again achieved truth, he has become enlightened, and our whole profession is now in danger. What to do? How to prevent people from going to this man?"

The oldest follower of the Devil said, "Don't be disturbed. We should go and we should organize a church around him. Don't worry. Then the church will become the prevention, then people will not be able to come to him directly. The church will be in between, and whatsoever he says will not be heard by the people directly. The church will first interpret it, and through interpretation you can destroy anything."

Truth can be destroyed most easily if you order it, organize it. When religion becomes a sect, it becomes a part of society. Whenever religion is alive and not a sect, it is against society. Jesus is against society, Mahavira is against society, Buddha is against society. But Buddhism, Jainism, Christianity are parts of society. They are no longer religions. Religion has to be rebellious. And this is the rebellion: religion tries to destroy the mechanicalness because the mechanicalness is your hell. Spontaneity is your heaven; mechanicalness is your hell.

I am not going to give you any new pattern – new or old. I am simply going to destroy the pattern and leave you alone to live without a pattern. A life without a pattern is a religious life. A life without any forced order is a religious life. A life without any discipline, but with inner awareness, is a religious life.

The last question:

Osho,
The Kenopanishad told us in the beginning that nothing is to be denied and that there should be total acceptance. But in the morning you said that prayer, idol worship, temples, churches, are all based on falsities –

on mental projection. This seems to be a denial.

It is not. It is simply stating a fact. To say that a dream is a dream is not to deny it. To say that a projection is a projection is not to deny it. To say that a false thing is a false thing is just to state a fact. It is not to deny it. Total acceptance doesn't mean that the falsity has to be stated as true, that the dream has to be called reality.

Total acceptance means that whatsoever is, is accepted. If the worshipper's mind is projecting deities, divine beings, this has to be accepted. It is a fact that worshippers have been doing that. And you are not told to go and try to destroy their projections; you are not told to go and destroy their idols and their temples. If you understand, the very understanding will change you. You will not create those projections. And if you want to create them, then you will know that these are projections and you can enjoy them as such.

It is reported of Naropa, one of the greatest Tibetan mystics ever born... He was a very absurd personality. I say absurd because he would do things no one would expect of a master. He was found in a pub drinking.

Someone said, "Naropa, what are you doing? You are enlightened, you have achieved the goal, and you are drinking?"

Naropa said, "This is a game. And when it is a game, I don't care this way or that. Once I have come to know that I am the eternal within, why be afraid of this alcohol? Why be afraid?"

I say absurd personality – but he is saying that this is alcohol and that whatsoever is created by alcohol is a dream. He is not saying this is reality; he is saying this is a dream. But he said, "I am not obsessed for or against. It happened that a friend invited me and I didn't want to say no. A friend invited me. For him this is real, for me this is a dream. But this is a dream for me, not for him. Why be bothered? It will be difficult for him."

I will tell you something else which will be nearer the point – less absurd.

It happened that Kabir's family became very much disturbed. The family was poor and whosoever would come to Kabir's house, Kabir would invite him for food. And at least two hundred people would come every day for his *darshan*, to see him. And he would go on inviting everybody for food.

Then his son, Kamaal, said one night, "Stop all this! We are poor. We have been begging, we have borrowed; now no one is going to give anything. What are you doing? You will reduce us to being thieves."

Kamaal was very angry. But Kabir laughed and said, "Why didn't you think of it before? Be a thief. This is a good idea!"

But Kamaal was also his son, Kabir's son, so he looked at him: Kabir, a mystic, saying this – to be a thief? He must not be in his senses, or he doesn't understand what he is saying. But Kamaal said, "Okay, if you say so, then I will go. I will steal, but you will have to come with me." Kamaal was thinking that now Kabir would come to his senses. Kabir going to steal…?

Kabir stood up and said, "Okay, I am coming."

Kamaal carried the whole thing to the very extreme. He was thinking that somewhere at the last moment Kabir would laugh and say, "I was just joking." But no. Kamaal entered a house, pulled out some things from the owner's treasure, brought them out, and Kabir was ready, waiting there. This was the point of no return; now there was no further possibility to change things. Now Kamaal asked, "What is to be done? Shall we take these things to the house?"

Kabir said, "Okay, but first you must go back, awaken the people of that house, and tell them."

Kamaal asked, "What way of stealing is this?"

Kabir said, "At least they should be told; otherwise they will be unnecessarily worried."

Those who write about Kabir have stopped narrating this story in their books because it is absurd. Kabir approving stealing? But what was the matter? In the morning Kamaal asked, "What is the matter now? Tell me the whole thing. You are in favor of stealing?"

Kabir said, "Everything belongs to God. No one else is the owner."

Look at this mind. For this mind everything is acceptable. There is total acceptance. Even stealing is accepted. But he says, "Go and tell the people so that they are not unnecessarily worried."

Kamaal said to him, "But they will think we are thieves."

Kabir said, "They are right. We are!"

Kamaal said, "But then the next day all your respect will go to the dust. No one will honor you."

Kabir said, "That's right! Why should they honor thieves?"

Total acceptance means not denying anything. When you accept, you accept with conditions. You say, "Okay, I will do this, if that is not going to happen. I can steal if God is not going to throw me into hell. I can steal if there is no sin in it. I can steal if people are not going to dishonor me for it." But what people will do has to be accepted also. Total acceptance is the most alive way of life. But then everything is accepted; whatsoever happens as a consequence is accepted. There is no denial on any point. That is the last, the ultimate way of life. Really, that is what a sannyasin should be. What a sannyasin should have is total acceptance.

But when we say that you can create dreams, we are not denying; we are simply stating a fact. If you like, you can create dreams. I can help you to create them easily. But remember, they are only dreams.

The problem arises when a dream becomes a reality. You can play with your Krishna, you can dance with him; nothing is wrong with it. Dance in itself is so good. What is wrong about it? You are not doing any harm to anybody playing with your Krishna, dancing. Dance and play! It will be good for you. But remember that this is not real. It is a projected thing; you have created it.

If you can remember this you will play the game, but you will never be identified with it. You will go on being aware that this is a game. A game is a game if you are not identified. If you are identified, it has become serious, it has become a problem. Now you will be obsessed.

Now get ready for the meditation.

...

CHAPTER 8

BEGINNINGLESS BEGINNING, ENDLESS END

If you think that you know brahman well, then you know little indeed, for the form of brahman that you see as conditional in living beings and gods is but a trifle. Therefore, you should inquire further about brahman.

I don't think I know it well, nor do I think that I don't know it, yet I know too. He amongst us knows it who knows that it is other than the unknown and the known.

Knowledge of the ultimate is paradoxical for many reasons. One, the very claim that one knows becomes a hindrance because the moment you say, "I know," you are not only emphasizing knowledge; you are also emphasizing "I" – and the "I" is the barrier. The ego is the subtlest barrier, but also the strongest. So when someone says, "I know," the "I" destroys the knowledge. The "I" cannot know him because he can be known only when you have disappeared completely. When you are not, only then he is. This is the first problem.

It is said that the oracle at Delphi declared Socrates to be the wisest man alive. Those who heard it went to Socrates and said, "The oracle has declared you to be the wisest man on earth."

Socrates is reported to have laughed and said, "They should

have done it earlier – then I would have been happy. Now it is too late. Go back and tell the oracle that now I am the most ignorant man on earth.

"When I was younger and full of ego, I was also of the same opinion as the oracle – that I knew – because the 'I' was so strong, it couldn't conceive that the ultimate mystery could not be known. The 'I' was so strong that I could not think that it was possible for me to be ignorant. Everything that was, was conceived by me as known, or at least as knowable. But as I grew in knowledge, in understanding, I became more and more aware of my ignorance. So now go back and tell the oracle that Socrates himself says that he is simply ignorant, that he doesn't know anything."

The people returned. They said to the oracle, "Socrates refuses to accept what you say, and when he himself refuses it means something. He says he is the most ignorant man."

The oracle laughed and said, "That is why I have declared him to be the wisest man – because only the wisest can know that he is ignorant."

This is the paradox: those who are ignorant always think they know. This is part of ignorance. To think that you know is part of ignorance; it comes from ignorance. If you are ignorant you will think that you know much. The more ignorant, the more you will think that you know. Ignorance is filled with knowledge. Ignorance, really, lives on knowledge, feeds on knowledge. The wiser you become, the more aware and understanding, the more you will feel how ignorant you are. And a moment comes when you feel that you don't know anything. Simply, you are ignorant. All the burden of knowledge is thrown away. There is no heaviness of knowledge on you. You have become so weightless that you can fly.

Knowledge is a burden. When you feel that you don't know, ego disappears; it cannot exist. It can exist only with knowledge. Really, whenever you claim knowledge, it is a claim by the ego:

"*I* know." The emphasis is not on knowing, the emphasis is on I. When you say, "I don't know," the emphasis is not on ignorance; now the emphasis is on egolessness. The moment you say, "I don't know," where are *you*, where is the I? It is no longer there. Now it is simply a word to be used. Now there exists nothing corresponding to it within you. This is the first problem.

One Christian mystic, Tertullian, has divided humanity into two classes. He said that one part of humanity is in one class – that of ignorant knowers; and the other class is of those who are knowing ignorants. The whole humanity is divided in two. There is an ignorance which knows, and there is a knowledge which is ignorance. If you claim knowledge you are ignorant. If you accept ignorance you become knowing, because in ignorance the I cannot exist. And when the I is not there the door is open: you can look at reality directly. You are the only barrier. When you are not there the barrier is not there; this is the first thing.

The second thing: the ultimate is not only the unknown; the *brahman* is not only the unknown – it is unknowable also. You can know it, but you cannot know it totally. That creates again a new puzzle. You can know it, but you cannot know it totally because you are just a part of it and the part cannot know the whole. How can the part know the whole totally? But also the part cannot be totally ignorant either because it belongs to the whole, it is part of the whole. So it knows in a way, it feels in a way, it understands in a way, but it cannot comprehend the total because the total is so vast.

A river dropping into the ocean comes to know the ocean; it feels the ocean, it lives in the ocean, it merges in it, but it cannot merge into the total ocean. It cannot spread to the total ocean; it cannot know the total ocean. It only knows a part of it.

When your consciousness falls like a river into the *brahman*, into the ocean of the ultimate, you will know him, but you will not know him in his totality. You cannot; there is no possibility. So the *brahman* is unknowable because the whole remains unknowable to the part; hence, the problem when someone comes to know. Someone becomes ignorant, egoless, and comes to know; then, too, he cannot say, "I have known the whole."

He cannot say, "I have not known," and he cannot say, "I have known." He can say, "In a way I know, in a way I don't know. In a sense I have entered into him and he has entered into me, but I am just a drop and he is the ocean. I know him, but still the total remains a mystery." Because of this, those who have known through their ignorance, through dropping themselves, are also in a difficulty over what to say about it. They cannot deny the knowledge, they cannot declare the knowledge. This has to be so. Because of this many have remained silent.

Buddha would never answer any question about the *brahman*. Wheresoever he would move, his disciples would spread the word: "Don't ask anything about the ultimate because Buddha is not going to answer anything about it."

Someone asked Buddha, "Why don't you answer?"

Buddha said, "If I answer, it is going to be false in some way or other. If I say, 'I know,' it is wrong – because how can a drop know the ocean? If I say, 'I don't know,' it is wrong, because the drop knows the ocean. The drop is just an atomic part of the ocean. The whole ocean is in the drop also. Really, knowing a drop of water totally, you know the ocean, because nothing else is there. The drop contains everything, but still it is a drop. So if I say, 'I know,' it will be wrong, because I am only a drop. If I say, 'I don't know,' it will be wrong, because I know. I am also an ocean – a minute ocean. So it is better to keep silent."

But even silence can be misunderstood, and it was misunderstood. People who were against Buddha started saying, "He is not saying because he doesn't know. He is silent because he has not yet entered the *brahman*; otherwise he should say." Look at the difficulty: if he says, "I know," then there will be difficulty; if he says, "I don't know," then there will be difficulty. If he keeps quiet, then people will misunderstand.

The ultimate cannot be conveyed in any way; whether you are silent or saying something, it remains unconveyed. It cannot be transferred; it remains untransferred. It cannot be communicated, it is beyond communication.

A third difficulty comes and makes it a problem again and that is: *brahman* means the ground, the source of everything. The source must remain a mystery; it cannot be decoded. Who will decode it? No one can stand outside it. For decoding you need someone who can be an observer – separate, neutral, looking at a thing from a distance. We cannot be at a distance from the ultimate. We are in it just like fishes swimming in a pool. Those fishes cannot stand aside, cannot observe the pool.

Kabir used to say that once a fish heard two scholars talking on the bank of a river, talking about what the ocean is. The fish became very much mystified; she started inquiring. It became an obsession for her – what the ocean was. She inquired from elders, and they said that they had also heard about it, but they didn't know what it was. They had never seen it – and they all lived in the ocean. But how can you see a thing if you live in it? They were born in it, but how can you know a thing if you are born in it? You are so much a part of it and it is so much a part of you that there is no distance, so you cannot know. Then the inquiring fish went on inquiring, moved on inquiring. No one could answer her, but everyone said that they had heard that there was an ocean.

Kabir says that this is the situation of man who goes on inquiring what God is, where God is, who God is. We are in him; hence, the difficulty. For a fish it is possible to jump out of the river or out of the ocean. Even for a few seconds the fish can jump out of the ocean and be on the bank and look at the ocean. But for man there is no such possibility. You cannot jump out of the *brahman*; there is no bank beside it. You cannot jump out; there is nothing out of it. Everything is in and nothing is out. That is what is meant by infinity.

You cannot go out of existence, or can you? – because the moment you go out of existence you are no more. You cannot go out – all is existence, everywhere is existence. Wherever you go existence is there, so no distance is possible. You cannot become an observer; you cannot look at *brahman*. The mystery cannot be decoded. The mystery is so basic, so ultimate, so universal, and you are just a fish in the ocean. The *brahman* cannot be known the way we know other facts because other facts can be observed by us.

Science decodes; science goes on decoding. But science can decode because science never takes on the ultimate question. It only takes on non-ultimate questions. It can come to know what hydrogen is; it can come to know what atomic structure is. You can observe. You can go into a lab and you can observe and you can penetrate into the mystery of things because no thing is ultimate. But how can you observe and experiment with the *brahman*? Where, how, is it to be penetrated? Wherever you go you are part of it, in it. The mystery cannot be decoded. The *brahman* remains mysterious – and if the *brahman* is an ultimate mystery, how can you say you have known? You can know something only when it is demystified. The moment you know, there is no mystery. That is why science is a mystery killer. And the more science grows and the more people are trained scientifically, the more they lose contact with mystery.

Science is a sure mystery killer, it goes on killing mystery. That is why the world has become so poor while science has made it so rich. The world was never so rich and so poor before. Everything has become richer. You are living in better houses, wearing better clothes, eating better food. Everything has become richer. Even kings would become jealous if they could be revived from the past. Even Ashoka and Akbar would feel poor before you because an Ashoka cannot have the shirt you are wearing, the bathroom you are using. These would be luxuries even for Akbar.

The world has become richer as far as things are concerned, but man has become poorer and poorer because there is no mystery. Life has become non-mysterious, dead. Only a mystery can be alive.

Look at children – they are more alive. Why? Why is an old man not so alive? It is not only a question of aging. The basic question is deeper. The child is alive because the child is living in a mystery: everything is mysterious for him – everything. The seed is sprouting. The child looks at the seed sprouting: it is so mysterious that he cannot believe that it can happen. A bird has alighted on a branch and is singing: it is so mysterious. The clouds moving in the sky and the rain falling, everything is mysterious. The child lives in a wonderland; hence, the aliveness – because everything is a challenge. Life is not flat, life has nooks and corners that are undiscovered. The child goes on jumping, inquiring, looking at everything. Everything is so mysterious because the child is ignorant.

Back in the days of the Upanishads everyone was so alive, everything was mysterious. There was wonder, and when there is wonder you are alive because there is a challenge to penetrate the mystery outside. Science goes on killing mystery; it goes on explaining everything. Whatsoever you do, there is an explanation – and once explained the mystery is gone, everything becomes flat. With nothing to discover there is no challenge. And when there is no challenge, life subsides; it cannot dance, it cannot explode. There is nothing.

For these last three centuries, humanity has been made so poor – unimaginably poor. Science has explained the world of things and psychology has tried to explain the world of the mind. If you fall in love it is a mystery. But go and ask Freud and he will explain the whole thing. He will say that this is nothing, just hormones in the body, and "Don't get too serious about it. It is just chemicals working – just particular hormones forcing you to be in love. This is nothing to get worked up about. Those hormones can be taken out of your body and the love will disappear, or an injection of those hormones can be given and you will fall in a deeper love. So it is hormonal. Don't get too much into it." And once explained, the mystery of love is gone.

Now they are teaching sex all over the world. It is good in a way, but only as an antidote. Because of the Victorian puritanic teachings it is good, as a reaction, to teach children about sex. But on a deeper layer it is very dangerous because once explained, the mystery of sex is lost. And this is happening particularly in America where now everything is known about sex. People are becoming disinterested in it. They will get disinterested when everything is known.

Masters and Johnson, two experimenters, have penetrated the mystery of sex through electronic devices. While a couple is making love, electronic devices inside the vagina go on recording what is happening; a graph is made. While a couple is making love, devices go on working which are recording what is happening to the blood, to the breathing, to the body, to the hormones. Then the whole mystery is clear, and then they say, "This is just a mechanical thing. It happens because of these causes."

Once the mystery about sex is gone your life will be just boring. While making love to your wife or to your beloved, you will know what is going on. The blood pressure is changing, the hormones are running: you will know everything. And then there is no need, really, to be involved in love, because love can be done by devices also.

Masters and Johnson have devised electronic penises and vaginas. And now they say an electronic penis, an electrical device, can give a deeper orgasm than any man can because it goes on vibrating – and it is only a question of vibration. Man has limited energy, but an electronic device has unlimited energy. Turn it on and it goes on vibrating. It can give a deeper orgasm to the woman. It can give multiple orgasms. And once a woman knows that an electric penis can give such a height of pleasure, then all lovers will be just pale before it. But this is dangerous. It is a penetration into a very dangerous terrain – once the mystery is known, the romance is gone.

Science has tried to demystify life in every way. I am emphasizing this fact so that, because of this background, you can understand the meaning of religion. Religion is to mystify life and science is to demystify it. Religion says that the mystery is so ultimate, nothing can be known about it. Whatsoever you know is just temporary and whatsoever you know is just shifting the problem. It is never solved; you only shift it a step back. Nothing is solved. All your explanations are just artificial – because the ultimate remains hidden and no explanation explains it. The why cannot be answered even if you answer the how.

For example, science can say that there is no mystery in water: it is just that hydrogen atoms and oxygen atoms meet and water is created; H_2O, and the mystery is solved. Two atoms of hydrogen and one atom of oxygen and the mystery is solved, but religion says this is only an answer to the how; the why is unexplained. Why do two atoms of hydrogen and one atom of oxygen make water – why? We have come to know how – if we arrange two atoms of hydrogen and one atom of oxygen, water will be created. We know the how, but the why remains unexplained and the why is the *brahman*.

Why is it happening that two atoms of hydrogen and one atom of oxygen make water? Why not three atoms of hydrogen? Why not four atoms of hydrogen and one atom of oxygen? Science says we are not interested in the why, we are only interested in the how. Religion says how is a superficial inquiry, because unless you answer the why, the how can be used but the mystery remains; the mystery is not destroyed. The why of existence is the *brahman*.

So science ultimately is reduced to technology because it is how – know-how. Science always goes on being converted into technology. You know the how, then you know the technique: you can use it, and the technology is created. So science just becomes a forerunner of technology, just a pilot to technology.

Religion is based in mystery, believes in mystery and believes that mystery is ultimate. You cannot destroy it, you cannot decode it, and that's the beauty of it. Once you feel that the mystery is ultimate and undecodable, you are like a small child filled with wonder. And when wonder grips you, only then are you alive to the maximum. When the wonder is not there, you are alive to the minimum.

You pass through life without wondering eyes; hence life appears so boring. It is not life that is boring, it is your eyes without wonder: they create boredom. You can regain the insight if you can regain a wondering mind, which goes on wondering to the very end, where it meets the ultimate mystery. There you can go on wondering and wondering and you can never solve it. A puzzle is not a mystery because a puzzle can be solved. A mystery is a puzzle which cannot be solved. Science is interested in puzzles which can be solved, which are solvable. Religion is interested only in the mystery which cannot be solved. And the more you penetrate, the more you know that it is impossible to solve.

Greek philosophers have said that philosophy is born in wonder. The Upanishads say that philosophy is born in wonder, and religion ends in wonder. Philosophy *is* born in wonder, but to the Greeks it is against wonder. It is born in wonder, but then tries to destroy it, tries to find answers, tries to find answers and explanations. Because of this attitude of Greek philosophy that philosophy is born in wonder, and the effort to overcome wonder, Western science was born. The source remains in the Greek mind. Western science is just the success of Greek philosophy. Philosophy is born in wonder, but ends in explanation: then it becomes science. Philosophy starts with wonder and ends in explanation, system, solution: it becomes science. When science experiments, comes to know the how, it becomes technology.

The Upanishads say religion ends in wonder, not that it begins. Wherever you begin, religion ends in wonder. The mystery remains there; it is never solved. This is the basic difference between the Indian mind and the Greek mind – and these are the two basic minds in the world. Because of the Greek mind Western science came into being and because of the Indian mind no science came into being: religion came into being.

All the greatest religions were born in the East. In the West there has never been a birth of any religion at all. All the great religions were born in the East and the deepest were born in India. Others that were born around India, but not exactly in India, are just echoes of the Indian. Christ was basically a Hindu; that's why Jews could not understand him, they had to kill him. All the deepest religions – Hinduism, Buddhism, Jainism – were born in India. And science basically originated from Athens; it is Greek.

The Greek attitude is that when you become aware of life you feel wonder. Then it is the duty of the human mind to destroy this wonder and to find explanations. The Upanishads say that wherever you find any explanation, penetrate deep into it – sooner or later you will come to the base where mystery is.

Explanation is only on the surface; nothing can be explained: this is the attitude of the Upanishads. Everything remains unexplained and will remain unexplained. It is only the human ego that thinks that explanations have to be found. Why the Upanishad's insistence on mystery? – because if there is mystery, only then can you be ignorant. Remember this: if there is mystery, ultimate mystery in the existence, only then can you remain ignorant. With mystery, ignorance inside the heart is possible. If everything can be explained, you will become knowledgeable. Then you will cling to knowledge. Then you will cling to knowledge and knowledge will become very, very important.

In the Western universities they have been teaching knowledge for centuries. Now in the East also, universities are teaching knowledge because they are nothing but copies of the West. Basically, originally, Eastern universities never taught knowledge. Nalanda and Takshashila were not teaching knowledge, they were teaching meditation. They were teaching a deep ignorance and a deep mystery around it. Now there exists no Eastern university. All of the universities are Western wherever they exist, whether in the East or in the West. They go on stuffing the mind with knowledge.

Whenever a student comes back from the university he is a stuffed being. He has no soul, he has only knowledge. And then he creates problems. He will create them because the university has given him only the ego – nothing else. He has not learned a single piece of humanity or humbleness. He has not touched a single point of non-ego. He has not looked from that window from where life is mystery. He is ignorant; he has not looked from that window. He has been stuffed with knowledge. Knowledge gives him the feeling that he is very significant and very important because he knows. The ego is strengthened, then the ego creates every problem that is possible.

The ego creates politics, the ego creates ambition. The ego creates jealousy, the ego creates a constant struggle, violence, because the ego cannot be satisfied unless it reaches to the top. And everyone is trying to reach to the top. A cut-throat competition arises in every arena of life. In economics, politics, education, everywhere, there is cut-throat competition. No one is interested in himself; everyone is interested in the ambition to reach to the top and no one thinks where he is going when he reaches to the top. What will you achieve just by reaching the top? Nothing is achieved. You simply waste your life.

Eastern universities were teaching a deep ignorance: the basic ignorance that man cannot penetrate the mystery because the mystery is ultimate. It is basic to nature – and man is just part of the same mystery. When these two mysteries meet – the mystery within man and the mystery within existence – when these two mysteries meet, there is ecstasy. Life becomes beautiful. It becomes an eternal music; it becomes a dance. You can dance only if there is mystery. The dancing god is needed – a god who can dance. And existence is dancing all around. Look! This is not a theory. Look at existence! It is dancing all around. Every particle is dancing. Only you have become stuck to the ground. You cannot move, you cannot dance because you know; your knowledge has become poison.

Now we will enter the sutra:

> *If you think that you know brahman well, then you know little indeed...*

Really, you don't know at all – not even a little, because you are still there claiming. The ego is still being maintained; the ego still remains the center. The ego is still asserting, saying, "I know." *If you think that you know brahman well, then you know little indeed...*

And if you say such a thing, it is only a thought, not an experience. You can think that you know, but this is not an experience. If you experience, then you will not be capable of saying "I know."

It is so vast: how can you know it? It is so endless, beginningless: how can you know it? The claim seems to be absurd – obscene. To know *brahman* seems to be just a stupid claim. Only idiots can claim it. The claim can come only out of ignorance because you don't really know anything, you just claim it.

> *If you think that you know brahman well, then you know little indeed, for the form of brahman that you see as conditional in living beings and gods is but a trifle.*

Even if you have come to feel the *brahman* in the manifested world – in the trees, in the hills, in man, in animals, in birds – if you have come to feel this life to be *brahman*, that too is a trifle, this is just a minute part of the unmanifested. The Upanishads say the *brahman* has two forms – the manifest and the unmanifest. The manifest has become the world, the unmanifest remains unknown. Many worlds have been born out of it, many have disappeared in it. This is not the first world, remember.

Christianity used to say just two centuries ago that the world was created four thousand and four years before Jesus Christ. Then there was great conflict between scientific investigation and this claim, because science came to know that this earth has been in existence for at least millions of years. There was conflict. Now, the more scientists know, the further back goes the beginning. But the Upanishads say that this is only one of the worlds: many have existed before it and have disappeared.

Existence is an infinite process. So there is no beginning, really, and there cannot be any end. How can there be a beginning? – because a beginning means that there was nothing before it. And how can this world come out of nothing? Only something can come out of something; something cannot come out of nothing. That is absurd. How can something come out of nothing? If it comes at all, there must have been something preceding it.

The Upanishads say that this is not the first world, this is not the first creation. It is only one chain in a long, beginningless, endless procession of existences. Worlds have been in being and then they have disappeared. Just as a child is born, then he becomes young, then old, and then dies. And the child is born of parents and those parents were also born of other parents. And this goes on and you cannot find the beginning.

The Upanishads have no concept of Adam and Eve, the first man and the first woman. They say there has never been a first woman and a first man. The first is just nonsense: we are always in the middle. The beginning was never there and so the end is not going to be there.

Just like a child, the earth is born out of parents. There may have been a collision between two big stars. When two parents collided, the earth was born. Now scientists say that something like this must have happened: a collision of two stars. The Upanishads seem to be true. When two stars, one feminine and one male, collide, the earth is born. The earth is alive; it is not dead. There are dead earths also. Now scientists suspect that the moon may be a dead earth. It may have been alive some time back.

This earth is alive. The greenery of the trees is just part of its life. Your consciousness is just a part of its growth. It has been evolving. It is young; it will become old. It will die, but somewhere else life will erupt. Now scientists say that there is at least a mathematical possibility of fifty thousand earths being alive in the whole of existence – fifty thousand planets alive! This is just a mathematical possibility. We have no contact with other living earths, but when one earth dies another is born. Somewhere birth happens, somewhere death; somewhere death happens, somewhere birth. Life goes on continuing. It is a continuity – an eternal continuity.

Whatsoever we know is always a very small, atomic part. Backwards, it spreads to a beginningless beginning; forwards, it spreads to an endless end. We are always in the middle. Only a particle of existence is known. And this whole existence, so vast, is still a part. The whole is also a part because it is the manifested.

Look at me: I am communicating something to you. Whatsoever I communicate is just the manifested part. There remains in my heart much that is uncommunicated: that is the unmanifest part. My silence is the unmanifest part; my words are the manifest part. In my words a part of my silence is being communicated, but my words are not my whole being. My words are just a part, and behind that part a deeper silence is hidden.

A poet is singing a song – a Rabindranath or a Shelley or a Yeats is singing a song: that song is just a manifest part of the poet's being, but thousands and thousands of songs can be born out of that being.

The Upanishads say this whole world, this universe, is just a song which has become manifest. In the heart of the divine infinite songs are waiting to be manifested. He has been singing many songs which have disappeared. He is singing this one right now; he will sing many. We can be acquainted only with one song, but not even with the one song in its totality – just with a part of its tune, just a fragment, just a word, a gesture. The infinite remains unknown around it.

The sutra says:

> *...for the form of brahman that you see as conditional in living beings and gods is but a trifle. Therefore, you should inquire further about brahman.*

Really, there comes no end to this inquiry. It goes on and on and on, and the more you inquire, the more abysses open. The more you inquire, the greater the doors that open and the mystery is not demystified: it deepens. The more you know, the more of what is to be known is before you. The wider your focus, the wider becomes your consciousness. Greater possibilities to be known open before you and this goes on and on and on; this play is endless.

So wherever you feel to stop, beware. There is no point to stop at. Wherever you feel, "Now I have achieved," beware. You are falling a victim to the ego again. There is no point where one can say, "I have achieved." The point is always being reached and reached, but it never reached.

That's the meaning of the infinity of the *brahman*. You never come to a point where you can say, "Now the journey is finished." The journey goes on and on and on. That journey is infinite life. You finish somewhere, but the journey never ends. Your ego is no more at a point. Really, at that point the real journey starts. But then it goes on infinitely. There is no end to it; there cannot be any end to it. You drop somewhere. When you come to realize that you are just a burden to yourself, you drop yourself and you move on. This movement is eternal.

I don't think I know it well...

The master says:

> *I don't think I know it well, nor do I think that I don't know it...*

This is the mystery. I cannot say that I know it well because much more is still to be known and much more will be there always to be known. This knowing of *brahman* is always a beginning and there is no end to it. You begin it once, then it goes on and on. So I cannot say that *...I know it well:* that claim will be wrong. *...Nor do I think that I don't know it...* But the opposite is also true. I cannot say that I don't know it – I know it also.

This is the difference between the Greek and the Indian mind. The Greek mind cannot conceive of this sentence. Impossible for

Aristotle to conceive of this sentence! Aristotle will say that this is a basic law of logic: that if you know, you know. If you don't know, you don't know and there can be no middle to it. If you are alive you are alive; if you are dead you are dead. There cannot be any middle to it – or can there be? Can you say, "I cannot say that I am alive and I cannot say that I am dead"? Then Aristotle will say you have gone mad. Either of the two is true; both cannot be true. Aristotle says both cannot be true; two opposites cannot be true. One will be true.

This seer of the Upanishads says, "I cannot say I know."

Then Aristotle will say, "Stop! This is finished. If you cannot say you know, drop the matter."

But the seer goes on and says, "I cannot say that I don't know."

This, Aristotle cannot approve. The founder, the father of Western logic, cannot approve. He will say, "Now you are going crazy." Can you say that you are in the room and out of the room? You cannot say this. You cannot say that you are in and out of the room. Either you are in the room or you are out of the room: both cannot be true. Can you say, "I cannot say I am in the room and I also cannot say that I am out of the room"? To us, also, Aristotle appears right, he appears true. To the common mind, to ordinary logic, he is exactly right, logical.

Indian seers are illogical in this sense. They go on saying opposites simultaneously, but they have something to convey through it. They are not really wrong; they have something to say and that something is so mysterious it can be conveyed only when opposites are used together. The mystery can be conveyed only through contradictions, through inconsistencies.

> *I don't think that I know it well, nor do I think that I don't know it, yet, I know too.*

I know in a sense and I don't know in a sense. I know because I am part of it; it is impossible not to know it. And I don't know it because I am only a part and it is impossible for the part to know the whole. Both are true, and if you can feel that both are true, then just between the two contradictions a new meaning will arise. You will feel what the *rishi* is trying to express and you will feel how difficult it is to express it. Too much is felt and the words cannot carry that much, so both the opposites have to be used to carry it.

For example, the Upanishads say the divine is very far, then immediately they say he is very near. How, if he is very far, can he be very near? Or if he is very near, how can he be very far? But they have something to say and it is very significant. Through this absurdity they are trying to convey something which is not easy to convey or which is even unconveyable. He is very far because you have forgotten him. That forgetfulness creates the distance. And he is very near because whatsoever you do, whether you forget him or remember him, you cannot be alive without him. He is the very beat of your heart. He is breathing in and out; he is you. You can forget him, but you still remain him. Hence, this contradictory way of expression: "He is far and near," and "I know him and I don't know him."

The Upanishads will not agree with Socrates. I told you that Socrates said, "Once I knew; now I say I don't know." He is again following the Greek trend of mind. He is very consistent. He says, "Once I felt that I knew. Now I feel it is wrong. Now I don't know." The Upanishads will say both are wrong. A third possibility is there when you say, "In a way I know; in a way I don't know."

First Socrates was claiming absolute knowledge, now he is claiming absolute ignorance – but in both the cases he claims the absolute, he clings to the absolute. He is not contradictory. Once he said, "I know"; now he says, "I don't know." Upanishadic seers say both simultaneously: "I know and I don't know." Try to feel the thing that is just in between the two, between the lines, just in the gap.

> *He amongst us knows it who knows that it is other than the unknown and the known.*

The known is your knowledge; the unknown is your ignorance. If you say, "I know," you have made him known. If you say, "I don't know," you have made him unknown. And he alone amongst you knows, who knows he is neither the known nor the unknown, but the unknowable. He is the mystery.

Only one who knows him as the mystery, as the mysterium, as the ultimate mysterious which cannot be solved, only *he* knows it.

Now get ready for the meditation.

...

CHAPTER 9

DEATH: THE CLIMAX OF LIFE

The first question:

> **Osho,**
> **In the fourth step of the morning meditation, in the effort to keep the body frozen or dead, one tends to become tense. As this is the step of relaxation and total let-go, how is one to relax and also be frozen at the same time? Rather than ecstasy, it becomes a tension.**

A dead person is totally relaxed. He cannot be tense. A dead person cannot be tense – or can he? He is relaxed because there is no ego to be tense. Only the ego can be tense. When in the fourth step I say be dead, it means to be so relaxed that you are just like a dead man. You are not to try to be frozen and dead. If you try, then you will get the reverse result. Don't try to be frozen; don't make any effort to be dead. Simply relax and be dead.

These are two different things. If you try to be dead, then your whole body will become tense. And when you are tense, you cannot be dead, you cannot relax. Simply relax the body as if it is no more, as if it has gone dead. Don't make any effort to make it dead. Simply relax, and feel that the body has gone dead: you don't have to do anything about it.

I have been telling you that even if you feel that a sneeze is coming, don't sneeze, don't cough. But if you feel an irritation in the throat, what can you do? If you try to prevent it, it will become more and more irritating. If you try to block it, it will become stronger because this is a sort of suppression. Then you will have to cough. If you feel a sneeze is coming, what should you do? If you hold it, it will become more forceful, it will come out with a greater force.

But there is a way: if you feel that your throat is irritated and you want to cough, relax the throat. Don't prevent it. Simply relax the throat; be indifferent to the irritation and relax the throat. Don't make it tense because the tension will create more irritation. Relax the throat and be indifferent. Feel as if you are not concerned, and within seconds the irritation will go. If you feel that a sneeze is coming, just be indifferent to it; don't do anything about it. Relax the part where you feel that the sneeze is hitting, and be indifferent.

In that indifference, out of a hundred times, ninety-nine times the sneeze will disappear. Out of a hundred times, there is only one possibility that the sneeze will come – but that too will not disturb you because you will be so indifferent that even if it happens you will feel that it is happening to someone else. You will be so unconcerned that even if it comes it makes no difference. You will remain unperturbed within.

And I am not saying to you don't sneeze because others will be disturbed – no. I am not saying don't cough because others will be disturbed. That is not the point. *You* will be disturbed. You will lose the whole point of the effort; the whole endeavor will be lost.

In the morning meditation, relax. After the third step, relax. One thing more you should remember is when I say "Stop!" in the morning meditation, or when the music stops, don't make your body comfortable. Don't try to take a posture; don't lie down. Leave the body as it is. Stop then and there, even if it is inconvenient and uncomfortable.

You were jumping and the posture is uncomfortable: remain

frozen in that posture, don't change it. The moment you hear that the music has stopped, you stop. Become dead. You can make your body comfortable, you can lie down, but this gap will have already disturbed the energy; this gap will have already changed the direction.

In the three steps you have created a vital force, a floodlike force. Now, just making your body comfortable, you have forgotten it: your attention is diverted. Don't do that. When I say, "Stop!" stop immediately, then and there. And don't try to deceive. Don't say to yourself, "No one is looking at me, so why not make the body a little more comfortable? It is no one's concern." Then you are deceiving yourself.

One thing more. In the second step, when you are expressing all the suppressed emotions, when you are going completely mad in catharsis, do one thing emphatically: contract your facial muscles and relax. Contract and relax. Your body is not as tense as your face is because your face is the focal point of all suppression. And your face is the most expressive; that's why the face becomes the most suppressive. It is through your face that you express or suppress. In the second step – remember it – go on expressing through the whole body, but remember also to make the face tense and relaxed, tense and relaxed. In that way, much suppressed emotion will be released more easily.

Relaxation is not something to be done; you cannot really *do* it. No one can do it because relaxation is against doing. You can simply stop doing and relaxation happens. So when I say "Stop!" and the music stops, stop completely as you are; don't do anything. Simply stop, stop all doing – not even a single movement. Then a very deep silence will happen to you and you will feel the difference. You have been making yourself comfortable; from now on don't make your body comfortable.

In the afternoon meditation also, after *kirtan,* when the music stops, stop as you are. Suddenly all the activity stops, and the whole energy moves only inwards; there is no opportunity for it to be diverted anywhere. And the same in the evening meditation we will do just now. When I say, "Stop!" stop completely as you are. And when the music starts again and you begin to express your ecstasy, only then start moving again. For the gap in between, remain in nondoing and the relaxation will happen.

The second question:

Osho,
Why is the ultimate experience so hard to attain?

It is not! It is not hard to attain. It is very easy. But because it is so easy, it has become hard. The ego is always interested in whatsoever is hard to attain because then the ego feels a challenge. The ego is not interested in doing whatsoever is easy; this is the problem. The ego is not interested in doing meditation; that is the only reason it appears to be so hard.

It is so easy – but so easy that there is no challenge in it. No ambition can be fulfilled through it; you cannot attain to any worldly power through it; you cannot attain to any worldly prestige through it. Really, you don't attain anything which is visible in the world. Rather, on the contrary, you go on losing and finally you lose yourself. It is hard because you are not ready to lose yourself; it is easy if you are ready to lose yourself. In a single moment it can happen. Otherwise, you will take lives and lives and lives and it will not happen.

The question is not of time; the question is deeper. The question is whether you are ready to lose yourself. But you can ask, "Why is it so hard to lose? Why are people not ready to lose more easily?" There is a reason, and the reason is that losing oneself appears to be deathlike and no one wants to die. Everyone wants to live – to live more. Everyone wants to avoid death.

Of course, no one can avoid it. No one ever succeeds in avoiding it. Death occurs. Death is the only certainty. All else is uncertain in life. Only death is certain. Death will happen whether you are trying to avoid it or not. You cannot escape it. In a sense it had already happened the moment you were born. Half of it has already happened and the other half will follow. And these two halves cannot be divided.

Buddha says again and again, "Once born, you will have to die" – because you have entered death with your birth, it is an entry. You are already dead in a way. You have started to die. The moment you are born, you have started to die. Your death process has started.

But we are afraid to die and we cling to life. Why do we cling to life and why are we afraid of death? You may not have thought about it. The reason why we cling so much to life and why we are afraid of death is just inconceivable. We cling to life so much because we don't know how to live. We cling to life too much because really we are not alive. And time is passing and death is coming nearer and nearer. And we are afraid that death is coming near and we have not yet lived.

This is the fear: death will come and we have not lived yet. We are just preparing to live. Nothing is ready; life has not happened. We have not known the ecstasy which life is; we have not known the bliss life is; we have not known anything. We have just been breathing in and out. We have been just existing. Life has been just a hope and death is coming near. And if life has not yet happened and death happens before it, of course, obviously, we will be afraid and we would not like to die.

Only those persons who have lived, really lived, are ready, welcoming, receptive, thankful to death. Then death is not the enemy. Then death becomes the fulfillment. If you have really lived and known what life is, then death is not the end of life. It is the fulfillment, it is the peak, it is the climax, it is the last thing that life can offer to you – and the best.

Life offers only two things: one is love, another is death – and both are dangerous because in both you will have to die. In love you will have to dissolve yourself. In death also you will have to lose yourself. And you are so afraid of death, of losing yourself, that deep down you have become afraid – afraid of love also. You go on talking about love, but no one is ready to love because love is deathlike. Love and death, these are natural phenomena.

If man simply lives naturally, love will happen and death will also happen and both will be peaks. Love is dying into the other person and death is dying into the universe. But love is not ultimate death; you will come out of it. You will come out of the other person again, there will be a resurrection. And death is also not ultimate because you will be reborn. You will come out of the universe again and you will enter a body and you will become embodied.

Meditation is ultimate death: it goes beyond both love and beyond death. You cannot come out of it; that is why it is the most dangerous thing. Even in death there is the possibility you will be reborn, that you will come out of it. You will dissolve and you will again integrate, you will again evolve. So death will just be a passage of change, but meditation is final death – ultimate, absolute death. You cannot come out of it; hence, the fear. And it looks so hard because of the fear; otherwise it is as easy as anything can be. But love is difficult, so meditation will be difficult. Death is difficult, so meditation will be difficult.

To me, therefore, love is very significant: if you can love, you can meditate easily. But the whole society is against love, the whole culture is against love. They take every precaution so that love should not happen. They have created marriage so that love should not happen. Through marriage they have tried to close the very door. Before you get involved in love – a death process – they have protected you. They have created all types of teachings, all types of nonsense in your mind, to make love immoral.

Basically, you are also afraid because in love you will have to lose your identity. You want to remain yourself so you go on protecting yourself. Even if you move in love, you move in a very protected way, very carefully. You remain an individual even in love. You remain an ego. So two egos meet, but the meeting is going to be only an appearance. They can come near, but the meeting never happens. They never dissolve into each other;

they never lose themselves into each other.

If you can love, meditation will be very easy. The world will be more religious if love is accepted, helped along, and love becomes a natural milieu around you. Then meditation will be very easy because through love, you will know a taste of what it means to be dissolved – even if only for a single moment. Then you can dare to be dissolved for longer moments.

And if you can love, you will not be afraid of death. Lovers are never afraid of death. If a person is afraid of death, you can be certain that he has not loved and he has not been loved. The fear of death shows that the life has been without love. Lovers are ready to die very easily. They can die for each other. They don't care much about so-called life because they have known a higher quality of life; they have known a higher life. They don't care about this life very much.

But look at persons who have never loved. They will always be afraid of death. Look at misers: they will always be afraid of death. And misers are those persons who have not loved anyone because if you can love a person you will never love money. Money is a substitute. When you cannot love an individual, when you cannot love a live person, you love dead money.

Misers, those who go on clinging to their possessions, are not even acquainted with what love is. Their whole love has gone to dead money. And why has it gone? There are deeper connections. A person who is too much attached to money will be afraid of death. Really, a person who is afraid of death will love money too much because money seems to be a protection against death. If you have money you feel protected. If you don't have any money you feel unprotected. Death can occur and you cannot do anything. With money you feel you can do something. Money will be helpful.

A person who loves will not love money because a person who loves will not be afraid of death. And if a person is not afraid of death, there cannot be any clinging, attachment, and mad obsession with money. It is impossible.

If you can love, then you will accept death very easily. It will be a deep relaxation, a long sleep, a beautiful dissolution into the existence. And if you can be receptive to death, meditation is as easy as anything. The problem arises because love is not there. When death has become a fear, then meditation will be difficult because it is love plus death: both. It is death as far as your ego is concerned; it is love as far as the divine existence is concerned.

I can define meditation in a mathematical formula: meditation is equal to love plus death – love of existence, of the total, and death to the ego. They are two aspects of the same coin because you can love the total only if you are ready to lose the individual. If you are ready to die, only then can you be reborn as the existence, as the *brahman*.

Jesus says, "Only if you lose can you survive. And those who try to survive will be lost." It is hard because you have not loved; it is hard because you have not lived. It is not hard by itself. Meditation by itself is very easy – a spontaneous phenomenon. If a human being evolves naturally, falls into love, knows what love is, knows what type of death and what type of life love is, comes out of it, knows the taste of being, of moving into death, then he will love death as it is – not as against life. Death changes the quality then. Then it becomes the last point in life, the highest peak, the climax of life. Then meditation is very easy.

Those of you who are ready to lose can understand it; it is very easy. Those of you who are not ready to lose... One friend came to me today. He said, "Whatsoever you say appears to be absolutely true. I am totally satisfied; my mind is in complete agreement with you. But don't tell me to do this meditation. Is it not possible," the friend asked, "that just by total agreement with your thoughts I can achieve enlightenment? Is it necessary to move into this meditation?"

What is the fear? You can agree with me intellectually, but you are not losing yourself. And, really, if you go deep and penetrate more, you will find the whole process is just the reverse. You agree with me intellectually because you have always been feeling that whatsoever I am saying is true. But really, you are not agreeing with me; I am agreeing with you. You feel me agreeable, so your ego is fulfilled. "Right!" you say inside your mind, "This is what I have been always thinking. Right! You are right, because this has been my idea." You feel fulfilled, satisfied. Your ego is strengthened. This is not going to lead you to enlightenment. Rather, it may lead you to deeper ignorance – because the ego…

What is the fear? Moving into meditation, the fear is you will have to lose the ego; you will have to lose your identity. And this is a sort of mad meditation. If I say to you just sit in a buddha posture and close your eyes, you can sit easily because you are not afraid. You can sit easily because nothing is expected, really. But in this mad, chaotic meditation in which you have to lose yourself, your identity, your image, then you become just crazy and you feel you are losing control, and sooner or later the group mind takes possession of you.

Then you are dancing, but you know very well, deeply, that *you* are not dancing. The whole group is dancing, and you have just become a part of it. You cannot stop it, really. A moment comes when you cannot stop it; you are no longer in possession. Something greater than you has taken the grip, something greater than you has taken control: that is the fear.

If you sit in a *siddhasan* – in a buddha posture, you are in control. But my meditation is throwing you out of control – really pulling the ground from beneath your feet. You are being pushed into an abyss, into a whirlwind where you are no more. Something deeper, something greater, something powerful has taken possession. Now it is not that you are dancing, something else is dancing; you are just a part in that greater dance. This gives you fear. This makes everything difficult.

So I will tell you: be ready to lose and it is easy. Resist, and it is difficult and hard. Resistance makes it hard; let-go makes it easy.

And the same friend has asked something more. He says, "It seems to me that it is part of nature's intention to make it very difficult and to require man to go through ages of development before he reaches it. Isn't there a divine purpose behind why it takes him so long to reach?"

Man's mind is very cunning. You can go on throwing responsibility on someone else: "It is nature's way to make it hard." You are making it hard; it is not nature's way. Nature's way is always simple and easy. Nature means natural, spontaneous, easy. In nature, nothing is hard. Only man complicates things, makes them hard and difficult. Nature is very easy-flowing. But you can deceive. You can say it is nature's way that meditation is difficult. Then you are relieved, then it is nothing on your part and you cannot do anything. It is nature's way, so what can you do?

You can just wait, or you can go on doing whatsoever you are doing. You need not meditate – you have thrown all responsibility on nature. But if this is really true, then meditation will happen. If you can really throw all responsibility on nature – remember, *all* – then meditation will happen; then there is no need to do anything. When you feel miserable don't ask anyone for advice. Feel miserable and know that it is nature's way. When you feel in pain, don't ask for remedies; know this is nature's way. If you can do this totally, there is no need for meditation; meditation has already happened.

But you are cunning. Only with meditation will you say this is nature's way and with nothing else. With everything else you will struggle, you will make effort. If you are poor then you will make every effort to become rich, and you will not say it is nature's way. You will not say, "When I become really capable, nature will make me rich." You will not wait for nature.

If you are really honest, then leave everything to nature. You need not meditate then, because this itself, this leaving everything to nature, has become the deepest meditation possible. But if you are not honest, then you can deceive yourself so that whatsoever you want to do you will do, and whatsoever you don't want to do you will throw on nature's shoulders. Beware of this trick. You are doing it here.

But I am ready. If you are totally throwing it on nature, then for you nothing is needed. But if you are not ready to throw it totally, then be kind to yourself: don't throw meditation. Don't say that nature must have some inner work and so nature makes it hard. Nature is not making it hard.

The same friend asks, "Isn't there a divine purpose behind why it takes so long to reach?" Not only are you throwing it on nature: you are trying to make it look very good and divine, as if there is some divine purpose behind it – that's why you are not reaching the goal; that's why you are not attaining to meditation; that's why *samadhi* is so difficult. No. You are creating barriers for some divine purpose. And in a way, there can be no divine purpose because existence is purposeless. It is a play.

Purpose is human: *you* have purpose. But existence cannot have any purpose. There is no sense in having any purpose. Existence is flowing – overflowing with its own energy. It is a festivity, not a purpose. It is a constant celebration. Existence is enjoying itself in so many forms. There is no purpose, and existence is not worried if you are not reaching to ecstasy, it is only your worry. If you are not reaching, you will suffer. Existence is not suffering because of your not reaching and existence will not force you to move into ecstasy. It is up to you.

Existence is a deep freedom. If you want to be in suffering, be in suffering. If you want to be in bliss, be in bliss. It is your own choice. But it is too much for our minds to think that everything is our choice because then we become responsible. If you come to think that you are the cause of your suffering, then you will feel very bad. It always feels good to make someone else the cause of your suffering.

But, remember, if someone else is the cause of your suffering, you can never become free. Then there is no liberation. But if you are the cause of your suffering, then liberation is within your hands; you can do something and change it.

I tell you: you are the cause of your heaven and of your hell. If you are in hell, you have chosen it to be so. And the moment you decide, you can come out of it. No one is even going to prevent you; no one will say to you, "Don't go." The gates are not closed against you. Really, there are no gates, and no Devil is standing at the door. You need not even have a passport to move out. It is simply your decision to be there.

You are in suffering because you have decided to be in suffering; you can come out of it the moment you decide to come out. You can be in bliss if you decide to be in bliss. Your decision is your being. You choose whatsoever you are. You have chosen it to be so; that's why it is so. Don't go on throwing responsibilities on something else – on nature, on God, on faith, on destiny. Don't go on throwing them.

But if you really feel that you cannot do anything, that you are helpless, then I say throw the total responsibility. These are the two ways. The first is: throw the total responsibility. Then you have nothing to do and everything will happen, because the moment you throw the total responsibility, the ego is also thrown, the ego cannot exist. If you give total responsibility to nature or to the divine force or to *xyz*, your ego is no longer there. And when the ego is not, the thing happens. But, if you cannot throw total responsibility, if you cannot surrender totally, if you cannot feel that you are totally helpless – remember the word *total* – then do something to dissolve this ego. Then effort will be needed. You will have to do either this or that, but don't move in between. And don't try to travel in two boats. You will be in difficulty; you will never reach anywhere.

This is my observation: if I say to people, "Leave everything to existence," they say, "How can I leave? How can I surrender? I don't know what existence is. Unless I know, how can I leave everything to it?" They say, "It is difficult." They say, "Please show us some way that we can follow."

But if I say to them, "Do this, follow this method and you will achieve," immediately they bring some objection. They say, "Man is helpless. What can we do? We are so helpless – just puppets in the hands of a destiny which is unknown."

If I say to them, "Leave everything to destiny," they say it is impossible. If I say, "Do something," they say it is impossible. The mind is cunning and always tries to escape. Be alert about it; only then can something happen to you. Otherwise, you can go on just wavering your whole life and nothing will happen.

You have wasted so many lives before. You are not here for the first time hearing about meditation; you have listened to it many times. It is not only that you are clever with me; you have been clever many times before. You have listened to Buddha, you have listened to Jesus, you have listened to Krishna. You were there – with different faces, of course, but you were there. You are very old, ancient ones, but your cunning is so deep that Buddhas fail; Christs come and go, and you remain unperturbed. No one can push you off your road. You continue; you bypass all.

While talking to you or while leading you into meditative states, I never think that you are new ones. You have done many things before, but never with your full heart. And unless you are total in something, nothing can happen. Be either totally with destiny, with the divine force, and then you are no more; or be totally with a technique, with a method, so that the ego can be destroyed by and by, slowly. Method is a slow thing; surrender is total and final. Surrender is possible in a single moment; method will take time. I am giving you method because I know you cannot surrender.

The last question:

> **Osho,**
> **I have always heard you speaking about surrender, and it seems to me that surrender is the only important factor in achieving transformation. Then how to surrender? What is the meaning, method and process of it? And what contribution does the active meditation make in reaching the state of surrender?**

The first thing to be understood about surrender is that you cannot ask how, because "how" brings the method, "how" brings the technique. Surrender is enough unto itself; it needs no technique. Asking how to surrender is asking how to love. And if you ask how to love, one thing is certain: love is not for you. How can you ask how to love? And if someone is trained, whatsoever he comes to know about love will be false. Training will make everything false.

It happened that one young man used to come to me to learn how to love and I used to tell him, "Go and do this and say this to the girl." And he would go and he would come and report back to me what had happened. But he was always a failure. He tried and tried with many girls and he was always a failure because something would always go wrong. He was ready and I would train him for something, but life never happens in that way. The girl would say something different and he was not ready to answer. Then he would be in difficulty. He would come back and he would say, "You told me to answer this, but she never asked."

So I told that young man, "It is going to be very difficult unless I train you both. But then it will become just a drama."

You cannot learn surrender. If you can do it, you can do it, and there is nothing more to it. If you cannot do it, leave it completely; then follow some method. Method doesn't need any surrender; method is a substitute. You want to do something because you cannot surrender, and by doing something the same phenomenon will happen in a long process that can happen immediately in surrender.

Surrender means you are feeling that you are not capable of doing anything, so you surrender. It is a total helplessness. You say, "I don't know." You say, "I'm not capable of doing anything, so I surrender. Now lead me wheresoever you would like to lead." And remember, this is going to be total. You cannot ask, after following two or three steps, "Where are you leading me?" You cannot say, "You are leading me up some wrong path," because you have surrendered. Now you are no more.

Surrender has its own beauty, but only very rare souls, very strong souls, can surrender. Remember, ordinarily it is the feeling that weaklings surrender. This is absolutely wrong. To surrender you need to be a strong person, very strong, because it is going to be such a total decision. And you cannot move backwards. You cannot take it back; you cannot say, "Now I take my surrender back." It is unconditional. Surrender cannot be conditional; you cannot say, "If this happens, only then will I follow you." If I take you to hell, to the very hell, you will follow me because it has been unconditional. You have given up your own decisions, now you are not going to decide.

Surrender needs very strong, absolutely strong souls. If the master says, "This is day," and you see it is night – but you have surrendered, you don't see now from your own eyes, you see from the master's eyes – he says, "This is day," you say, "Yes sir, this is day." You don't allow your ego to come in; you don't allow your intellect to come in. You put aside everything. If you can do this – there is no "how" to it, remember – it happens.

Surrender is not a doing; doing is contradictory. You cannot do it. Doing is contradictory to surrender. Surrender is a happening. You can ask, "How does it happen?" Don't ask me how it is done. You can ask me, "How does it happen?" It happens when you have tried and tried and failed and failed; when you have tried every path and it has led nowhere; when you have tried your intellect in every way and it has always led to some cul-de-sac; you have tried to do whatsoever you can do and nothing has happened – and you have come to a conclusion that you are not enough, that you are helpless. When you have come to conclude this, that you are helpless, in this helplessness surrender happens. Then you can surrender.

So the first thing: surrender has no "how" about it – no. It has no technique. It *is* the technique itself; it has no other technique. If you can do it, you can do it. If you cannot do, forget it: it is not for you. But don't be worried, don't feel hopeless, because there are techniques and you can try them. And if you try techniques, there are two possibilities: either you will succeed – if you succeed there will be no need to surrender – or you will fail, and then it will not help you.

Buddha tried for six years. He tried every method. One of his contemporaries, Mahavira, was also trying – in the same days, at the same time, in the same part of the world, in Bihar. These two greatest souls were working for their enlightenment in the same period. Mahavira was working on certain techniques for twelve years. Buddha was also working on similar techniques for six years. After six years Buddha came to conclude that no technique can be helpful. Everything failed, so he surrendered. He surrendered to the universe. He said, "Now I have nowhere to go. Now I have nothing to achieve. Now I end my search. Whatsoever happens, now I am not interested in the future in any way. I am neither for life nor against."

He was in such total frustration that you cannot even say that he was hopeless because you can be hopeless only when a certain hope is still hidden. You can feel hopeless because you still go on hoping. He was not even hopeless. Hope was gone, even hopelessness was gone. He was simply without hope. The future was no longer there; he was a total failure. Buddha was a total failure after six years and in that total failure surrender happened. He relaxed under the *bodhi* tree that night without any desires, not even for nirvana, *samadhi*, ecstasy, godliness – no desire at all.

You still desire, you still hope, you still feel something is possible, because your desire shows that you are still not totally a failure. But Buddha came to conclude that nothing was possible. He relaxed under the *bodhi* tree because now he could not be tense. When you are really a failure, how can you be tense? A man who is successful can be tense, a man who is trying to succeed can be tense, a man who has failed but still hopes can be tense. But a man who has failed so totally that now there is no hope, who doesn't even feel frustrated, hopeless, who has simply left the whole game, cannot be tense. For Buddha, there was no worry. How can worry exist? There was no ego because ego exists only when you are trying to succeed.

Suddenly in the morning, when he awoke from the night, there was no dream, no desire, no idea of the tomorrow. And in the morning he opened his eyes – his eyes were totally vacant. There were no clouds of desire and dreams. He saw the last star setting and as the star disappeared, he disappeared. And when there was no star on the horizon he was also not there. It is said that he laughed. He laughed within himself because he had tried so much and nothing had happened, and now he was not trying at all and everything had happened. He was in ecstasy. He was in such ecstasy that he is said to have said, "Nirvana has happened, enlightenment has happened – and such an enlightenment that has never been known before."

Then he tried to preach effortlessness, but no one would listen to him. How can you believe that without effort everything can happen? And it had not really happened without effort. Effort had been there. Through the effort happened the failure, and through failure happened this ultimate state of consciousness.

Mahavira also succeeded – the other seeker in the same part of the world. He was doing certain techniques and he succeeded. He succeeded in dissolving his ego through techniques. That's why Jainas and Buddhists are bonafide enemies. They cannot come to any reconciliation, they cannot come to any compromise, because they are so absolutely opposite. Mahavira succeeded through technique, so the whole teaching of Mahavira is of method. Buddha succeeded through failure, so his whole teaching is of effortlessness: "Don't do anything."

These are the two dimensions. Both are good, but my suggestion is: first try to follow technique. If you succeed, it is okay. If you fail, then surrender will be possible. Then too it is okay. I am for both; that's why I look contradictory.

One young man came to me today and said, "You are so contradictory that it is impossible to follow you, and you contradict yourself so much that you just confuse me." So I told him not to listen to me. "Just close the eyes and don't listen to me. Just meditate." Because if you feel that whatsoever I say is contradictory... And you will feel! Your intellect will feel. It *is* contradictory.

Unless you come to know that all the contradictory ways can lead to the same point, you will not be able to feel the inner consistency within the contradictions. They are contradictory, and they are not. They are because what Buddha says is consistent, what Mahavira says is consistent. But I am saying both things simultaneously. It has never been done really; it looks contradictory. But you need not think about it; just follow one thing.

If you can surrender, surrender; don't ask how. If you ask how then you are not meant to surrender yet. You are asking for a method – then follow the method. Either you will succeed or you will fail: both are good. Through both you will reach.

Now get ready for the meditation.

...

CHAPTER 10

THE ETERNAL PLAY OF EXISTENCE

He knows it who knows it not, and he knows it not who knows it. To the man of true knowledge it is the unknown, while to the ignorant it is the known.

Indeed, he attains immortality who realizes it in and through every bodh – pulsation of knowledge and awareness. Through the atman he obtains strength and vigor and through its knowledge, immortality.

For one who realizes it here, in this world, there is true life. For one who does not so realize it, great is the loss. Discovering the atman in every single being, the wise ones, dying to this world of sense-experience, become immortal.

Knowledge of the *brahman* is impossible, but knowing is possible. Knowledge and knowing are basically different. A very subtle difference has to be understood. Knowing is always in the present, knowledge is of the past. Whenever you say, "I have known," it means the experience has become past, it has become part of your memory. When you say, "I am in a process of knowing," the experience is still continuing; you are still in the experience. It is not part of your memory. Your being is still involved in it.

When you think about the world, the knowing stops. It

becomes knowledge. That accumulated knowledge is known as science. Whatsoever man has known becomes science. Science is knowledge. Religion never becomes science because religion is an eternally continuing process of knowing. You never come to a point where you can say, "I have known." The *brahman* never becomes the past; it is always the present. The ultimate cannot be reduced to the past; it cannot be reduced to knowledge. It is always a riverlike flow of knowing.

So you cannot say that you have experienced godliness because that means it is now a past thing and that you have transcended it – you have already experienced it and gone beyond. You cannot go beyond godliness, so you can never say meaningfully that you have known, that you have experienced. You cannot put it in the past; it cannot be made part of your memory. You can be in a process of experiencing – but it is never experience, it is always experiencing: a lived process, never a dead memory.

It is just like this: you cannot say, "I have breathed." You are breathing. Breathing cannot become past. If it becomes the past you will be no more. There will be no one to say that he breathed. Breathing is always a process, continuous. You are always breathing – it is in the present. You cannot say, "I have lived," because then who are you? You are life, but you cannot say, "I have lived." Life is a continuous process. It is always here and now in this very moment. The ultimate means the ultimate life, the ultimate breathing, the ultimate experiencing, the ultimate knowing.

So the first thing to be understood is that the *brahman* cannot be reduced to knowledge. So whosoever says, "I have known," the Upanishads say is ignorant. He is insensitive to the great mystery of life. Whosoever says he has known has not known. He may have known through the scriptures; he may have known through others; he may have gathered information. But he has not known, because one who knows will know that God can never be reduced to knowledge. It remains a process.

God is not a thing. A thing can be known. God is a process. A thing means something which has stopped. A process goes on and on and on. In the ordinary mind we always think of God as a thing. God is not a thing, it is a flow, a continuum. It goes on eternally, never stops, never can stop. Nonstopping is the very nature of it, so how can you know a process? The moment you say, "I have known," you have stopped – and the process goes on. You have stopped in your knowledge and the process goes on: you are lost, your contact is lost. Now you are no longer in touch with the process.

You will have to move with the process. You cannot stop. Stopping is not possible with the divine. You can stop, but the divine cannot stop. And when you stop and the river goes on, you have lost contact with it; you are no longer in living touch.

So those who say they have known have lost contact. Really, they have not known. They have gathered information. Intellectually they have conceived, but they have not lived, because one who lives will come to know that this is a river, eternally going on and on. You have to flow with it. A single moment of stopping and the contact is lost. You can never say, "I have known." You can only say, "I am knowing."

Knowing is an open thing; knowledge is closed. Knowledge has come to a full stop. Knowing is a growing thing, it grows. Knowledge is dead, it has already stopped. It is not breathing now, the blood is not flowing in it; the heart has stopped beating, it is dead. Knowledge is a corpse, and if you carry knowledge you are carrying a corpse, a dead body. That is why pundits, scholars, those who think they know, are dead men. Even sinners have entered the divine, but it is unheard of that any pundit has ever entered the divine. A sinner can enter, but a man who is knowledgeable, who thinks he knows, cannot enter.

In the eyes of the Upanishads the real sin is knowledge, because that is the only barrier. But it is very subtle, and you have to understand the meaning. Knowing is allowed; knowledge is not allowed. Move with the divine moment to moment, alive, in touch, open. Don't say, "I have known." Simply say, "I am aware, experiencing, knowing. Everything is open, and I don't know what is going to be revealed the next moment, so I cannot close, I cannot say now it is finished, the end has come." There is no last chapter, there is no last page. The scripture is endless. You cannot close it and every moment something new is revealed because the divine or existence or *brahman* is every moment new, fresh, young. Only we get old, and we get old because of knowledge.

It is not simply the body which gets old. The body will get old, but your consciousness need not get old. If it gets old, it means you have gathered knowledge. Then the weight of knowledge makes you old. Otherwise your eyes will remain innocent, virgin. You will be open; that openness is virginity. You will be seeking and searching. You will be inquiring and meditating and contemplating – and you will be always ready for the new to happen because it is happening every moment. Existence is never old. If existence is old then some day it will have to die because oldness leads to death.

The *brahman* is always young, evergreen. Old age is not known there, that is why there is no death to it. Existence is always green, alive, pulsating. With knowledge you become old. The moment you say, "I have known," you have stopped knowing. You think you have experienced and the experiencing stops. From that moment on you are not growing. You are a dead seed.

The Upanishads believe in knowing, not in knowledge. What is this knowing? – and what is the process of knowing? With knowledge you gather the past. In knowing you disperse it – you go on dispersing it. Whatsoever is known must be thrown away so that you are open again to know anew. You must die to the past; only then can you be alive to the present.

We all live in the past – that which is no more, that which has gone, that which is dead. We live in that past; that's why we are so dead. Life is always in the present and mind is always in the past; that's why mind cannot know life. There can be no meeting ground. There is no common ground where mind can meet life. Hence, the Upanishads are against mind.

Mind is always the memory – that which you have lived, that

which is past, that which is no more. Mind is just the past dust gathered upon you. Throw it away. Wash it away so that you are fresh, young, and you can meet the present, the ever young – the ever-young *brahman*.

In knowing, the past has to be constantly renounced. This is the basic renunciation. Die to the past so that you can be alive in the present. You cannot do both. If you are alive in the past, then you will be dead in the present. If you want to be alive in the present, be dead to the past. Each moment go on throwing the past dust. Don't allow it to gather. Go on renouncing it, go on throwing it. It is of no use. You have already used it, now it is just a dead shell. The bird has flown away from it. Don't go on collecting dead shells. They will become the imprisonment; they will hamper you. They will become so weighty that they will not allow you to move.

To me, a sannyasin, one who has renounced, means not that he has renounced wealth, not that he has renounced his house, not that he has renounced family, but one who has renounced the past – because that is the basic burden. That is your family; you go on living with the dead.

I have heard...

Once it happened that Jesus was walking on the road. It was just morning and the sun was just about to rise, and he saw a fisherman throwing his net on the lake. So he said to that fisherman – he came near him and said, "Why are you wasting your life just catching fishes? Follow me. I will show you how to catch the kingdom of God in your net."

The fisherman looked back. There was a different type of light in the eyes of Jesus. The fisherman was hypnotized. He threw down his net and followed Jesus. But just as they were passing out of the village a man came running and asked him, "Where are you going? Your father has died." His father was ill, very old. Any moment it was expected that he would die.

So the fisherman said to Jesus, "Jesus, allow me a few days so

I can go back and pay my respects to the old man who is dead and do all that is needed and expected from a son."

Jesus said, "You need not go. The dead will bury the dead." To Jesus the whole village was dead. So he said, "They will bury the dead; you need not worry about it."

Why did Jesus say that the dead will bury the dead? Because all those who live in the past are dead. Only those who live in the present are alive. Life means the present, the here and now. It is a very fleeting moment. You can catch it only when you are totally unburdened; otherwise you will miss. If your mind is moving toward the past you will miss the fleeting moment of life. It is so momentary, it is so fleeting, that if you are attached to the past you will go on missing it.

And this is happening. Even when you are not thinking of the past, you are thinking of the past reflected in the future. But you are never in the present, that much is certain. Either you are in the past which is no more, or in the future which is yet to be. Both are not, both are nonexistential. One is dead and one is not yet born. And whatsoever you think of the future is just a reflected past, a projected past, because what can you think of the future? You can think of tomorrow only in terms of yesterday because you don't know any other language.

You loved someone yesterday, now you think to love him tomorrow. It is going to be just the past again repeated with some modification. And those modifications also come from past experience. But nothing new can be projected into the future. Only the past can be projected. So you move like a shuttle between the past and the future, and in this constant movement the fleeting present, that which is life, is missed. And only through life can you enter the *brahman*.

The Upanishads say don't be attached to knowledge, don't be attached to memory, don't be attached to the past. Go on dying to it so that you are ever young, fresh, virgin. Again and again you are open. No past becomes an imprisonment around you.

You always move on and leave the dead shells to the past.

The sutra says:

He knows it who knows it not...

He knows it who knows it not... He who has not made it a knowledge – only he knows it who is still in the process of knowing, who is still searching, inquiring – who is still not closed, who is still going onward, still flowing. And this is going to be eternally so. No one ever reaches the goal; no one can reach the goal. Life really has no goal. It is just an eternal play – beginningless, endless. Man creates the goal. Why?

Man creates the goal because then he can be at ease. The goal is achieved – now you can relax. Now you can be dead; now you are not needed. But life has no goal. Rather, it creates many goals, but those goals are just temporary. Every goal is just a means to a further goal, and ultimately there is no goal; otherwise the *brahman* would have stopped at any moment, because the goal had been reached.

Existence has been existing beginninglessly. You would think that at any time the goal might have been achieved, everything would have stopped. But it has not happened so; it will never happen. The goal is a human creation. Life is goalless; that's why it is eternal. If there is a goal then life cannot be eternal, because when the goal is achieved life is dead. All goals are just temporary. When you can realize this you have realized the *brahman* – the purposeless energy moving goallessly, moving everywhere, but not moving to somewhere – moving toward nowhere. The movement is beautiful in itself; it is blissful in itself. The bliss is not somewhere in the goal, it is here and now, just in the movement, just in the pulsation of being alive.

When you look at a Buddha sitting under a *bodhi* tree, or you look at a Jesus on the cross, or you look at Mahavira standing under the skies, a question must arise in your mind: "What are they doing?" It cannot be conceived that Buddha is thinking about some business – he has no business. He is not thinking about his family – there is no family. Thinking about the future? – what can he think about the future? What is a Buddha doing under a *bodhi* tree? He is not doing anything. He simply is. The very happening of life, the breathing in and out, the very pulsation of being alive, is blissful. He is not doing anything else. He is simply in bliss.

But whenever you think about bliss, you always think as if bliss is something which he possesses in his hand. It is not something, it is just a way of existing – the right way of existing. There is no past and no future. Just under the *bodhi* tree, this very moment, the Buddha is simply alive. The heart is beating, the breath is coming in and out, the blood is circulating, and everything is alive, pulsating. He is not moving anywhere, he simply is. In this isness is bliss.

Hence, the continuous emphasis that when you don't desire you will be blissful. Why? – because desire leads you somewhere else. Desire doesn't allow you to be here. Desire says go on somewhere else; the goal is there in the future. Desire creates the future and forces you towards the future. When you are nondesiring, when there is no desire, you are here and now. You are under the *bodhi* tree, you have become a buddha.

A buddha means a state of consciousness – a state of consciousness which is not going anywhere to achieve any goal. Because of this realization, Buddha said, "There is no God." Just because he was so compassionate towards you he said there is no God, because if he says that God is, then you will make a desire out of him. You will want to achieve him. You would like to reach God, you would like to know God, so you will create a desire.

So Buddha says there is no God: drop all spiritual desire. Not that there is no God, but he says this just to help you drop all desiring and all future. Otherwise you go on changing the future. Sometimes the desire is worldly and sometimes it becomes spiritual, but the desiring remains the same.

Buddha says there is no *moksha;* there is no state of total freedom somewhere in heaven. There is no *moksha*. Not that there is no *moksha*, but he says this just to help you drop it; otherwise you will start desiring *moksha*, the liberated state – and desiring is the bondage. So when you desire *moksha*, liberation, you are still in bondage. He says this just to help you to drop all desiring so that you can be here and now.

People go on coming to Buddha and they ask, "What will happen when we die?"

Buddha says, "Nothing will happen. You simply die."

They are asking him to create a future even beyond death. They are not satisfied; this much future in their lifetimes is not enough. They want some future beyond death so they can project their minds more and they can desire and they can plan what to do after death. They go on insisting. In every village where Buddha moves they go on insisting, "What will happen to the enlightened one, to you, when you die?"

Buddha says, "Nothing will happen. I will simply die. As the flame of a lamp ceases to be, I will cease."

They are not satisfied; they feel uneasy. They say, "But where will the flame go? Will it meet the *brahman*? Will it become cosmic? What will happen to the enlightened soul?"

Buddha is hard. He says, "Nothing. Just a flame is put out. Do you ask where the flame has gone? No one asks where the flame has gone because everyone knows it has just ceased."

The word *nirvana* means cessation of the flame. Buddha never uses the word *moksha*, he never uses *heaven*, he never talks about paradise, he never uses any word that can create future. He simply says nirvana. Nirvana means the flame has ceased. Don't ask what happens, "Why? Does the flame really cease to be?" It never ceases to be, but just through his compassion he is telling a lie because the truth will create a desire in you.

If he says there will be bliss – *sat-chit-anand* – if he says there will be bliss and existence and consciousness, or if he says that there will be a kingdom of God, then a desire will be created. And if the desire is there, there is not going to be any kingdom of God. Cessation of desire will bring you here and now. There is no possibility to move into the future; you are thrown back to the present. And once you are thrown back to the present you are in paradise. You will be in the divine, you will become one with the *brahman*.

The Upanishads say: *He knows it who knows it not*...Don't create any memory; don't help create the past. Go on dropping it. You have used it, why go on carrying it? Don't make it a knowledge.

People come to me and say, "Yesterday the meditation was just wonderful." You have become non-meditative because of yesterday's meditation. Now that man will go on looking for yesterday to be repeated today. He will wait. He will not be meditating; he will not be totally in it. Part of his mind will be looking backwards to see when that will happen again – and it will not happen. In the meditation, his mind was totally in the moment; now it is not. Now he is looking backwards; he has brought in a new thing. Now the situation is not the same. He is not totally in it; he is expecting a result. It will not happen and then he will come to me and say, "What has gone wrong? Yesterday it happened, but today it didn't happen and I am feeling very frustrated."

The mechanism is simple. Yesterday it could happen because you had no past about it. Remember, you had no past about it, no expectation about it. You couldn't project any future because you didn't know anything. You were ignorant, so it happened. You were simple, innocent, in the moment – just doing it without any expectation for a result because the result was unknown.

Now it is known. It has happened, it has become the past. Now it is your knowledge. Now this knowledge will become the barrier. Now you can do whatsoever you like, but it is not going to happen. Knowledge becomes the barrier; the past becomes the barrier to the present. So if it happened yesterday, forget it. Drop that yesterday.

Remember one thing more: you will be frustrated if it is not happening. And you will be frustrated even if it happens again, because it will be just a repetition. You will get fed up. You will get fed up even with your meditation if it goes on repeating, being the same. Drop the past, because if the past is there it is not going to happen. And even if sometimes it happens, it is going to be just a repetition of the past and you will get bored. In both ways the past goes on interfering with the present.

Why do you feel it is a repetition? You feel it is a repetition because you go on comparing with the past. If you drop the past it is always new; it is never a repetition. Repetition means you are constantly comparing it with the past experience. Drop the past completely and you will be open to the present; whatsoever happens will be new and you will never get bored.

Everyone is bored because of this nonsense going on – bringing in the past again and again. You kissed your beloved yesterday and now you kiss her again and you compare. The very beauty of the kiss is gone because it is just a repetition. Sooner or later you will get fed up. Sooner or later you would like to escape from your beloved. She will look like an enemy because now she has become a situation in which everything has become a repetition. Forget the past. It is killing you. It is killing your love, it is killing your life, it is killing every possibility. Drop the past. Don't make it a knowledge. Be fresh again and again. Every moment move and don't carry the past.

> *He knows it who knows it not, and he knows it not who knows it.*

He knows it not who knows it, who says, "I know." This is the indication that he has stopped knowing. Knowledge is complete; the book is closed. This man is dead. A dead man cannot be in contact with a live force.

> *To the man of true knowledge it is the unknown, while to the ignorant it is the known.*

Go anywhere on the earth: there are churches, temples, *gurudwaras,* mosques. There, everyone is worshipping; the whole earth seems to be religious. Everyone "knows" about God and life is such a misery, such a suffering. Everyone "knows" about God – not only knows: everyone argues about him.

There are two types of ignorant people: one who says there is a God and they argue for it, and another who says there is no God and they argue against it. But both believe that they know. Theists, atheists, both believe that they know. In one thing they both agree – that they have knowledge. Not only this: they try to prove that they have the true knowledge.

The Upanishads say that only ignorant people can claim that they know: the divine has become known, the mystery is solved; now there is no mystery but a theory, a philosophy, a scripture; now there is no mystery and everything is known. Only ignorant people can do this. They can kill the mystery by asserting that the ultimate is known. Those who are wise will insist that the mystery remains a mystery. Even if you come to face it, encounter it, even if you come to meet it, the mystery is not solved. On the contrary, it is deepened more. It becomes more mysterious, it goes on becoming more and more mysterious. The more you know, the more it becomes unknown.

This is the mystery of religious knowing. The more you know it, the more it becomes unknown – the more you feel how it is impossible to know, difficult to know. The more you know it, the more you become aware of your incapacity, your helplessness, your ignorance. The more and more God becomes unknown, the nearer you approach. And when someone really enters the divine, he comes to know that it is unknowable – not only unknown. Then he comes to realize there is no possibility to know. What does it mean? It means there is no possibility to be finished with it. It is going to be an eternal concern. You cannot finish, you cannot say, "Now I will drop this religious inquiry, I can drop this religiousness. The thing is finished." No, it cannot be finished.

People come to me and they go on asking, "When will it happen that the search ceases, that we reach, that the ultimate happens?" They are in such a hurry. It is not going to end anywhere, remember. It is not going to end. This quest is eternal. You will go on growing. You will go on growing into deeper awareness, into deeper bliss. But still something always remains hidden, and you go on uncovering it. But it is never uncovered completely; it cannot be so. This is how the very nature of the ultimate reality is.

But teachers have been saying, "Don't worry. Sooner or later you will reach." I myself go on saying it. People come to me and they say, "We have been meditating for so long. When will it happen?" I say, "Wait! Soon it will happen." But these are all lies. If I say that it is not going to happen ever, you will simply drop the whole effort; you will feel hopeless. So I will go on saying it is going to happen.

It is happening already, but it is not going to happen in such a way that the journey ends. And one day you yourself will become aware of the beauty of this non-ending process. Then you will feel what an ugly question you were asking. You were asking how to end all this. The very question is ugly and absurd. You don't know, but what you are asking is against yourself – because if it ends, you end with it. If there is no search, nothing to be revealed, nothing to be loved, nothing to be known, nothing to be entered, how can you be? If you were in such a state, you would want to commit suicide.

Bertrand Russell has somewhere joked. He said, "I cannot believe in the Hindu conception of liberation – of *moksha* – because," he says, "in *moksha*, the Hindu conception of liberation, you will be freed of everything: nothing is to be done, nothing will happen. You will be sitting and sitting and sitting under *bodhi* trees, and nothing will happen because everything has ceased." So Russell says, "That will be too much. It will become a burden, and the liberation will become a new type of bondage. Everyone will get fed up, and everyone will start praying: 'Send us back to the earth or even to hell.' Even hell will be better because there will be something there to be done, there will be some news. But in *moksha* there will be no news, no events, no happenings. Just think: eternally no happenings, no movement – what type of *moksha* will this be?"

Really, when Hindus talk about this *moksha*, or Jainas talk about this *moksha*, that doesn't mean that such a *moksha* exists or such a state exists. This is just to help you, because *you* cannot conceive of the eternal process. So they say, "Yes, don't be worried. Sooner or later everything will stop and then you will not have to do anything." But you don't know what type of misery this will be. This will be more miserable than the earth is.

Moksha is not a static thing. It is a dynamic process. And *moksha* is not some geographical place. It is a way of looking at things, it is an attitude. If you can be alive moment to moment, you will never ask when all this is going to finish. The very question shows that you are not alive and you are not enjoying life as it is. If you enjoy life, you will not ask when it is going to end, you will not ask when you are going to be freed of it. Then you are already free. In the very enjoyment the freedom has come. Whether it ends or not is not a concern at all. If it ends it is good. If it doesn't end it is also good. Then you accept it totally.

The sutra says: *To the man of true knowledge it is the unknown, while to the ignorant it is the known.* It is only ignorance which can claim such a thing. And the more stupid the mind, the more arrogant will be the claim, the more dogmatic will be the claim.

But even that dogmatic claim may impress you. There are religious fanatics all over the world who go on claiming. And their claims impress people because just by their aggression, their dogmatism, their absolute definiteness, you are overpowered. You think this man must have achieved because he is claiming so boldly. You are so uncertain about yourself that anyone, any stupid man, can claim anything with certainty and you will be impressed. But remember this: only for ignorance does such certainty exist. A man who is wise cannot be dogmatically certain. He cannot assert anything absolutely; he cannot assert anything in an imperative way.

For example, if you ask Mahavira anything he will look very

uncertain. He is not, but he is a wise man. If you ask him, "Is there God?" he will say, "Maybe, maybe not." This is the mind that doesn't claim – because if he says, "He is," it becomes a claim; and if he says, "He is not," it still becomes a claim. He says, "Maybe, perhaps." *Syad* is his word – perhaps, maybe.

You will not be impressed by him. That is why such a great man has so few followers; Jainas are not more than thirty lakhs. Twenty-five centuries have passed. Even if one Adam and Eve were converted by Mahavira they would have created such a number. Only thirty lakhs, three million people in twenty-five centuries – and they too are Jainas only by birth, because to be a Jaina means to be in the attitude of perhaps, maybe.

Why does Mahavira go on saying maybe, whatsoever you ask? Even if you ask if there is a soul, he says, "Maybe, maybe not." Why this insistence? Because he never claims knowledge and he allows everything to remain unknown – that is why the insistence on maybe, because then things remain unknown, uncertain, vague, and you can inquire. When everything is certain, inquiry ceases. If he says, "Yes – there is a God," or, "There is soul," or, "There is bliss," inquiry has stopped.

Now what can you do? Either you can follow him or not follow him, but he says, "Maybe." He leaves everything open. That is the meaning of *syad*: everything is open. He doesn't force anything upon you. He doesn't say yes dogmatically, he doesn't say no, because his aggression may impress itself upon you, it may become fatal to you – just listening to him. And Mahavira is such a person that you will be impressed, you will be magnetized just listening to him. If he says, "There is," it may become knowledge to you and you may go on believing that there is. That will be destructive: to create knowledge is to be destructive.

But only those who are very sensitive can understand Mahavira. Those who are insensitive, ignorant, stupid, will think, "This man doesn't know. Our village pundit is better. At least he says, 'Yes, there is a God, and I can prove it. I can give you proofs from literature – from the Vedas, the Upanishads. I can argue that there is a God and I can convince you.' And this man Mahavira says, 'Maybe.' What does he mean? Has he known or not?" People go on asking Mahavira, "If you have known, then why not say yes? Or if you have come to know that there is no God, then why not say no? Be clear."

Why do you ask for clarity? You ask for clarity so that you can follow blindly. You ask for clarity so that nothing is left for you to work out. You are lazy, so you ask for clarity. Mahavira will not give you clarity. Really, whenever you come across such a person as Mahavira he will create more confusion in you because out of confusion inquiry is born. Out of certainty comes only ignorance.

This sutra says that the ultimate is the unknown to the wise, to those who know, *...while to the ignorant it is the known*. Don't be too certain. Remain uncertain. Uncertainty means fluidity; uncertainty means every alternative is possible. You are not a fixed entity. The future is not going to be just a repetition of the past. Something new is possible every moment. Remain vague. Don't insist on consistencies. Even if there is apparently a contradiction, don't try to choose in haste. Wait, weigh, and even in the contradiction try to find something which joins the two opposites. That third thing will be nearer to truth than any polarity.

The whole emphasis is to remain in a state of receptivity for the unknown to happen to you. Be sensitive, fluid, impressionable, as if some guest is to come and you are waiting. The door is open. Even the breeze passing through the trees or the breeze passing through the dead leaves – and you jump to the door. The guest may have come; you are alert.

The guest has not come yet. You are simply waiting. In this alertness, one comes to know the ultimate core of reality. The guest never comes really. He is always coming, he is always coming – coming and coming and coming. He is always nearer and nearer and nearer, closer and closer, but he never really comes. You always remain in waiting. This waiting is beautiful. It is bliss – if you can wait. But then you need a very sensitive mind. Mediocre, stupid minds won't be of any help there because a stupid mind will say "Now come in; otherwise I am going to close the door and rest. I have waited long enough."

There is a poem by Rabindranath Tagore, one of the most beautiful ever written. The poem is known as "The King of the Night":

There is a temple, a big temple, with hundreds of priests to serve the deity there. One night it happens that the chief priest has a dream. He dreams that the king, the deity, has appeared to him and he says, "Tonight I am coming."

He awakes feeling very disturbed. He is very worried whether this dream is just a dream or a vision: "Is this just dreaming, my mind dreaming? Or is it really an intimation? Is the deity, the god of the temple, really to come? Or is it just my own imagination?"

He is afraid to tell the others because they will think he has gone mad. They will say, "The deity has never come. We have been worshipping the stone deity since the temple was built and he has never come. You have been dreaming. You have fallen prey to your own imagination." But then he is also afraid that if he doesn't speak up and suddenly the deity comes and they are not prepared to receive him, then what will happen? So he thinks it is better to be foolish and speak.

So in the morning he gathers all the priests and he says, "The deity has appeared in a dream and he says this night he is coming: 'Wait and be ready to receive me.'"

They all start laughing, and they say, "This is a dream. Don't believe in dreams; don't be foolish. If the news spreads, then people will laugh if the deity doesn't come."

So they decide that they should not tell anybody, but they should prepare just in case. So they clean the whole temple. They prepare everything. But they know that it is just a dream, so it is half-hearted, it is just in case. They do everything – but it is not done with love, it is not with waiting. They already know it is a dream. The dream has not opened them. They are knowers and they know the history: it has never happened. They know the scriptures, they are great scholars, so they say, "It has never happened and it is not going to happen."

Scholars always think that the future is just the past repeated again and again, it is never new. But still, not to take a chance, the priests prepare. They clean, they decorate; much food is prepared for the coming god. But they know that this is for them also. This is for them *only;* the god is not coming. So their hearts are not ready, only the temple is ready. And when the hearts are not ready, what can a temple do? So they wait. Night falls, it becomes dark. The road is dead, no one is moving, everyone around has gone to sleep.

Then they say, "It is enough. We have waited long just for a dream. We are foolish. Now we must eat the food we have prepared. The whole day has been an unnecessary fast." So they eat and they enjoy, and then they fall asleep. They are tired from the whole day's work of cleaning and decoration, so they fall asleep.

Just at midnight they hear in their sleep that a chariot is coming near the temple. The noise comes; one priest hears it and he says, "It seems the king, the god, has come. I hear the wheels of the chariot making noise."

Somebody else says, "Don't be stupid and don't disturb our sleep. We have been waiting too long; it is enough. Now don't disturb." So they fall asleep again. Then someone hears footsteps. Someone is coming up the steps of the temple – the temple has many steps.

Someone again says, half asleep, "It seems the king has come. Someone is coming up to the door – and the very sound of the feet is so qualitatively different – it cannot be that of a man."

But then the chief priest himself says, "Don't be foolish! Don't disturb us the whole night. We have been working the whole day. If he had to come he should have come by the evening. No need – it has never been heard that he comes at midnight."

Then someone knocks at the door and someone hears again that someone is knocking on the door. Then a priest becomes absolutely mad and says, "Stop completely! This is nothing but a breeze striking on the door." So they sleep.

In the morning they all weep and cry and scream because the chariot had come. There are marks on the road, and the god had come up to the temple. On the steps in the dust there are footprints. But now nothing can be done. The moment, the opportunity, is lost.

This is the whole situation. Really, he is always coming, his chariot is always near the door. He is knocking continuously, but you are closed. Be open – that is the basic message of the Upanishads. Don't be knowledgeable. Don't cling to the past, to the history, to the memory. Be open and wait for the unknown to happen. And whenever it happens don't try to make it known. Whatsoever happens, throw it away and be ready again. Something new will happen again. The *brahman* remains unknown continuously.

> *Indeed, he attains immortality who realizes it in and through every bodh – pulsation of knowledge and awareness.*

No knowledge is ultimate. Every knowing is just a pulsation – just a pulsation, a vibration. Don't make any vibration the ultimate. In deep meditation you will come to feel a great silence: this is just a pulsation. Don't think this is *brahman. Brahman* is always more. Whatsoever happens, he is always more. Don't identify any happening with the *brahman*; otherwise you will stop.

In meditation, many times a deep bliss will happen to you; you will be washed away. But don't say this is the *brahman* because the moment you say this is *brahman* you are closed. It is just a pulsation of *bodh,* just a pulsation of knowing, just a pulsation of consciousness, but just a wave. Never transform any wave into an ocean. Remember, when you make a wave into an ocean it has become knowledge and then you are closed. Let every wave be just a wave and wait for the ocean.

And remember, the ocean never comes; it is always the waves

which are coming. The ocean comes through the waves, but it is always the waves which are coming. The ocean never comes. So don't fix yourself and don't say that this wave is the ocean. The moment you say it you are closed.

Many people have reached deep ecstasies and then they stop because then they say, "This is *brahman*; the ultimate has been achieved." Remember, it is never achieved. It is simply achievable but never achieved; approachable but never approached.

The journey remains, and it is beautiful that the journey remains. Whatsoever knowing comes to you, the Upanishads say it is just a pulsation of knowledge and awareness. And if you can feel this pulsation of knowledge and awareness, you will attain immortality. Why? You become mortal, you become prone to death, because you cling to the dead – the dead past. If you don't cling to the past there is no death for you, it cannot happen. The body will disappear, but that is not death. It becomes a death because you have become too much obsessed with the body – because you have lived in the body in the past.

When a person has lived a hundred years in his body, in that hundred years' experience of living in the body he has become obsessed with the body. Now he thinks he is the body. A hundred years of routine, habit, has created this false notion that he is the body. That is why he feels that death is coming.

Children are less afraid of death than old men. Why? – because they are still new to the body. It has not become their experience and knowledge. They are fresh. Children can play with snakes without any fear. They can play with poison, they can move into any danger. They are not afraid. Why? – because they are still fresh to this new abode. They are not clinging to it too much. It has not yet become a past. But sooner or later, when they have lived in it for many years, they will cling to it. Then they will be afraid. Then they will be afraid of death because in death the body will die and they have come to feel that they are the body.

A person who lives moment to moment, who goes on dying to the past, is never attached to anything. Attachment comes from the accumulated past. If you can be unattached to the past every moment, you are always fresh, young, just born. You pulsate with life and that pulsation gives you immortality. You are immortal, only unaware of the fact.

> *Indeed, he attains immortality who realizes it in and through every bodh. Through the atman he obtains strength and vigor and through its knowledge, immortality.*

The more you know life, the inner life, the atman, the more you know that you are immortal. There is going to be no death: you are deathless.

> *For one who realizes it here, in this world, there is true life.*

For one who realizes it here, *in this world, there is true life.* So don't hanker after any other life; don't hanker for something to happen after death. If it cannot happen here it will not happen ever. If it can happen it can happen here and now. This earth, this life is the present. Don't condemn it for another life. There is no other life. Life is always *here;* life is always in this moment. Don't postpone it because through postponing you may miss the opportunity.

> *For one who realizes it here, there is true life. For one who does not so realize it, great is the loss. Discovering the atman in every single being, the wise ones, dying to this world of sense-experience, become immortal.*

Go on dying to the past, and you will not have any world around you with which you are attached, obsessed. Dying to the past, you die to this world. Remember, this world is created through your experience; it *is* your experience. Dying to experience, you are so young that you don't create any world around you. The real world is not the problem – the world around your mind is the problem.

I have heard…

Once it happened that a house was on fire. The master of the house was weeping and crying, and beating his chest. His whole life was destroyed. Then suddenly a man came and said, "Why are you weeping? Don't you know? Your son has settled yesterday; the house has been sold."

The tears disappeared – the man even started smiling. He said, "Is it so?" The house was still burning, but now his inner house was not burning. This house was not the problem, but an inner attachment.

Then the son came and said, "Yes, we were just going to settle, but it is not settled yet."

The man's tears started flowing. He was weeping and beating his chest, but the house was completely unaware of what was happening to this man.

Within minutes everything changes – the inner world changes. If the house were not his, then he would not have any problem. The problem was not the house, but that "the house is mine." That "mine" creates the inner world.

If you go on throwing the past away, then nothing is yours. Then nothing is your possession; you always remain without any possession. That is what sannyas is. Not that you will not use a house, not that you will not use clothes, not that you will not live in this world – but nothing will be your possession. The world of the inner mind disappears. Then the real world is beautiful. All ugliness is projected by your mind, by the dead past; then life becomes ugly.

With the living present, life is just beautiful and blissful.

Get ready for the meditation.

…

CHAPTER 11

BE ALIVE TO THE PRESENT

The first question:

> **Osho,**
> **You said that to live moment to moment, one must throw away one's dead past and dead memories. Does it mean that all the memories have to be dissolved and destroyed to transcend the mind? But one needs a strong mind and an intense and sufficient accumulation of memories to function in this world.**

To die to the past does not mean that you will not be able to remember it. It does not mean that all your memories will be dissolved or destroyed. It only means that now you don't live in those memories, you are not identified with those memories. You are freed from them. They will remain, but now they will be just a part of your brain, not part of your consciousness.

The brain is a mechanism, just like a tape-recording machine. The brain goes on recording everything. The brain is the physical part. It will go on recording, and your memories cannot be destroyed unless the brain is destroyed. But that is not the problem. The problem is that your consciousness is filled with memories. Your consciousness goes on identifying itself with the brain and the brain is always stirred by your consciousness – and memories go on flooding you.

When it is said, "Die to the past," it means don't be identified with the brain. You can use the brain; then it is just an instrument. When you need it you will use it – and you *will* need it. You will have to go back home; you will have to remember where you live – where your house is, what your name is. You can use these memories, but use them; don't be used by them. That is the problem.

While you are here you need not think about the house where you live in your town, but you go on thinking about it. You need not remember your wife while you are here, but you go on talking with her even though she is not here. When you go back home you must recognize that she is your wife, but there is no need to be bothered with her now. She must not come into the mind; the mind must not go on functioning unnecessarily. It must not bring in the past; it must not flood the present with the past.

The memory remains. It is not being destroyed. Through meditation the mind is not destroyed. You simply start transcending it. It remains a storehouse; you need not live in it. If you live in the mind then you are mad. You need not live in a storehouse. When you need something, you go into the storeroom, bring that something out and use it. The storehouse is not a living-room, but you have made it one. Your storehouse of memory has become your living room; you live there. Don't live there, that is the whole meaning. Be in the present and whenever the past is needed, use it. But don't allow it to go on continuously overflooding you. That overflooding of the past makes your consciousness dim and dull. Then you cannot see with clear eyes, you cannot feel with a clear heart. Then nothing is clear, everything becomes confused.

When you are not identified with the mind you will have a very clear memory. Right now you don't have a really good memory because you are not your master. Your mind is just a mad mechanism. When you need to remember something it doesn't come, and when you don't need it, it goes on coming:

you are not the master. You cannot be the master if you become identified with the slave. If you become too much attached to the slave, the slave will start mastering you.

So if you die to the past you will not become less efficient in the functioning of your mind – you will become more efficient. A master is always more efficient. When he wants to remember, he remembers; but when he doesn't want to remember, he doesn't remember. When he says to the mind, "Function," it functions. When he says, "Stop," the mind stops. I have to use memories. For instance, I have to talk to you; I have to use words, I have to use language. But I use them only when I am talking to you. The moment I am not talking the mind stops. Then there is total vacuum – void. Then there is no cloud.

It is just like your legs: when you want to walk you use your legs. But if you go on moving them while just sitting or standing, people will say you are mad. Then you may say, "What can I do? My legs go on moving; I cannot do anything." And if someone says to you, "Stop this," you will say, "If I stop, then when I want to walk what will I do? I will become less efficient. If I stop, then I will lose the capacity to walk, so I have to use them constantly." Remember, if you use them constantly, when the time comes to walk, you will feel tired. You are already tired.

While sitting there is no need to use the legs. While not talking there is no need to use words. Don't verbalize within. While not using the past there is no need to allow it to flood you. Dying to the past means becoming master of your mind. Then you will be more efficient. But that efficiency will be of a different quality – a totally different quality. There will be no effort in it.

Whenever you want to remember now, you have to make an effort because you are so tired; your brain is so tired, continuously working. There is no stop for it, no relaxation. Even while you are asleep and the body is resting, the mind continues to work. Dreaming, it is working – constantly working. It is a miracle that you are not mad. Or maybe you are already mad but you are not aware; or maybe, because everyone is mad like you, you cannot compare and you don't know what is happening to you.

Don't be afraid, your efficiency will be increased. And the quality will be different because there will be no effort. When you need, you can use your mind. It is just an instrument; just like your hands and legs it is a physical part of you. Memory is a physical thing, remember; so if your brain is destroyed you may be alive and conscious but you will lose your memory. If a particular part of your brain is destroyed, then a particular type of memory will be lost.

One of my friends, a doctor, fell from a train. He fell on his head and something was destroyed. For three years all memory was lost; he couldn't even recognize his father or mother. He was alive, fully alive, conscious; but he couldn't read, couldn't write, because all memory was lost. He started from *ABCD* again, and only after three years was he able to use his brain again. But then he was just a child of three years; all the medical knowledge, all the degrees that he had were lost because particular tissues, particular nerves in the brain, were destroyed and with them all memory was lost or cut off.

Now, in China, they use brainwashing. They give some electrical stimulation to particular parts of the brain; just by electrical shock they destroy the inner memory. So if you are a religious man they will give your mind a shock treatment and all your memories – that you are religious, that you go to this church or you read this holy book, or you belong to this sect – will be destroyed. Then you can easily be converted into a communist because then you don't know who you are.

And now these techniques have become available to the whole world. Every government has the secrets. And the most dangerous thing that is going to happen soon all over the world will be not physical violence, but, rather, psychological violence. You need not murder a man; you simply destroy a particular memory in him. He is brainwashed, now he will have to learn from *ABC*, so he cannot fight with you. If you want to convert him into a communist or an anticommunist, first destroy the memory; then he becomes like a child, helpless. Then start the training again. Now a new memory will be created, a new learning, a new conditioning.

The atom bomb is not as great a danger as these secrets because the very soul of man can be enslaved through them. If Jesus is born now in Soviet Russia or communist China, they will not crucify him; first they will try to destroy his memory. They cannot be successful with Jesus, but they can be successful with you. They cannot succeed with Jesus because he is already unidentified with the memory. If you destroy the memory nothing is really lost because he lives in his consciousness, not in his memories. But you don't really have any consciousness separate from the memories, so if your memory is destroyed your consciousness is destroyed. You don't know how to function without the memories.

So for the new generation, the coming world, meditation is a must because only that can protect you from political dictatorship – nothing else. They will not put you in jail or send you to Siberia – no, those things are just out of date now. They will simply put an electrical instrument around your head. They will give particular electric shocks to the brain, and you will become just like a child. They will wash away the memories, just as you can erase on a tape recorder. There, just electrical stimulation is used, and whatsoever is recorded is erased; then you can record again. The same is possible with the brain because the brain is a mechanism.

And when I say die to the past, I mean don't get so attached to the brain that you don't know that you can exist without the brain. Knowing this, realizing, "Without the brain I can exist; I am consciousness and not the memories; memories are just my instruments," you will become free from your own mind. And once you are free from your mind, no one can make a slave of you. Otherwise, everyone is trying to manipulate you to make you a slave.

Religions, so-called religions have done that. They go on manipulating your mind. When you were just a child they started teaching you that you are a Hindu or a Christian or a Catholic or a Protestant. They went on teaching you from the very childhood when you didn't know anything; when you were not alert; when you were not aware; when you couldn't recognize what is true and what is false. When you could not think, they started to teach you, to condition you. They made a Christian out of you or a Hindu or a Jaina or a Mohammedan. These are slaveries.

Now there is no need to get hold of children; even an old man can be made a child again by just washing his mind. Then he will have to learn from *ABC*. And when you learn from *ABC* you cannot argue, when you have to learn from *ABC* you cannot disbelieve. That is why every religion wants to get hold of children and every religion tries to force some type of religious education because only in childhood…

Really, if you cannot get hold of a child before seven years of age, you will never get hold of him. Only before seven years of age can you make a slave of him. Then he will never know that he is a slave because slavery goes deeper than his awareness. You cannot think that being a Christian you are a slave or being a Hindu you are a slave – or can you?

Society has played a trick upon you. When you were not fully alert they conditioned your mind. Now when you think, the conditioning has gone deeper than thinking. Whatsoever you think, that conditioning colors it. Even if you become anti-Christian and you were taught to be a Christian, your anti-Christianity will carry your Christianity with it. Even your anti-Christianity will be colored by the conditioning that was given to you. You will be obsessed with the same thing in the reverse order.

Friedrich Nietzsche was against Christianity, particularly against Christ. But he was brought up as a Christian. His whole life he struggled; his whole life he went on writing against Christ. But he was so much obsessed with Christ that as he was going mad, in the last stage of his life before he became mad, he started signing his name "Anti-Christ, Friedrich Nietzsche." That conditioning had gone so deep. You can become anti, but you cannot be indifferent.

Die to the past. Be alive to the present, to the moment you are in – it will not destroy your mind. Really, it will give a rest to your restless mind. Your efficiency will grow, and there will be no effort. You will not need to remember. You will simply remember because it is the functioning of the mind; you need not make any effort.

I have been traveling all over this country for fifteen years, and I have known thousands and thousands of people. Even after ten years when I return to the same town, I remember the faces, I remember the names. Even I was surprised: What is the reason? – and I had not made any effort. But I am interested in people, that is all. If you are really interested in something you will remember it; there is no need to make any effort.

Remembering is a mechanical functioning of the memory. If you are really interested in a person you will remember the face even after many lives. I remember many faces after many lives. You cannot forget them because there is no question of forgetting. The mechanical part of your brain just goes on recording everything. The only thing that is needed is your interest.

When you are interested, your mechanism is focused on the person; it records just like the lens of a camera. If you are interested in a face the camera moves, it records. If I am interested in what you are saying my mind is focused; it records, it goes on recording. There is no need to make any effort. If you are not interested, then it will not record because then it is not focused.

So if you forget things it is because you are not interested. If you forget things it is because your mind is confused. If you forget things and cannot remember and are not efficient, it means that while you are seeing a face many memories inside go on moving. Your mirror is not vacant; your lens is already overcrowded.

Someone is saying, "My name is Ram," and you nod your head, yes, as if you have heard it. But your mind is filled with so many things you have not heard. And then you say, "Why have I forgotten the name?" Really, you never heard the name. You were not interested in the person – not so interested that your mind became silent.

Whenever you are interested the mind is silent – your whole being is open. The memories go on being recorded and, whenever you need something, it will come up. But it is not so easy with you. Whenever you need something everything gets entangled because your mind is so full. Nothing is clear-cut; everything penetrates, trespasses, every other thing. Nothing is clear. The clarity is not there; only confusion is there. Because of that confusion you are not efficient. You will be more efficient – and without any effort – if you become alert to the moment and don't allow the past to go on overburdening you.

The second question:

Osho,
I feel and realize the futility of desiring. There seems to be no ambition in me. But yet there is a thirst, a yearning, and an inner sense of unfulfillment. Please explain whether this too is a part of desiring.

Yes, this too is a part of desiring – the negative part. Everything has two parts, the positive and the negative. The positive part of desiring is to desire something, to be ambitious. To be aware of the object of desire is a positive desire. The negative desire is: one is not aware of the object of desire, but one is aware only of the thirst of desire – the yearning.

These are the two parts. The subjective feeling of unfulfillment is the negative part of ambition and being obsessed with an object of desire is the positive part of ambition. Both are ambition. And if you intellectually understand that desire is futile, the negative part will remain with you – if you *intellectually* understand that desire is futile and this is not an existential experience.

You have been hearing, you have been listening and you have been reading. And buddhas and christs have been talking to the world and they have been saying you are in misery because of desire, that you are in suffering because of desire – and they say they are in bliss because of desirelessness. And you have seen them: you have seen their eyes, you have seen their faces, you have seen the grace, the bliss, the ecstasy that just moves around them. Even in their shadow the ecstasy, the dance is there. You have seen them and you have heard them and they say if you desire you will be in suffering, if you don't desire you will be in ecstasy and bliss.

Now intellectually you can understand this, that desire creates tension, desire creates the future, desire creates expectations, and when desire is not fulfilled you are in misery. Or even when it is fulfilled you are not in bliss. When it is fulfilled you feel that this is nothing – this is nothing compared to the dream, compared to the hope. You fall in love with a person, a girl or a boy, you fall in love with a house, you fall in love with a car, and you think, "If this woman is achieved I will be in absolute bliss." But this is your dream; no woman can fulfill it.

This is just fantasy; no real woman can fulfill it. Every real woman will be just a faint thing compared to it. But there is no fault on the woman's part. This is your mind which goes on fantasizing. You create a fantasy, a romance, and you move high in the heavens. Then you meet the woman. If you cannot achieve your desire, if you cannot get possession of her, you will be in misery, because you had a dream and the dream remained unfulfilled. You will feel a constant pain in the heart.

But I tell you, if you meet her, if you can get her, you will be in a deeper misery, because at least the dream remains intact if you have not met her – you can go on dreaming. But if you meet her you will see that no woman lives in heaven. As you live on earth, she lives on earth. She is as earthly as you – even more. Woman is more earthly than man. She will shatter all your dreams. And when you awake from your dreaming, you will be in misery. Whether your dream is fulfilled or not, misery will be the result. Out of dreaming only misery results.

This you can understand. Your experience can also be helpful.

Intellectually you can understand, and then you can come to conclude that it is futile to desire – to be ambitious is futile; it leads to misery and hell. But this will stop only positive desiring; the negative will remain. Really, you are still desiring – you are now desiring the state of non-desire. You are *still* desiring – now desirelessness. Desirelessness has become the object of desire. You will feel a yearning, a search, a thirst and an unfulfillment.

What is to be done now? What can be done? Intellectually nothing will happen to you, you will go on changing the object of desire and the negative part will go on pushing you into new desires. *Live* it. Don't believe in Buddha, don't believe in Jesus, don't believe in me. Live it. Desire and live, and experience desire in its totality. And don't hurry, don't make any haste to conclude. Your misery is because you make such hurried conclusions.

You are so susceptible to believing anything because you don't want to go through experience. Experience may be painful – let it be. But only experience can help you. Premature conclusions, premature beliefs, will be of no help. You are simply wasting opportunities. Desire and desire intensely, I tell you: desire intensely and suffer!

Buddha comes to his conclusions not because of previous buddhas. The Upanishads were in existence; he could have read them. He was well educated, well cultured, he knew all the scriptures, but they didn't help him. He moved through desire, he moved through experience; he suffered, he went through the fire. And only through his own experience did he come to conclude that desire is futile.

Your conclusion is not *your* conclusion; that is the problem. Your conclusion is borrowed. You are really afraid to go through suffering, so before going through suffering you start believing. But suffering is a discipline. The only real discipline is suffering. Nothing real can be achieved without it.

And you are acting like small children: in their books, the answers are given in the back. Small children will just look at the answers. They get the answers, but they don't know the process.

The problem is given and the answer is given in the last chapter. They look at the answer and they know the answer, but this is not *their* answer. They know the problem and they know the answer, but they don't know the process – how the answer is achieved.

You have been looking at the answer without going through the process. Answers are there. Buddhas have existed; they have said everything that can be said and you can memorize the answers, but without the process you will not be transformed. So forget the answers; that is what the Upanishads say. Knowledge is the barrier: forget knowledge. If you are ignorant, then you are ignorant. Start from your ignorance; don't start from anybody else's knowledge.

It is better to start with your ignorance because then that can lead you towards knowledge. But you always start with somebody else's knowledge. Then you move in a false world, then you go on accumulating conclusions – you know everything without knowing anything. You are in such a hurry. You say, "I don't want to go through the process; I want the answer."

The answer can be given to you – but unless you move through the process, the answer will not be a lived answer. Unless lived, it is futile. You know desire is futile, you know anger is poison, you know greed leads to misery – you know everything. But that knowledge is of no use. Throw it. It is rubbish.

Just be aware of your state of mind: the yearning is there, the thirst is there, the unfulfillment is there. That means you are ready to desire. Now desire, and don't listen to the buddhas: they are dangerous. Desire! Move! You will have to move your own way; you will have to suffer your own way. Nobody can escape suffering. The law is universal. Nobody can come to shortcuts; there are none. You will have to move your own way, you will have to pass through your own hells.

When you have passed through them, transcended them, have become richer, experienced them and a maturity has happened to you – only then will desire fall. Desire will disappear and then there will be no negative part to it. Then the total desire will disappear because you will come to realize that this is nonsense. "I have been creating my own hell." And this is not intellectual, this is not in the mind. Your total being, your whole being, will come to conclude and this conclusion will be through your experience, not through anybody else's.

Then desire disappears without giving birth to another desire in a different guise. Otherwise you will go on changing the object. Sometimes you desire wealth and then you feel misery. Then you conclude desire is misery, so you start desiring godliness or you start desiring heaven or you start desiring liberation or you start desiring meditation, ecstasy – but you go on desiring. And if you go on desiring, you are simply changing the shape of the desire, the object of the desire. But the desire remains the same: you are not changing, you remain the same. You are moving in a pattern, in a circle. You are not moving anywhere.

Hence, I go on saying again and again, be aware – beware of buddhas, christs, krishnas. Beware of me, because I go on saying things to you which you can believe and then it is dangerous. When I say something try to understand it; don't conclude through it. Conclusion must come through your own life; only then will it be a mutation. And don't be in a hurry. There is no hurry; time is eternal.

Experience! Be authentic to your experience and allow the conclusions to come only through your own individual particular search. The truth will happen to you, but it will not happen to you if you go on borrowing it from others. That becomes a substitute truth. It creates more problems than it solves.

Your problems, as I see them, are ninety percent because of your borrowed knowledge. Only ten percent of problems are true. Ninety percent are false because they don't belong to you at all. First you start believing in a thing and then problems arise out of that belief and this is a problem. This is a borrowed problem because you have believed, you have concluded intellectually, rationally, that desire is futile. If this is really your conclusion, then how can unfulfillment exist there? – unfulfillment is the seed of desire.

When you are unfulfilled it means desire: you want to seek fulfillment somewhere – desire is there. When you are unfulfilled it means you are not that which you would like to be, you are not there where you would like to be. Then desire, find, seek, move! Unfulfillment means discontent with yourself. Fulfillment means: I am what I am; I am where I should be. Or whatever I am, I am absolutely content with me – fulfilled. Then there is no movement of desire.

Movement is there, but that movement is of life, not of desire. I will go on moving; each movement will happen through my life energy, not through desire. Desire is through mind. Life goes on moving and I will move like a river. The very energy of life will create movement, but the movement will not be according to desire. I will not desire first and then move. Try to understand this distinction.

I am speaking to you. This speaking can be of two types: it can be a sheer movement of life energy, or it can be part of a desire, a plan. If I desire it, then I will have to rehearse it. Then before coming to you, in my mind I will desire you to be present. Then in my mind I will think what to say, what not to say, how to say, how not to say. Then I will plan – then I have moved into the future. Then I will repeat it. Then if it is not up to the standard I had planned I will feel frustrated.

I have heard…

Once Mark Twain was coming back from a lecture hall where he had spoken. When he came back, his wife asked him, "How was the lecture?"

Mark Twain said, "What lecture are you asking about – the one I rehearsed before, or the one that I actually delivered, or the one that I wanted to deliver and was delivering in the car while coming back?"

If I think about it beforehand it is desire. If I simply come to you and it is a response, not planned, not thought about – it is a sheer movement of life energy, there has been no planning for it

– then it is life moving. If there has been planning, then it is mind, desiring.

Movement will be there, but it will be unplanned, spontaneous. Desire cripples movement. It doesn't allow life energy itself to move. It plans, it chooses, it decides beforehand. You have decided before the actual situation. You will always be in difficulty because it is never going to be exactly the right response – because you cannot conceive of the situation beforehand. It always remains unknown. You will feel frustrated.

A mind which desires will always feel frustrated. A mind which doesn't desire, which simply moves wheresoever the *brahman*, life, leads – whether right or wrong, whether to hell or heaven... Wheresoever the life energy leads, the one who is desireless moves within. Nothing can frustrate such a being. How? How can you frustrate him? And nothing can make you fulfilled. How can anyone make you fulfilled? With desire there is no meeting with fulfillment. With nondesire there is no meeting with frustration.

Be true and authentic to yourself, and if you have not overcome desire don't believe that you have overcome it; that is not going to help. Know that you have not overcome. Know that ambition is there; know that as you are, you are unfulfilled. You need something else. That need for something else – whether vague or not, whether you know it or not – makes no difference. You are not at this moment whole and total, at ease with yourself. You are not at home. Your home is somewhere else; you are searching for it.

Know it because this knowing will be good and helpful. Know it and move into desire. Suffer it! Feel the pain of it, the frustration of it, and allow life itself to come to a conclusion. Please don't conclude; allow life itself to come to its conclusion. And when life comes to its conclusion, desire falls without any substitute desire being created there. It simply falls. Just like dead leaves fall from a tree, desire falls from you – desire in total. Then there is no negative part hidden behind it. And when you are in that state of nondesiring, all that is blissful happens to you, all that is ecstatic happens to you. You flower for the first time, you bloom for the first time. And when there is no unfulfillment, you are fulfilled *as you are.*

But before that happens, if you go on borrowing it will be difficult: you are creating unnecessary barriers for yourself. The conclusions may appeal to you, but that appeal is of no meaning. I can convince you about something, but that conviction carries no meaning because it has been forced by me. I can argue, I can convince, and you may feel that it is right. But that feeling will not help unless your life energy concludes it, unless it is an inner conviction that arises within you – not forced from without.

That is why I say buddhas are dangerous – because they are so convincing. When you move around them there is every possibility you will become a victim, every possibility you will get convinced. Their very being is convincing. That is why so many religions are created, so many sects are there – because whenever a buddha happens, an enlightened one, necessarily you get convinced, you get hypnotized – and you borrow conclusions. And then for lives together you go on with those borrowed conclusions; they become a burden.

Die to that burden. Be authentic to yourself and try to find out where you are. Even if it is hell, accept, "I am in hell." The very acceptance that you are in hell will create the situation where you can move out of it. But you live in hell and you go on believing that you are in heaven. This is sheer nonsense and nothing can come out of it.

The last question:

Osho,
Last night you said that sometimes you lie and offer condolences for our frustrations. Then when are we to believe you and how are we to know if you are talking to us in truth or in trick?

Never believe me; don't believe me at all. Be alert. Whatsoever I say may be all lies; it may all be just tricks to give you consolation – just to help you to take a step ahead. Don't believe me! And it is difficult for you to decide when I am speaking truth and when I am speaking a lie. That is why I say wholesale: Don't believe me – because how can you decide? You don't know what truth is; hence, how can you decide?

If you know the truth already, then there is no reason for me, no use in telling you any lies. But because you don't know and you cannot understand the language of truth, it will be absurd for you. You can understand only the language of lies.

But lies are of two types: lies which can lead you to further lies, and lies which can lead you beyond them. For example, we are sitting here. If you have not known the outside ever, you don't know flowers are there, trees are there, and the moon is in the sky. And if I tell you, "Come out. The moon has risen and it is a full-moon night, so come out" – you will not believe me. You will say, "What is night? What is the moon? What is the full moon?"

And there is nothing in this room by which I can show you that it is like this. I have known the moon, and I have known the flowers and the open sky, and I want to share my bliss with you. I want you to also come out, so I create a device, I use a lie: I say the house is on fire; you can understand that. You become afraid, you start trembling. And I create such a conviction in you that the house is on fire, that you start escaping from the room.

Of course, outside you will understand me. You will not say, "You lied." You will be grateful; you will laugh. You will say, "There is no fire, but now we can understand." Only fire could have brought you out – nothing else – because that language you can understand. Suffering you can understand, bliss you cannot understand.

Hence, buddhas go on saying life is misery. It is not! They go on saying it is *dukkha* – misery, suffering, anguish. They are saying that the house of life is on fire: escape from it. And they convince you because they have that freshness which comes to persons who have come out of the house. They have that perfume that comes to persons who have come out into the open sky; they bring that flavor. You get convinced because you see that they must be true and that they have attained something. That attainment creates conviction, and when they say the house – the life – is on fire, you try to escape out of this house.

When you get out, you know it is a full-moon night – life was not a suffering. Life appeared to be a suffering because you became imprisoned in a cage.

Life is vast, so you cannot know when I am lying or when I am saying the truth. And if you ask me to tell you when I am lying or when I am saying the truth, then the whole point will be lost. And even if I say that this is a lie and this is a truth, how can you believe me, whether I am still lying or not?

So it will be easier for you, if you can believe me, to believe totally. Or if you cannot believe me, then don't believe me at all. This will be easy: either think that whatsoever I am saying is true or whatsoever I am saying is a lie. These are the two possibilities. Both ways you will be helped. I say that both ways you will be helped. You will not be in confusion.

If you believe me totally: "Whatsoever this man says is true," it will help you. Not that whatsoever I say will be true, but ultimately you will find that it was the only thing that could have been helpful to you. But this you will come to know only afterwards.

If you don't believe me at all, that will also be good. That too is not easy. The easier course would be to believe some things and not to believe some things. But if you believe me totally, or not at all, in either case you will become total. In one case you are surrendered to me and you say, "Whether you lie or not, that is your business: I believe." You become total; you are not divided. Or if you say, "Whether you say a truth or a lie, I don't believe you – you are a liar," then too you are total, and totality helps.

The easier course is to believe in some things and not to believe in some things. Why is it easier? It is easier because with whatsoever you want to believe you will think, "He is true," and with whatsoever you don't want to believe you will think, "He is lying." That will not be of much help – of no help really. So don't choose. My advice is, don't believe at all – but if you think that the other will be good then believe totally.

Now get ready for the meditation.

...

CHAPTER 12

THE GREAT CIRCLE OF BRAHMAN

The story goes that brahman obtained a victory for the devas. Though the victory was due to brahman, the devas became elated by it and thought: "This victory is due only to us; this glory belongs only to us."

Brahman came to know this, their vanity. He verily appeared before them, but they did not understand who that Yaksha – demi-god – was.

They addressed Agni: "Oh Jataveda, please find out who this Yaksha is." "Yes," said Agni.

Agni hastened to the Yaksha. The Yaksha asked him who he was. Agni replied: "I am verily Agni; I am also known as Jataveda" – near-omniscient.

"What energy do you possess, you of such fame?" asked the Yaksha. "I can burn everything – whatever there is on this earth," replied Agni.

The Yaksha placed a straw before him and said: "Burn this." Agni approached it with all speed; he was, however, unable to burn it. So he withdrew from there and returned to the gods saying, "I could not ascertain who this Yaksha was."

Then they addressed Vayu: "Oh Vayu, please ascertain this, who this Yaksha is." "Yes," said Vayu.

Vayu hastened to the Yaksha. The Yaksha asked him who he was. Vayu replied, "I am verily Vayu. I am also known as Matarisva" – carrier of the atmosphere.

"What energy do you possess, you of such fame?" asked the Yaksha. "I can verily blow away everything – whatever there is on this earth," replied Vayu.

The Yaksha placed a straw before him and said, "Blow this away." Vayu approached it with all speed; he was, however, unable to blow it away. So he withdrew from there and returned to the gods saying: "I could not ascertain who this Yaksha was."

Then the gods addressed Indra: "Oh Maghavan – rejoicing one – please ascertain who this Yaksha is." "Yes," said Indra, and hastened to the Yaksha. But the Yaksha disappeared from his view.

And in that very spot he beheld a woman, the wondrously effulgent Uma, the daughter of the snow-clad mountain, Himavat. And of her he asked: "Who could this Yaksha be?"

In deep silence there is no ego. It exists only when you are disturbed. It is part of disease. When you are deeply silent, you are, but there is no feeling of the "I." It cannot exist in silence. When you are totally calm and quiet, the "I" is not there. But when you are disturbed, the more disturbed you are, the more you will have the feeling of the ego.

The ego is a disturbed, diseased state of the mind. The ego is not healthy. It is an illness. You become aware of it only when you are not in total harmony. When you are in harmony, you are, but there is no I, no feeling of I. "Am-ness" is there, being is there, but without a center.

This is one of the most significant phenomena to be understood. For instance, you become aware of your body only when it is ill. If you are really healthy you don't have a body at all; a healthy body is bodiless, there is no feeling that it exists. Your head exists only when there is a headache: if the headache is not there, the head is not there. Can you feel your head? If you can feel it, it means there is some heaviness. Something is disturbed, something is ill. You become aware of your stomach when it is disturbed.

This is the definition of health: that if the body is not felt you are healthy, if the body is felt you are unhealthy – because only pain is felt. Whenever there is some pain, you feel it. Pain is needed to feel the body and pain is needed to feel yourself. And that pain creates the I, that suffering, anguish, anxiety, creates the I.

So if you are egoistic, remember, that shows that your inner harmony is lost. You cannot do anything about the ego directly – unless you regain the inner harmony. If you start doing something about the ego directly, nothing will happen. On the contrary, you may get more disturbed. All the religions say, be egoless. They mean, be harmonious. Their insistence to dissolve the ego is an insistence to dissolve the disturbance – become a rhythm, become an inner silence. They insist for health.

The Sanskrit word for health is very beautiful: the word is *swastha* – it means to be in one's self. When you are in your self, there is no ego. The English word *health* is also beautiful from a different viewpoint. It comes from the same root as the word *whole* comes from – wholeness. When you are whole, you are healthy; when you are fragmented, divided, split, you are unhealthy. When you have a feeling of wholeness – no division, undivided, one –

you are healthy. The word *holy* also comes from *whole*. When you are really whole, you are holy, you are pure, innocent.

The ego exists when you are fragmented, divided, split – when you are not one. When your parts are in conflict and there is a disharmony within, turmoil, anguish, the ego exists. The greater the anxiety, the greater will be the ego. If you try to fulfill your ego you will get more and more disturbed – and the last state of ego is madness. If you really try to fulfill the ego you will become mad.

In the East, madness is not such a problem as it is in the West because the whole Western mind depends on the ambition to fulfill the ego. American psychologists say that now three persons out of four are mentally ill. This is too much – unbelievable. And if it is true, then the fourth is just on the boundary line, because the fourth is a part; he lives among these three. He cannot be really healthy – just so-so, just on the boundary line. Any moment he can fall into madness.

Many modern psychiatrists are of the opinion that the whole of humanity is mad and the difference is only of degrees. If you are not mad, that only means you are simply normally mad – not abnormally mad. You are just within the limits – mad within limits. You can function, that's all, but any moment you can cross the boundary. Any happening, any accident – your wife dies, your money is lost, your bank becomes bankrupt, your house is on fire – and you can cross the boundary in a single moment. There is not much distance to travel and you can go mad. You were already mad, but just waiting for the boiling-point. It can come any moment.

Why is this happening so much in the West? Why is everyone going for psychoanalysis? Really, those who cannot go for psychoanalysis are thought to be poor now. Those who are rich, those who can afford it, go for it of necessity. It is a very costly affair. It is a luxury because psychoanalysis takes years – two years, three years, even five years, and it is a very costly treatment. Only the very rich can afford it. But the profession is growing, and now psychiatrists are very rich. They are getting richer every day.

The human mind gets more and more disturbed if you try to fulfill the ego because for a greater ego to exist you need greater disturbance, greater illness, disease, greater fragmentation, division. When your fragments of being are in deep conflict they create the tension. In that tension ego can exist. Fight is needed for the ego – a battleground: your being must become a battleground.

This can happen in two ways: either you can fight with others or you can fight with yourself. You can fight with others in a competitive world. You are ambitious, others are also ambitious. You want to be fulfilled as an ego, others are also on the same route. Then you fight with them. This is the worldly way to achieve the ego – the political way or the economic way.

But there are religious ways also. You stop fighting with others; you divide yourself and you start fighting with yourself. You fight with sex, you fight with anger, you fight with the body, you fight with the world – this world of "sin" – you divide yourself. You divide yourself into body–mind, body–soul. Not only that: you also divide your body into the lower body and the higher body. Through these divisions you can fight with yourself.

So remember, there are worldly egos and there are spiritual egos. A man who achieves riches, achieves prestige, becomes powerful, has ego. But don't think that a person who is struggling spiritually doesn't have one. He may have a subtler ego – a deeper, a more refined ego, but he has one. Your so-called saints are all egoistic. They achieve their egos through austerities – through *tapa,* through arduous effort. They have their own victories over themselves. They have no enemies outside, but they have created the enemy within. And then they fight with it, and when they win over it, they have a very egoistic feeling. They feel power.

The second thing to be understood: whenever you feel powerful, remember you have attained a crystallization of the ego. And whenever you are powerful, you cannot meet the divine, you cannot meet the truth, because power exists in conflict, power exists in fight. Power is created through war, through violence, through aggression. Power is against love, power is against silence, and power is against the total.

You cannot meet the *brahman*, the absolute, if you feel yourself to be powerful. You can only meet the total when you feel yourself to be totally powerless, helpless, no one, nobody. If you are feeling powerful in any way, you are creating a barrier. When you are powerful you are blind to the total. And you will be so much disturbed through your power, so much in inner turmoil, that you cannot have that silence which can become a meeting, a communion with the total. Hence, the emphasis of all religions on dissolving the ego: only then can you enter the divine.

Jesus says: "Only those who are like children will enter my kingdom of God." Why "like children"? Children are helpless; they are not powerful. Children are still part of the cosmic whole. They have not yet become egos. They don't yet have a crystallized center of the ego; they are still undivided. That is why children are so beautiful. It is difficult to find an ugly child and it is difficult to find a beautiful old man.

Why? Every child is born so beautiful. Why does every old man go on becoming ugly? Something goes wrong somewhere. Every child is beautiful. The beauty comes from wholeness. The child is whole, undivided. He has no fragments, no division. He is not schizophrenic, he is not fighting anything. He is simply living, breathing, with no fight. The world is not yet a struggle. And he is not fighting with himself either – he is not yet religious. He is simply a natural being just like animals, birds, trees, rocks. He is part of the cosmic whole.

He will come out of it. We will bring him out of it; we cannot leave him like that. And even if we leave him he will come out of it, because he has the potentiality to be divided, he has the potentiality to become an ego. And it is part of the ultimate education that he must become an ego, because unless you have an ego you cannot lose it.

The child is pre-ego. His innocence is natural, but a natural innocence can be disturbed any moment. When he becomes knowing, he will become cunning. When he becomes more alert about his individuality, he will become egoistic.

This is the meaning of the biblical story, that Adam and Eve were innocent in the Garden of Eden and God prohibited them from eating the fruit of the tree of knowledge. Why was the fruit of the tree of knowledge prohibited? – because the moment you know, you are separated. Knowledge separates.

The child is innocent because he is ignorant. He doesn't know where he ends and where you begin. Child psychologists say that in the beginning the child cannot even feel where he ends and where his mother begins. He feels everything as one. For nine months in the womb he exists as one with his mother. He breathes through his mother, he lives through his mother. Even after being born, when he has come out of the womb, deep in his mind he goes on existing as one with his mother. He has no ego and he cannot feel that he is separate yet. By and by he will know that he is separate, by and by he will become aware of *you*.

Remember, the consciousness of the "you" comes first, and then he becomes aware of "I." When he starts feeling "you" as separate, then reflectively he becomes aware that he is separate, he is not you. The mother goes away and he is still there. Now he becomes aware of the distance and now he starts feeling the I. But that I is not very solid. In the beginning children always address themselves in the third person. If the child's name is Ram, he will say, "Ram is feeling thirsty." He will speak in the third person; he will not say, "I am feeling thirsty." The I is not yet solid, it is not yet assertive. He still feels that "Ram" is feeling thirsty – as if Ram is a "you," not an "I."

Children always speak in the third person. They say, "Ram is feeling sleepy. Do that – Ram will feel good. Don't do that – Ram will feel bad." They address themselves as if they are addressing someone else. The I is not yet solid. It will become more and more solid the more they come to an awareness of others. The others exist first and then you start existing. It is a reflection. "I" is an inverted "you."

Adam and Eve were prohibited from eating the fruit of the tree of knowledge, but they had to eat it. It is part of maturing. They were innocent: the moment they ate the fruit they became alert and aware. Suddenly they started hiding their bodies. Now Eve was aware of Adam, Adam was aware of Eve. Clothes came into existence through the ego. They became aware of themselves as separate. Before that they were just part of each other; they never knew that they were separate. They became separated. And this happens to every Adam and Eve. It didn't happen only once: whenever a child is born, he comes out of the Garden of Eden.

In the mother's womb a child is in the Garden of Eden, one with existence, with no responsibilities, with no worries, with no ego. He exists, but without any center. Then he is born. Really, the story, this biblical story of Adam and Eve, is the story of every child's birth. He is thrown out of the mother. Adam and Eve were thrown out of the Garden of Eden and every child has to be thrown out. Then the ego grows; it goes on growing. And with it the pain goes on growing.

Hence, every old man goes on thinking in terms of childhood as paradise. It was! In this sense it was a paradise because you were not yet an ego. You had not tasted the fruit of knowledge; you had not come to know yourself as separate. With separation problems arise: you become anxious. With separation, death arises.

It is said in the biblical story that death didn't exist before. When Adam and Eve ate the fruit, death came into existence. Before that they were immortal. Every child is immortal. He is not aware of death because death can become meaningful only to the I, to the ego. When you have a conception that you are separate, immediately the problem arises whether you are going to be here forever or whether you will die. The trees are immortal. Not that they don't die – they die, but they have no awareness of death. The animals are immortal. Not that death is not going to be there – death will be there, but they are not aware of it. They have no egos, so how can they feel, "I am going to die"? I must be there before I can feel that I will die. Death is part of the ego.

So now, let me tell you: death arises out of disease, illness. And death is the last thing, the climax – where ego ends. Ego creates death around you, and the fear. And this is the paradox: the more fearful you feel about death, the more you try to be powerful, because you think that if you are powerful, then you can do something about death. At least you can postpone it; you can push it away a little.

But the more powerful you grow, the more death becomes significant. The more powerful you grow, the more you become afraid of death, because with the power grows the ego. If you are rich, politically powerful, you will be more afraid of death. If you are poor, with no power, you will not be so afraid of death.

Western people, when they come to the East, simply cannot understand why people in the East are so indifferent to death. They are so powerless. They don't have very fixed and solid egos so they cannot be so much afraid. You become more afraid. You become afraid in proportion to what death is going to take away from you. If you don't have anything, what can death take away from you? A poor man is not so afraid of death. Really, death cannot take anything away from him. He may attain something through death, but he cannot lose.

The richer you grow, the more afraid you are because all your riches will be taken away, and whatsoever is achieved will be taken away. The more power you have, the more you feel powerless before death because it will make you impotent again. All the glory and all the power will go and you will die like any beggar.

Death is absolutely communistic: it equalizes all. The lowest, naturally, cannot be much afraid. The highest will be afraid because he will be pulled down. Death will take your presidentship, your prime-ministership. All death will take from the beggar is his beggary. The president and the beggar will become equal in death. Of course, the president will be more afraid. He has a deeper fear than a beggar can have.

The West has become very much afraid of death. It has become an obsession – bound to be because now the West is more powerful; they have something to lose. And when Westerners see the indifference in the East, they cannot understand why people are so indifferent to death. This is the reason: they don't have much to lose. They are existing on the lowest rung, so death cannot be a fall to them. They are already fallen; they are already existing in their graves.

What I intend to say is: power gives you ego, ego creates a lust for more power and this becomes a vicious circle. And when you are powerful you become afraid of death. When you become afraid of death you cannot enter the divine, because the divine is a sort of death. Really, to enter the divine, to enter the whole, means to lose yourself as an individual – to become a child again.

But this childhood, this second childhood, is qualitatively different from the first. The first childhood was animal-like; the second childhood is godlike. The first childhood was bound to be disturbed; the second childhood cannot be disturbed. By "second childhood," I mean a state where you have consciously – through understanding, through meditation, through surrender – lost yourself again into the total. The circle is complete; you have become a child again. Hindus have called such a person in second childhood *dwij* – twice-born. This is a new birth. The old is dead. The man is again a child.

A saint, if he is really a saint, must become a child again. And Jesus says that only children can enter into godliness – can enter into the kingdom of God. Unless you become like Adam and Eve again, unless you throw the fruit of knowledge that you have eaten out of your system, you cannot enter the garden. If you can understand this, then this parable will be easy for you to follow.

This is a parable – one of the most loved. This parable is easy, but the implications are very complex. First I will read the parable, and then we will discuss it.

> *The story goes that brahman obtained a victory for the devas. Though the victory was due to the brahman, the devas became elated by it and thought: "This victory is due to us only; this glory belongs to us only."*

It always happens so. Whatsoever you attain is attained by your inner spirit, not by your ego. But the ego always exploits the victory. It says, "I have done this." And, really, *nothing* is ever done by the ego. The ego is the exploiter – exploiter par excellence. Even things like birth are exploited by the ego. You say, "This is my birthday" – as if you have done something about your birth. "*My* birthday! I was born on this day," as if "I" did something. The birth happened. It is a happening, not a doing. But your ego exploits even that.

You say, "I breathe." It is absolutely wrong. Breathing happens; you are not breathing. Breathing goes on without you. You can interfere, but you cannot breathe. Breathing is a natural thing. The *brahman* breathes through you. If it was so, as we say, that "I breathe," then death would become impossible – because if you can go on breathing, what can death do?

But you cannot go on breathing. If the breath goes out and doesn't come back, what can you do? You cannot do anything, because really, if the breath goes out and doesn't come in, you are no longer there to do anything. You don't exist; you are out of existence. Breathing is not something which you are doing. It is something which is happening to you: a greater force – life, you may call it. The Upanishads call it *brahman*, the *élan vital* of Bergson – call it whatsoever you like to call it.

Life breathes through you, but the ego goes on exploiting everything and goes on saying, "I am breathing." You fall in love and you say, "I love." Really, it is never anything on the part of *you*. Or can "you" love? If I say, "Love this woman," you will say, "How can I love if I have not already fallen in love?" What will you do? You can imitate love, you can act, but you will not be involved in it unless the life force has thrown you into it. Unless it happens to the life force that you are in love, you cannot love.

The whole of life is really a happening. Birth, death, love, all that is significant, is a happening. And if you move deeper, then even trivial things are happenings. You say, "I have built this house," but even birds are making their nests. Really, it is something that the life force is doing, not you. Don't think yourself very intelligent, very powerful, very clever, because you have built this house. Even birds are making such beautiful nests – without any training, without any knowledge, without going to any college. It is instinctive. Life makes its abode.

You go on accumulating riches and you think *you* are doing it. No. The life force goes on accumulating. Even animals accumulate. Even they try to possess; even they make arrangements for the rainy season.

If you look deep, then you will find a subtle phenomenon happening within you. Everything is done by the life force, and everything done by the life force is exploited by the ego. And ego says, "I am doing this," and then feels very elated.

This is the parable: *The story goes that brahman obtained a certain victory for the devas...* For the deities. In Indian mythology all the forces of nature are deities. Fire is a deity – a natural force; air is a deity – a natural force. Every natural force is conceived as a *devata* – as a deity. *...the brahman obtained a certain victory for the devas...* For the deities.

Though the victory was due to brahman, the devas became elated by it and thought: "This victory is due to us only, this glory belongs to us only." And this is a constant parable – the story that is happening to you.

The air, the fire, all the natural forces, are also working because of the deeper original source of the *brahman*. Otherwise they cannot work. Nothing can exist and nothing can be active unless the *élan vital,* the *brahman,* is active in it – the substratum, the original force.

But you are not aware of it. On the surface you go on doing things and you go on thinking that you are doing it: "I am the cause of it, I am the source of it." You are not the source of it. It is just like the Ganges flows to the sea. The Ganges must be thinking that she is flowing to the sea. Is she really flowing, or is she just part of a greater circle? She will flow to the sea, and then through sun rays the water will rise again and the water will become clouds. And the air will take those clouds to the Himalayas and they will rain there on the Gangotri – on the source of the Ganges. And the river will be created and it will move; it will flow, moving. It will fall into the sea because it is natural for water to move downwards.

It is not the Ganges flowing to the sea. It is just a natural law, part of the divine, that water moves downwards. So from the Himalayas, the water will move downwards – not that the Ganges is moving; the Ganges cannot have an ego, cannot be allowed to have an ego. It is part of a great circle. Again the water will fall into the sea, and again the clouds will come, and again they will pour water down the Ganges, on the Gangotri, and the river will go on flowing. It is a great circle. Clouds, Gangotri, Ganges, the sea – clouds, Gangotri, Ganges, the sea: it is a great circle. You are also just a part of a great circle. That great circle of energy is called *brahman.*

But the part goes on thinking, "I am doing it." So the *devas* became elated and they thought: The "*...victory is due to us only, this glory belongs to us only.*"

And one more point, by the way: whenever you get defeated you never say, "This defeat is due to us only." Whenever you are dishonored you never say, "This dishonor belongs to me only." This is strange. If glory belongs to you, then why not dishonor? If victory belongs to you only, then why not defeat? Whenever you are defeated you say, "Circumstances, situation, the way things are, destiny, the gods, are against me."

Whenever you are defeated, why do you throw the responsibility onto something else? – because through defeat ego cannot be fulfilled. Only through victory can it be fulfilled, so defeat has to be thrown onto the *brahman*. If the gods were defeated, they would certainly have said, "The *brahman* is against us, destiny is against us, fate is against us. That is why we have been defeated." But you are victorious, then it is because of you.

Look at the trick of the ego. Neither is because of you, or both are because of you. Decide and the ego will die. If you say, "Both are not because of me: a greater force is working and I am just a particle, an atomic thing, just a cell, just helpless. Things are happening to me – I am not a doer, so whether victory comes or defeat, both belong to the ultimate," your ego will dissolve. Or say, "Both belong to me. Victory and defeat, honor and dishonor, both belong to me." – then too your ego will disappear, because both are contradictory. They negate each other. Victory will give you a little ego and defeat will take that little ego away, and you will be just without the ego.

These are the two ways. Hindus have followed the first. They say victory and death and everything belongs to the divine, to the order of the cosmos. Jainas and Buddhists have followed the second. They say there is no God: "Everything belongs to me – the defeat and the victory, the loss and the gain, the birth and death, everything belongs to me." Then these two contradictory things negate each other and the ego is dissolved. In both cases the happening is the same. The ego can persist only if you go on giving all the victories to it and go on giving all the defeats to the world or to the destiny or to the *brahman*. Then the ego can exist. This is how the ego exists.

The parable says:

> *Brahman came to know this, their vanity.*

He came to know about their egos, that now they are feeling very elated and they are saying they are victorious. It is because of them – victory belongs only to them.

> *He verily appeared before them, but they didn't understand who that Yaksha – adorable spirit – was.*

The second part of the parable: whenever the original, the cosmic source, feels that you are feeling elated, you are feeling egoistic, it appears before you – but you cannot recognize it. The ego will not allow you to recognize it; it will close your eyes. This force comes to you also, not only to those *devas*. This is a human story, a very psychological parable. Whenever you feel elated, there are happenings around you which, if you can recognize them, will pull you back down to the earth. But you never recognize them, you cannot. Your eyes are not now in reality. Now you are living in a fiction.

So the *devas* couldn't recognize who this adorable spirit was. The *brahman* was standing before them, the ultimate energy was standing before them, but they were closed. They were in their heads, they were in their egos, enclosed, encapsulated. They couldn't see, they couldn't understand. Whenever you are in some egoistic mood you cannot see anything: you are blind. Whenever you are victorious you cannot see, you cannot understand. You lose all your senses. Even your common sense is lost. You are really mad in your victory, in your success.

> *They addressed Agni...*

...the deities addressed Agni, and they said, "Please find out who this spirit is, who has appeared in this form."

> *"...who this Yaksha is."*

Agni said, "Yes, I will try to find out."

> *Agni hastened to the Yaksha,*

...to the spirit who had appeared. The Yaksha is the form the *brahman* had appeared in.

> *The Yaksha asked him who he was. Agni replied...*

Agni means fire.

> *Agni replied: "I am verily fire – Agni; I am also known as Jataveda" – near-omniscient."*

> *"What energy do you possess, you of such fame?"*

...asked the spirit. "*What energy do you possess, you of such fame?*" Fire has been very significant and in the old days, fire came to be the top deity, because man lived in darkness, lived in caves, lived in forests – it was dangerous. There were animals, and in the dark they would attack and the night was very fearful. And then Agni, the fire, helped them to come out of the darkness. Even night became not so dangerous. So Agni came to be the top deity. Fire was worshipped all over the world; fire became the symbol of God.

Hence, the deities asked fire to go first and inquire, "Who is this spirit who has appeared before us?" And the spirit asked: "*What energy do you possess?*" The emphasis is on *you*. "*What energy do you possess, you of such fame?*"

> *"I can burn everything – whatever there is on this earth,"*

replied the fire. The emphasis is on "*I* can burn everything."

> *The Yaksha placed a straw before him and said, "Burn this."*

The *brahman* placed a straw before him and said, "Burn this."

> *Agni approached it with all speed...*

... with full vigor, with totality, with whatsoever he had.

> *...he was, however, unable to burn it.*

Because it is not Agni that burns: it is the cosmic force through Agni that burns. Without the cosmic force, Agni cannot burn, fire cannot burn. And when the *brahman* was standing there before him, Agni was impotent because the source was not behind it. Now there was only ego; the source had disappeared. Only the exploiter – that which has never done anything but which goes on thinking, "I can do this and that."

Agni could not burn the straw...

> *So he withdrew from there and returned to the other gods saying, "I could not ascertain who this spirit was."*

He didn't say that he had been a failure, that he couldn't burn it. He simply said, *"I couldn't ascertain who this spirit was."*

This is how the ego functions. Even if the divine is standing before you, you will go on saying: "I couldn't ascertain who this spirit was." Even if life reveals to you that your ego is impotent, you will not realize it. Life goes on revealing to you that your ego is impotent – is it not so? Every moment life goes on saying to you, "Don't claim. You are not the doer." But you never look at it.

> *Then they addressed Vayu:*

... the air force, the deity of air,

> *"O Vayu, please ascertain this, who this Yaksha is." "Yes," said Vayu.*

> *Vayu hastened to the Yaksha. The Yaksha asked him who he was. Vayu replied, "I am verily Vayu" – air. "I am also*

> *known as Matarisva" – carrier of the atmosphere.*
>
> *"What energy do you possess, you of such fame?" asked the spirit. "I can verily blow away everything – whatever there is on this earth," replied Vayu.*
>
> *The Yaksha placed a straw before him and said, "Blow this away." Vayu approached it with all speed; he was, however, unable to blow it away.*

...with all speed... Your ego can act with all speed, but nothing will happen out of it. Your ego can do something with all speed, all effort, but nothing will happen out of it. Remember this; it will be helpful.

People come to me and they go on saying, "I am making such an effort to meditate, but nothing is happening." Nothing will happen because the "I" is making the effort. You are not allowing the divine to happen within. *You* are trying to do something.

You are impotent. Whatsoever potency you have comes through the original source, from the cosmos, from the *brahman*. It doesn't belong to you. You are just a vehicle. So when the I starts trying something, then nothing happens.

In Zen monasteries they teach the seekers only one secret, and the secret is: do something without bringing the I into it. If you can do something without bringing the ego into it, everything will happen.

Herrigel, one German thinker, was in a Zen monastery in Japan. He was learning archery there, and the master said, "Allow the life force to aim and allow the life force to release the arrow. You don't do anything."

It was difficult, really impossible – and particularly for a German mind that is basically intellect-oriented. That is why the experience of Germany has proved so fatal: too much intellect, too much ego, too much effort. Finally the ego came to a point where it said to the German people, "Now you can be victorious all over the world." Hitler was just the expression of all the whole German mind – ego-oriented.

Herrigel was unable to understand: "If I don't release the arrow, how can the arrow be released? If I am not making an effort, then there will be no effort at all."

And this is how we would also feel. For three years he was there with the master. He learned the art completely – as completely as possible. His aim was a hundred percent accurate. The arrow would always reach the target. But the master went on shaking his head. He said, "This is nothing."

A hundred percent results, and the master would say, "This is nothing; you have not learned anything. You are still releasing the arrow. And we are not interested in the target, we are interested in you. We are not interested in the other end, we are interested in you. *You* are the target. That target is not the target. When the arrow is released without you, when the life force has taken possession of you, only then..." – because archery is not the point: meditation is the point.

"Even if you miss," the master said, "even if you miss the target completely – that is irrelevant. But you should not miss the original source."

Herrigel was desperate. And the more desperate he was, the more effort he made. The more he tried, the more the master would say, "You disappoint me."

Then a day came when Herrigel thought, "This is impossible, this cannot happen. Three years is too long a time, making so much effort every day." He felt frustrated. He said to the master, "Now allow me to leave. I think this is not for me. It seems impossible to conceive. I have done whatsoever I could but nothing happens."

The master said, "Because you were doing whatsoever you could, you were not allowing the life force to do anything. *You* are the barrier."

Herrigel decided to leave. The day he was leaving, he came

just to say good-bye to the master. The master was training another disciple. Herrigel just sat there. For the first time he was indifferent because now he was leaving, and he had left the whole effort, and there was no point in it. So he sat silently and just saw the master without the eyes of desire, ambition, achievement; just saw the master, and for the first time in three years he realized that the master was not releasing the arrow. It was the life force. The arrow was released by something which was not coming from the ego. It was coming from a deeper energy.

He stood as if hypnotized. He came near the master, he took the bow from his hand and he released the arrow, and the master said, "Right! You have done it." And Herrigel writes, "I now know the difference between when the life force releases it and when you do it."

"What energy do you possess, you of such fame?" asked the Yaksha. Vayu tried to show his energy. *Vayu approached it with all speed; he was, however, unable to blow it away. So he withdrew from there and returned to the gods saying, "I could not ascertain who this Yaksha was."*

And it was so clear. There was no need to ascertain. The whole thing was so clear. Vayu tried to blow away a straw and he could not. And the fire tried to burn a straw. He could have burned the whole earth, and a single straw was not burned. The thing was so clear: the Yaksha was the original source of energy.

But they couldn't recognize that the energy had been taken away, that now they were just vehicles – empty. The fire could not burn a straw, Vayu could not blow a straw. It was so clear to realize that the original source had withdrawn. But they couldn't recognize it.

Ego is really so blind that it never recognizes its impotency. Even when the source has moved away, it goes on thinking in old terms. Even when everything is defeated and everything is a failure, it goes on thinking in old terms.

Then the gods addressed Indra...

Indra is the chief of the gods in Indian mythology. Then they asked Indra:

> *"Oh Indra, please ascertain who this spirit is." "Yes," said Indra, and hastened to the Yaksha. But the Yaksha disappeared from his view.*

When Indra approached the Yaksha, the Yaksha disappeared from his view. The word *indra* is very meaningful; it comes from the same root as the word *indriya. Indriya* means the senses, and *indra* means the chief of the senses – the head. What is the chief of the senses? The mind. All the senses – your ears, your eyes, your hands – are just subordinate to the mind. Mind is really Indra in the body, so mind is the chief deity.

Eyes belong to fire and all your senses belong to some deity, but your mind belongs to Indra. Indra means the chief of the *indriya* – of all the senses. So when all the deities, senses, failed, they asked the head, the brain, the mind. But what happened? This is beautiful, this parable is just wonderful. When the senses approached the deity, the ultimate, the *brahman*, he was there – but when mind approached, he disappeared.

With mind you cannot see him, with mind he is not approachable. When mind tries to find out who the ultimate source is, it becomes invisible. It is not visible for the mind. For the intellect, the ultimate becomes invisible. That is why science never finds any divine element. Science cannot find it because science is the Indra – the mind, the intellect, the reason.

The spirit disappeared from Indra's view. If you bring your mind to find, there is nothing to find. It disappears. One more point is to be understood. You can feel godliness through the body, you can feel godliness through taste, you can feel it through smell, but you cannot feel it through the intellect – through the reason. Even through the senses it is approachable. If you become

e sensitive you can touch it. But through the intellect it is
ɔlutely unapproachable. Intellect is not the door at all.

ɩf you have a sensitive body you can live in godliness, you can athe it. But no matter how keen an intellect you have, you ɪnot touch it, you cannot come near it. If you simply bring :ellect in, it is no longer there; it simply disappears.

> *And in that very spot he, Indra, beheld a woman, the wondrously effulgent Uma, the daughter of the snow-clad mountain, Himavat. And of her he asked, "Who could this Yaksha be?"*

With the mind, if you bring mind in, if you bring reason in, the ultimate disappears. And what happens? This parable gives many clues, many dimensions. When the ultimate disappears, then only sex remains the source of all. Then you feel as if sex is the source of all energy. When you cannot feel the divine as the source, you feel sex as the source of all energy.

Science proved that there is no God; and then came Sigmund Freud, and he said there is only woman – or you can say there is only man if you are a woman. Science cleared the ground – God became invisible. Whenever there is no God, only sex remains to be the God. Then you feel everything is because of sex; Freud says so. If Freud could have known about this parable, he would have understood. This parable is a criticism, a deep criticism, his whole ideology. When there is no God, sex becomes the God.

A beautiful woman appeared before Indra, and he asked that woman, "Uma, who was this who has disappeared?" Now psychologists are asking sex: "What is the origin of life?" They are penetrating into sexual energy and trying to know something about the original source of life through sex, through the door of sex.

With intellect, you cannot penetrate deeper than sex. Sex is, of course, part of that great energy. But with mind alone you become acquainted with the part, not with the original source. And mind gets entangled with sex. The whole Western mind is now entangled with sex and it has become a labyrinth. You cannot move out of it. Wheresoever you move, you come back again and again to it.

Everything is now reduced to sex. Freud says if a mother loves a child it is sex; if a father loves his child it is sex. If a father loves his daughter it is heterosexual; if the father loves his son more it is homosexual.

Just now, a few days ago, I was reading a book – the book is written by a psychoanalyst – and he says it is possible that Jesus was a homosexual because he always moved with his twelve apostles – with boys. Always moving with boys means homosexuality. Somewhere I have read some other psychoanalyst who wrote that Buddha's monks must have been homosexual because they were always living in the company of men. Everything is reduced to sex if mind is the approach.

Before Indra, before mind, the ultimate disappeared. *And in that very spot he beheld a woman, the wondrously effulgent one, the daughter of the snow-clad mountain, Himavat. And of her he asked: "Who could this Yaksha be?"*

This is what we are asking – asking sex what this life is.

Now get ready for the meditation.

...

CHAPTER 13

MAN CAN BE TRANSCENDED

The first question:

> **Osho,**
> **In the West, psychoanalysis has grown through Freud, Adler, Jung and Wilhelm Reich, to solve the problems arising from the ego such as frustrations, conflicts, schizophrenia and madness. In comparison to your meditation techniques, please explain the contributions, limitations and incompleteness of the system of psychoanalysis in solving the human problems rooted in the ego.**

The first thing to be understood is that any problem rooted in the ego cannot be solved without transcending the ego. You can postpone the problem, you can bring in a little normality, you can create a little normalness about it, you can dilute the problem, but you cannot solve it. You can make a man function more efficiently in the society through psychoanalysis, but psychoanalysis never solves a problem. And whenever a problem is postponed, shifted, it creates another problem. It simply changes its place, but it remains there. A new eruption will come sooner or later and when the new outbreak of the old problem comes it will become more difficult to postpone and shift it.

ıoanalysis is a temporary relief because psychoanalysis conceive of anything which transcends ego. A problem ıolved only when you can go beyond it. If you cannot go it, then *you* are the problem. Then who is going to solve ı how is one going to solve it? Then you are the problem; blem is not something separate from you.

a, Tantra and all meditation techniques are based upon a nt ground. They say the problems are there, the problems ɪund you, but you are never the problem. You can transcend you can look at them like a watcher is looking down from ll into the valley. This witnessing self can solve the problem. ; just by witnessing a problem, it is half solved already. This is se when you can witness a problem, when you can observe it tially, when you are not involved in it – you can stand by the ınd look at it. The very clarity that comes out of this witnes- gives you a clue, gives you the secret key. And almost all pro- ıs are there because there is no clarity through which to ɪerstand them. You don't need solutions: you need clarity.

A problem rightly understood is solved, because a problem ses through the nonunderstanding mind. You create the pro- ɜm because you are not understanding. So the basic thing is ɔt to solve the problem; the basic thing is to create more under- ɪanding. And if more understanding, more clarity is there, the ɪroblem can be encountered impartially, observed as if it doesn't ɔelong to you, as if it belongs to someone else. The problem can only be solved if you can create a distance between the problem and you.

Meditation creates a distance, it gives you a perspective. You go beyond the problem. The level of consciousness changes. Through psychoanalysis you remain on the same level. The level never changes; you are adjusted on the same level again. Your awareness, your consciousness, your witnessing capacity, doesn't change. As you move in meditation you go higher and higher, you can look down at your problems. They are now in the valley, and you are now on a hill. From this perspective, this height, all the problems look different. And the more the distance grows, the more you become capable of observing them as if they don't belong to you.

Remember one thing: if a problem doesn't belong to you, you can always give good advice on how to solve it. If it belongs to someone else, if someone else is in difficulty, you are always wise. You can give very good advice. But if the problem belongs to you, you simply don't know what to do. What has happened? The problem is the same, but now you are involved in it. When it was someone else's problem, you had a distance from which to look at it impartially. Everyone is a good advisor for others, but when it happens to oneself then all your wisdom is lost because the distance is lost.

Someone has died and the family is in anguish: you can give good advice. You can say the soul is immortal; you can say nothing dies, life is eternal. But when someone has died whom you loved, who means something to you, who was near, intimate, you are beating your breast and crying and weeping. Now you cannot give the same advice to yourself – that life is immortal and no one dies, ever. Now it looks absurd.

So remember, while advising others you may look foolish. When you say to someone whose beloved has died that life is immortal, he will think you stupid. You are talking nonsense to him. He knows what it feels like to lose a beloved. No philosophy can give consolation. And he knows why you are saying this thing: because the problem is not yours. You can afford to be wise; he cannot afford it.

Through meditation you transcend your ordinary being. A new point arises in you from where you can look at things in a new way. The distance is created. Problems are there, but they are now very far away – as if happening to someone else. Now you can give good advice to yourself, but there is no need to give it. The very distance will make you wise. So the whole technique of meditation consists of creating a distance between the problems and you. Right now, as you are, you are so much entangled with your problems that you cannot think, you cannot contemplate, you cannot see through them, you cannot witness them.

Psychoanalysis helps just for readjustment. It is not a transformation; that is one thing. And another thing: in psychoanalysis you become dependent. You need an expert and the expert will do everything. It will take three years, four years, or even five years if the problem is very deep, and you will become just dependent – you are not growing. Rather, on the contrary, you are becoming more and more dependent. You will need to see the psychoanalyst every day or twice a week or thrice a week. If you don't go to him you will feel lost. If you stop psychoanalysis you will feel lost. Psychoanalysis becomes intoxicating, it becomes alcoholic.

You start being dependent upon someone – someone who is an expert. You can tell your problem to him and he will solve it. He will discuss it, and he will bring the unconscious roots out of you. But *he* will do it; the solving will be done by someone else, not by you.

Remember, a problem solved by someone else is not going to give you more maturity. A problem solved by someone else may give him some maturity but it cannot give you maturity. You may become more immature. Then whenever there is a problem, you will need some expert advice, some professional advice. And I don't think that even psychoanalysts grow mature through your problems because they go for psychoanalysis to other psychoanalysts. They have their own problems. They solve your problems, but they cannot solve their problems. Again the question of distance.

Wilhelm Reich himself tried again and again to be psychoanalyzed by Sigmund Freud. Freud refused to psychoanalyze him, and all his life he felt hurt because Freud refused him. And Freudians, orthodox Freudians, never accepted that Reich was an expert because he had not been psychoanalyzed.

Every psychoanalyst goes to someone else with his own problems. It is just like the medical profession. If the doctor himself is ill he cannot diagnose himself. He is so near that he is afraid, so he will go to someone else. If you are a surgeon you cannot operate upon your own body – or can you? The distance is not there. It is difficult to operate upon one's own body. But it is also difficult if your wife is really ill and a serious operation is to be done – you cannot operate because your hand will tremble. The intimacy is so much you will be afraid, you cannot be a good surgeon. You will have to take advice; you will have to call some other surgeon to operate on your wife.

What is happening? You have been operating; you have done many operations. And now what is happening? You cannot do it on your child or your wife because the distance is so little – as if there is no distance. Without distance you cannot be impartial. A psychoanalyst can help others, but when he is in trouble he will have to take advice, he will have to be psychoanalyzed by someone else. And it is really strange that even a person like Wilhelm Reich goes mad in the end.

We cannot conceive of a buddha going mad – or can you conceive it? And if a buddha can go mad, then there is no way out of this misery. It is inconceivable that a buddha goes mad.

Look at Sigmund Freud's life. He is the father and founder of psychoanalysis; he went on talking about problems very deeply. But as far as he himself was concerned, not a single problem was solved. Not a single problem! Fear was as much a problem for him as for anybody else. He was so afraid and nervous. Anger was as much a problem for him as for anybody else. He would get so angry that he would fall unconscious in a fit. This man knew so much about the human mind, but as far as he himself was concerned, that knowledge seemed to be of no use.

Jung himself would fall unconscious when in deep anxiety; he would have a fit. What is the problem? Distance is the problem. They had been thinking about problems, but they had not been growing in consciousness. They thought intellectually, keenly, logically, and they concluded something. Sometimes those conclusions may have been right, but that is not the point. They did not grow in consciousness, they did not become in any way superhuman. And unless you transcend humanity, the problems cannot be solved; they can only be adjusted.

Freud, in the last days of his life, said that man is incurable. At the most we can hope that he can exist as an adjusted being; there is no other hope. This is at the most! Man cannot be happy, Freud says. At the most we can arrange it so that he is not very unhappy. That's all. But he cannot be happy; he is incurable. What type of solution can come out of such an attitude? And this is after forty years' experience with human beings! He concludes that man cannot be helped, that man is naturally, by nature, miserable, that he will remain in misery.

But Yoga says that man's problems can be transcended. It is not that man is incurable, it is his minimal consciousness that creates the problem. Grow in consciousness, increase in consciousness, and problems decrease. They exist in the same proportion: if there is a minimum of consciousness, there are a maximum of problems; if there is a maximum of consciousness, there are a minimum of problems. With total consciousness, problems simply disappear just like the sun rises in the morning and dewdrops disappear. With total consciousness there are no problems because with total consciousness problems cannot arise. At the most psychoanalysis can be a cure. But problems will go on arising; psychoanalysis is not preventive.

Yoga, meditation, goes to the very depth. It will change you so that problems cannot arise. Psychoanalysis is concerned with problems; meditation is concerned with you directly. It is not concerned with problems at all. That is why the greatest of Eastern psychologists – Buddha, Mahavira or Krishna – don't talk about problems. Because of this, Western psychology thinks that psychology is a new phenomenon. It is not.

It was just in this century, in the first part of this century, that Freud could prove scientifically that there is something like the unconscious. Buddha talked about it twenty-five centuries before. But Buddha has never tackled any problem because he says problems are infinite. If you go on tackling every problem, you will never really be able to tackle them. Tackle the man himself. Just forget the problems. Tackle the being itself and help the being to grow. As the being grows, as a person becomes more conscious, problems go on dropping; you need not be worried about them.

For example, a person is schizophrenic, split, divided. Psychoanalysis will deal with this split – with how to make this split workable, with how to adjust this man so that he can function, so that he can live in the society peacefully. Psychoanalysis will tackle the problem, the schizophrenia. But if this man comes to Buddha, Buddha will not talk about the schizophrenic state. He will say, "Meditate so that the inner being becomes one. When the inner being becomes one, the split will disappear from the periphery." The split is there – but it is not the cause, it is just the effect. Somewhere deep in the being there is a duality and that duality has made this crack on the periphery.

You go on cementing the crack, but the inner split remains. Then the crack will appear somewhere else. Then you cement that crack; then the crack will go on appearing somewhere else. So if you treat one psychological problem, another problem arises immediately; then you treat another and a third arises.

This is good as far as the professionals are concerned because they live off it. But this is not a help. The West will have to go beyond psychoanalysis, and unless the West comes to the methods of growing consciousness, of inner growth of being, of expansion of consciousness, psychoanalysis cannot be of much help.

Now, this is happening already: psychoanalysis is already out of date. The keen thinkers of the West are now thinking about how to expand consciousness and not about how to solve problems – about how to make a man alert and aware. Now this has come; the seeds have sprouted.

The emphasis has to be remembered. I am not concerned with your problems. There are millions and millions, and it is just useless to go on solving them – because you are the creator and you remain untouched. I solve a problem and you will create ten. Your problems cannot be defeated because the creator remains behind them. And as I go on solving, I am just wasting my energy.

I will push aside your problems; I will simply penetrate you. The creator must be changed. Once the creator is changed, the problems on the periphery drop. Now no one is cooperating with them, no one is helping to create them, no one is enjoying them. You may feel the word *enjoy* strange, but remember well that you enjoy your problems; hence you create them. You enjoy them for so many reasons.

The whole humanity is sick because of basic reasons, basic causes, which we go on overlooking. Whenever a child is sick he gets attention; whenever he is healthy no one gives him any attention. Whenever a child is sick, the parents love him – or at least they pretend. But whenever he is okay, no one is worried about him. No one thinks to give him a kiss or a good hug. The child learns the trick of how to get attention. Love is a basic need and attention is a basic food. For the child, attention is even more potentially necessary than milk. Without attention something will die within him.

You may have heard about new experiments in one English laboratory, Delabar, where they are experimenting with plants. Even plants grow faster if you give them attention by looking at them lovingly. Two plants are used for the experiment. Give one plant attention, love – just a smiling, loving approach – and don't give any attention to the other. Give everything else necessary: water, fertilizers, sun rays; give everything equally to each, but to one give more attention. To the other don't give any attention; whenever you pass nearby don't even look at it. And one grows faster, brings bigger flowers, and the other grows in a delayed way and brings smaller flowers.

Attention is energy. When someone looks lovingly at you he is giving you food – a very subtle food. So every child needs attention; but you give attention only when he is ill, when there is some problem. So if the child needs attention he will create problems, he will become a creator of problems.

Love is a basic need. Your body grows with food, your soul grows with love. But you can get love only when you are ill, when you have some problem; otherwise no one is going to give you love. The child learns your ways; then he starts creating problems. Whenever he is ill or with a problem, everyone gives attention.

Have you ever observed? In your house the children are playing silently, peacefully. Then if some guests come they start creating trouble. This is because your attention goes to the guests and now the children are hankering for attention. They need your attention, your guests' attention, everybody's attention towards them. They will do something, they will create some trouble. This is unconscious, but it becomes a pattern. And when you are grown up, you still go on doing it.

For women, it is true that ninety-nine percent of their illnesses, their mental problems, are basically love needs. Whenever you love a woman, she has no problems. Whenever there is some problem in love, many problems arise. Now she is hankering for attention. And psychoanalysts are exploiting this need for attention, because a psychoanalyst is a professional attention-giver. You go to him: he is a professional. For one hour he looks at you attentively. Whatsoever you say, whatsoever nonsense, he listens as if the Vedas are being preached. And he persuades you to talk more, to say anything, relevant or irrelevant, to bring your mind out. Then you feel so good.

You know, ninety-nine percent of patients fall in love with their psychoanalysts. And how to protect the client–expert relationship is a great problem because sooner or later it becomes a lover's relationship. Why? Why does a woman patient fall in love with a male psychoanalyst? Or the reverse: Why does a male patient fall in love with a woman psychoanalyst? The reason is for the first time so much attention is given. The love need is fulfilled.

Unless your basic being is changed, nothing will come out of solving problems. You have an infinite potential to create new ones. Meditation is an effort to make you independent, first; and second, to change the type and quality of your consciousness. With a new quality of consciousness old problems cannot exist: they simply disappear. For instance, you were a small child; you had certain types of problems. When you became older they simply disappeared. Where have they gone? You never solved them, they simply disappeared. You cannot even remember what the problems were that belonged to your childhood. You have grown and those problems have disappeared.

Then you were a little older, you had different types of problems; when you become old they will not be there. Not that you will be able to solve them – no one is able to solve problems – one can simply grow out of them. When you are old you will laugh at your own problems which were there, so urgent, so destructive that you had many times contemplated committing suicide because of them. And then when you have grown old, you will simply laugh: Where have those problems gone? Have you solved them? No – you have simply grown. Those problems belonged to a particular state of growth.

Similar is the case as you grow deeper into consciousness. Problems go on disappearing. A moment comes when you are so aware that problems don't arise. Meditation is not analysis. Meditation is growth. It is not concerned with problems; it is concerned with the being.

The second question:

> **Osho,**
> **Last night you said that we should either believe in whatsoever you say as true, or we should disbelieve you totally, taking what you say as untrue, and that both ways will help us. But what is to be done by those persons who are not capable of being total in either way? Is there any third alternative possible in this matter?**

There is none and there cannot be. The third is your state

already; there is no need. The first two are the alternatives to come out of that; the third you are already – confused. You can come out of this confusion only with a *total* effort. Why is it difficult to be total either in belief or disbelief? Why is it easy to be in the middle? – because if you are in the middle, then no change is needed: you are already there. And if you go on thinking about what to believe and what not to believe, your mind remains the same. This is because it is *your* mind which chooses what to believe and what not to believe. You choose according to your mind.

Then how can this mind change? If your mind is the chooser, it will choose something which can become a food to it. It will go on discarding all that can be destructive to it or that can help it to change. The mind tries to remain in the status quo. It wants to remain static, because with change there is pain, insecurity. You will have to adjust everything again; every arrangement will have to be made again. It will be difficult.

So mind is basically orthodox, even the minds of those who think themselves revolutionary. Mind is orthodox, so every revolution becomes an orthodoxy in the end and all the revolutionaries turn out ultimately to be dogmatists. Every revolution ends as a static society. Why does this happen? – because the very nature of the mind is to be orthodox, to cling to the old. So if I say something which will help you remain as you are, you can choose that. You will say, "This is true." To that which will lead you to a transformation – to an unknown state, in insecurity, on an uncharted path, on an unknown journey and voyage – you will say, "This is not true."

So you can go on choosing; this is what you have been doing. So I say to you, "Be total!" Then change is bound to be there, the revolution will happen. When I say, "Believe totally in me," or, "Don't believe at all," I don't say, "Believe in me," I say, "Be total." Half-hearted, you will never move anywhere. And how can you decide what is true and what is untrue? There is more possibility that whatsoever you think is true will be untrue, and vice versa, because if you already know what is true, then there is no need –

no need to come to me or anybody else. There is no need at all! But the mind goes on playing tricks.

One young man was here today to meet me. I told him, "Take a jump – take a jump into sannyas."

He said, "I have been listening to J. Krishnamurti and I cannot be committed to anything." But he is not aware that he is already committed to J. Krishnamurti.

J. Krishnamurti says, "Don't be committed," so he is not committing himself. He has taken the advice; he has already become a follower of J. Krishnamurti. But his mind is working a trick. It is thinking that now there is no need to follow anybody.

You have already become a follower, but this is unconscious. You are not clear about what has happened to you. And this will not be of much help because this is unconscious. Unless it becomes conscious… I say, if you feel that Krishnamurti is right, then be committed to him consciously and totally. But make it conscious because only that which is conscious can be of help in transmutation, in transformation. That which is unconscious cannot be of much help. Or, if you think that don't need to commit yourself to anyone, then you will have to safeguard your independence in many ways. Then there is no need to go to J. Krishnamurti or to me or to anyone else because the very effort of going shows that you need help – that someone else is needed.

But you can go on playing with yourself; you can go on thinking, "I am just listening. I will choose: whatsoever is true I will believe; whatsoever is not true I will not believe" – as if you have a criterion to judge what is true and what is not true. How will you judge it? Either you know it, then there is no need to go; or you don't know it, then you cannot judge.

Buddha used to say, "Don't ask me questions. Rather, do whatsoever I say, and after a year of doing I will allow you to ask questions. But for one year, just do whatsoever I say. For just one year don't be a chooser; follow me totally. And after one year, when you have become clear, conscious, then you can ask, and then you can choose because then you will have something like a criterion to judge by – a touchstone." But it almost always happened that after one year's deep meditation, when Buddha would say, "Now you can ask and now I allow you to choose," the man would say, "Now I have nothing to ask and now I have nothing to choose."

When I say to you, "Take a jump into sannyas," I mean this: for the time being don't be a chooser. This is not going to be for your whole life, but for the time being don't be a chooser so that your mind is not allowed to come in. And do whatsoever I say. After a year of sincere effort of doing, I will allow you to choose. Then you can choose, then you can think. Then you have something by which you can judge. Right now you cannot judge, but you go on judging.

I am happy with both types of people: those who can say, "I believe totally" – I can work with them – and those who say, "I don't believe at all" – I can leave them to themselves. But for the confused types who go on saying, "Some things I can believe and some things I cannot believe," nothing can be done. They go on hanging around me and I cannot help them. They are unnecessarily wasting their time because they cannot take my help. They won't allow it. They are wasting time; they are missing an opportunity. Something would have been possible very easily if they were available, but they are not available. And they say they will judge. They can go on thinking, but they will never come to any conclusion.

You cannot come to any conclusion because your mind is confused. And if you choose out of confusion, you will be more in confusion. Any conclusion out of confusion will lead you into more confusion. A confused mind cannot choose. That is the meaning of surrender: when you feel you are confused, you go to someone; you feel he has a clarity. I say, you *feel*, not you think. If you feel that someone has a clarity that you don't have, then surrender. This is risky, dangerous, but one has to take the risk because without risk there is no possibility.

If you are too wise and clever and you don't want to take any risk, you will miss for your whole life and you will not come to any point of realization. Risk is basic. It is risky – because you cannot be absolutely certain whether the person to whom you are surrendering is really true or not. It is risky, but try it. If he is not true, then too you will have gained something because he cannot lead you anywhere. If he is not true and you risk your total being to him, you will become aware of what an untrue master is and you will never fall in the same trap again. But if he is true, then you will come to a new dimension of being. Nothing is lost; the risk is worth taking.

But you are clever – your cleverness is your barrier. Be a little foolish and take a jump. Don't be so clever – you have already missed much by being clever. There are certain points where only fools, madmen, lovers, can enter; there are certain doors. Clever men never go there. It happens that through certain risks fools prove to be wise and the wise prove to be fools because fools can take the risk and the so-called wise cannot take it.

There is no alternative, no third alternative; these are the two possibilities. The third alternative you are already. So if you think that the third is good, remain whatsoever you are; don't think of any change.

If you think that whatsoever you are is too much of a misery, a hell, then take a jump out of that hell. And the jump is always into the unknown, so risk is there; it is implied. Be a little daring, a little foolish.

When Buddha left his palace he was foolish. Even the driver who led him out of his kingdom told him. The name of the driver was Chhanna. Chhanna said to Buddha, "You are committing a foolish act. It is too risky: losing an empire, losing a kingdom, for something which is very vague. No one knows whether any soul really exists. It is foolish to lose that which you have for that which is uncertain."

Buddha would not listen to him. That man was old, wiser, and he said to Buddha, "You are young, and because of your youth you are not yet mature enough to understand what you are doing. Turn around! Everyone is trying to get into that palace which you are leaving. And where are you going – to be a beggar? If beggars could have achieved, then the whole world would have been beggars. And there are beggars on the streets and they have not achieved. Where are you going? You are taking a risk."

Leaving the known for the unknown is always a risk. Buddha said, "I am fed up with the known. I have known it; now there is nothing more to know. So allow me to take the risk. Even if I lose, I lose nothing because I don't have anything. If I gain, I gain everything. The risk is worth taking. I cannot lose anything because I don't have anything. I have lived with those palaces and those beautiful wives, I have known them. Now nothing is there to know. No mystery is there. Now it has become a boredom, a repetition, a habit. I have become a mechanical thing. Now there is nothing to go back to. I will take the risk. If I lose, I lose nothing because I don't have anything."

What have you got that you are so much afraid of surrender? What have you got? You are just like a naked man who is afraid of taking a bath in the river because he is thinking, "Where will I go to dry my clothes?" And he is nude, he has no clothes, but he is not entering the stream to take a bath because he is afraid that there is no place where he can dry his clothes. What have you got to lose? And there is every possibility to gain. But I say "possibility": that is the risk.

Religion is not for weaklings, it is only for those who have a strong will to move into the unknown. Weaklings always remain confused because they go on traveling in two boats simultaneously – in two directions. They cannot move in one boat because they are afraid. And they are very clever, so they think that if one goes wrong at least the other will always be there. So they travel in two boats, but they never reach anywhere because you cannot travel in two boats.

There is no third alternative. You will have to decide this or that; only then does a revolution set in. The old will have to die for the new to be born and there can be no compromise.

The old cannot continue in some form in the new; it has to be dropped completely. Religion is both a death and a rebirth. And when I say to you: "Choose one," be total in your choice, it is going to be a death – that is the fear. But unless you die you cannot be reborn.

The last question:

> **Osho,**
> **I am feeling completely helpless about everything – life, health, meditation – and even helpless to surrender totally. Everything I can do is always partial. Unconscious factors control much and my efforts and attempts at no-effort are powerless against them. I feel that I want to leave it all to you but that too is only possible as much as I am consciously capable. And then too I am aware the ultimate happening may or may not happen in this life and that I cannot ask when it will happen if I leave it to you. Can I just adopt an attitude of leaving it all to you even though I am aware of the possibility that the happening could take lives anyway? Is this still surrender even though nothing happens as a result of it?**

Three things: one, by "total" I mean whatsoever is possible; I don't mean the whole. You cannot surrender the whole right now, because you are not the whole. So how can you surrender the whole? By "total" I mean that which you can do: don't withhold anything. That which you can do: your whole capacity – not your whole being because you are not that, so how can you surrender it? But let all that you can do be included in the surrender.

It is going to be partial – partial in the sense that your whole being will not be involved in it. You have an unconscious part. You cannot bring that into it; it is impossible for you. You don't even know what it is, where it is, how it functions and how it can be brought into the surrender. You cannot do it. Don't leave anything undone of whatsoever you can do. By "total" I mean surrender with all your conscious capacity. Through this surrender, by and by, the inner being will come up and will be included in it.

In the beginning it can only be in this way. So don't wait until you are ready to surrender the whole being because then there will be no need to surrender – because when you have already become whole there is no need to surrender. Surrender is a technique to become whole. So take a jump as you are and as much as you can; that is all.

Secondly, don't be worried about when it will happen. It can happen the next moment, it may not happen for lives together. It depends. If your jump is intense, total, if you have put into it whatsoever you could, it can happen the next moment. But if you withhold something, then it will take time. It can take lives together. But even if it happens after many lives it is early because you have already been alive for millions of lives and it has not happened yet.

So even if it takes a few lives it is not too much – it is early. Don't be worried about it because that worry will become a barrier to total surrender and that worry will create an inner condition. Knowingly or unknowingly you will be expecting it to happen soon. That will become a desire and that desire will become a barrier.

So don't think about what will happen; don't make a condition. Let it happen unconditionally. Say deeply within your heart, "I am not. Whether it happens or not, I am still ready to surrender." Then it will happen very soon. It can happen in the very surrender itself; it may not take a single moment.

I will tell you a story, one very old Hindu parable:

Two sannyasins are meditating under two trees, and Narada passes by. Narada is a messenger between the two worlds, "this" and "that"; he moves between both. He goes on carrying news from here to there and from there to here.

He passes the first monk who is very old, who is doing deep austerities and who has been working for salvation for many lives. The monk asks, "Narada, are you going to the other world? Then ask the divine how much time I still need, how much more time I will have to exist in this body. It has been too much. I have been working for many lives. Now how much time is left for the ultimate transformation? Please ask for me."

The way the old monk asks this is very tense, full of lust, full of conditions, as if he is complaining. He feels he has been making arduous efforts for too many lives – that some injustice has been done to him. The tone, the very way, is of complaint.

Narada passes by the second tree. A young man is dancing there, singing, celebrating his ecstasy. He doesn't even look at Narada. Narada stands there. The young man sees him, but he goes on dancing. So Narada asks him, "Don't you have any question? The other monk under your neighboring tree has asked. Would you also like me to bring you news about when your salvation is going to happen?" The man goes on dancing and he doesn't say anything.

Narada goes to the other world. He comes back. He says to the old monk, "I asked God, and he said three lives more."

The old monk was chanting on his *mala*, his beads. He threw down the beads and said, "Three lives more!" He got very angry and disappointed.

Narada reached the other tree. The young man was still dancing. Narada said, "Though you didn't ask me to ask, still I asked. But I am afraid to tell you, because that old man has thrown his beads and is so angry and disappointed. I am afraid to tell you."

The young man said, "You can say it because whatsoever is, is blissful and whatsoever happens is good. You can tell me; don't be worried."

So Narada said, "I asked God and he said that you will have to be born as many lives as there are leaves on the tree under which you are dancing."

The young man became so full of ecstasy. He said, "Just this many leaves? So few? – because the earth is so full of leaves, infinite leaves." He again started dancing and it is said that immediately, that very moment, he disappeared from the earth.

This is surrender. This is total acceptance – no complaints, no conditions, no expectations. Immediately he was liberated; that very moment he was liberated.

I don't know about the old monk; nothing is said. But I don't think three lives will be enough for him. He must be somewhere here, still working.

Now get ready for the meditation.

...

CHAPTER 14

KNOWING ALL THROUGH THE ONE

"That Yaksha was brahman," said Uma. "It was through the victory of brahman, indeed, that you achieved this glory." It was from that – from the words of Uma – that Indra understood that the Yaksha was brahman.

Therefore, verily, these gods – Agni, Vayu, and Indra – excel all other gods, for they approached the Yaksha nearest; they were the first to know him as brahman.

And, therefore, indeed, Indra excels the other gods, for he approached the Yaksha nearest; he was the first to know him as brahman.

This is the teaching regarding that – brahman. It is like a flash of lightning; it is like a wink of the eye. This is with reference to the adhidaivatam – its aspect as cosmic manifestation.

Now its description with reference to the adhyatma – its aspect as manifested in man: mind proceeds to brahman in all speed, as it were. By his mind also, this brahman is remembered and imagined as always near.

The mind is abstract. It cannot touch, it cannot see, it cannot hear. It can only think. Thinking is abstract. Thoughts move just in a vacuum. Thoughts have no substance. They cannot be touched, cannot be heard, cannot be felt. So mind is the most abstract faculty in man and when this abstract faculty tries to reach the truth, it can only think about it. It cannot realize it, it cannot feel it. It can only contemplate about it. The approach is going to be indirect. Senses are direct; mind is indirect.

Indra represents the mind; Agni represents the eyes; Vayu, air, represents the ears. Remember this. Ears are the part which is related to the cosmic existence of air. Eyes are the part in man related to the cosmic existence of fire or sun.

Vayu approached *brahman*, Agni approached *brahman*: they could hear, they could see. They could be in more substantial touch with the ultimate reality, but they couldn't recognize. The *brahman* was present, but the senses could not recognize who he was. For the recognition the mind is needed; only mind can recognize. But then a problem arises: mind cannot approach directly. Mind approaches indirectly. Mind cannot penetrate reality because mind is an abstract sense. It can only think. Through thinking it can recognize, but then the reality disappears. It becomes only a thinking inside. Indra could recognize, but not directly, because when Indra approached, the *brahman*, the spirit, disappeared.

So the first thing to be understood is that mind is an indirect process. Senses are direct: I can touch you with my hand, but I cannot touch you with my mind. I can see you through my eyes, but I cannot see you through my mind. Mind is enclosed within me and there is no bridge from the mind to reach you directly. If the mind wants to reach you directly, some medium will be needed. If the mind wants to see you, it will see through the eyes. To touch you, it will touch through the hands. A medium, an agency, a mediator, will be needed. Mind needs a mediator.

So whatsoever knowledge mind can give, it can never be immediate. This is one of the findings of the Eastern mind, that mind cannot give you immediate knowledge of anything. A mediator will be there and knowledge will come through a means, through a medium. There is no direct penetration from the mind into reality. Senses are direct, but they cannot recognize. Mind can recognize, but it is indirect. So unless mind and senses are both in a deep harmony, you cannot know reality.

Agni approached alone, Vayu approached alone, Indra approached alone. They all were failures. *Brahman* was present to Agni, but then Agni had no mind to think, to recognize, to remember; he couldn't come to any conclusion as to who he was. Indra could recognize, but he had no direct possibility to know who he was. The *brahman* disappeared before the mind.

So the first thing: if mind is the way to know the reality, the reality will disappear. That is why for science there is no *brahman*. Science is Indra – mind working. So science goes on denying. Science says there is no spirit in you, no *atman*, and no *brahman*, no cosmic soul in the universe. This is a mental approach – abstract. But a very deep phenomenon happens in this parable: *brahman* disappears and a woman, one of the most beautiful of women, Uma, appears.

Whenever the mind tries to penetrate the mystery of life, *brahman* will disappear and sex will appear. For the mind, sex is the nearest to *brahman*, the closest possibility to know the life force. Why? Sex is the nearest to the mind for many reasons. One, *brahman* is the cosmic life force and sex is your individual life force. *Brahman* is outside you; sex is within you. To feel *brahman*, senses will be needed. To understand sex, you can close your eyes and understand it. It is a reality within you. Or, you can say that the *brahman* has penetrated you in the shape of sex. It has become sexual energy within you. It is the individual counterpart of the cosmic life force.

You can understand *brahman* through the mind only as sex. So whenever abstract thinking reaches to its climax, *brahman* disappears and sex becomes the sole reality. It has happened many times before; it is happening right now in the contemporary world. It happened in India and because of that happening Tantra was born. Tantra means to forget the *brahman* completely; just penetrate the sexual energy to its very core and you will come to *brahman*.

Tantra was born because India reached to an intellectual climax, to the same climax that now Western countries have reached. India has known that climax – the climax of abstract thinking, the climax of scientific thinking, the climax of conceptualization and philosophy. India reached to a very sophisticated state of mind where the *brahman* disappeared and the life force became the sex force – appeared as the sex force.

Tantra preaches that there is really no God to be approached directly. Unless you penetrate the mystery of sex, unless you go deep into it, you cannot know *brahman*. And it is also symbolic that sex appears before Indra in the form of Uma. Uma is the consort of Shiva, and Shiva is the greatest tantric. Uma is the counterpart. In that deeper experience of the life force, Shiva is male, Uma is female. To Shiva, Uma is the source of the life force, the door toward cosmic phenomena. To Uma, Shiva is the door to the cosmic phenomena. And when Uma and Shiva meet in a deep orgasm, they lose themselves and only the cosmic energy vibrates.

You have seen the *shivalinga* – it is not alone, it is also with the *yoni* of Uma. The *shivalinga* is placed in the *yoni* of Uma. The *shivalinga* is phallic, and just underneath is the pudendum – the *yoni*. The *shivalinga* is the symbol of sexual orgasm and meeting. Through this meeting the individuals disappear and the cosmic is revealed.

Before Indra, Uma appeared; before mind, sex appeared. This is how I decode it. And Indra asked Uma, "Who was this spirit?" When mind reaches to its climax, it can only ask sex energy, "Who is this cosmic force?"

Inside man, mind is one pole and sex is another pole. You exist between two poles. In your head is the thinking force, the reason, the mind. And just on the other pole is sex. On your backbone these are the two poles. Scientists say that your brain is just an extension of your backbone, the spine. On one pole exists sex energy, on the other pole exists reasoning. These are the two poles of your spine, and your spine is your existence. You exist through your spine. When reason comes to its climax, you become polar. You have moved to one extreme, and it is absolutely abstract. And sex is the most substantial; it is not abstract at all.

Through eyes you can see, through hands you can touch, through ears you can hear; but through the sex center you penetrate most deeply. No eyes can penetrate that much, no hands can touch that much, no ears can hear that much. Through sex, you penetrate into the mystery of the other to the very depth. Sex is a deeply penetrating force. Mind never penetrates anything directly; sex penetrates only directly. Sex has no abstraction about it; mind has no substantiality about it. So sex is the earth within you; mind is just the sky. Sex is the root within you; mind is the flower.

So whenever mind wants to know what the life force is, what the *brahman* is, there is only one way and that is to come back to the roots, because those roots are in the cosmos, those roots are deep in the cosmic life energy. Through sex, mind can move backwards to the very source. If you go on thinking, then you move around and around in the mind and there is no way to go out. You can create big philosophies, great systems, but they will be all concepts, words, verbalization; they cannot be realities. Mind can know only if mind falls back to the roots, goes down to the very source. And through that source the *brahman* can be known.

Now, through Western search, the world has come again to a point where mind has become supreme. Hence, so much interest, so much research and so much philosophizing about sex in the West. God has been pushed aside. Now the basic problem in the West is not God: the basic problem is sex. And if this mystery can be penetrated, only then can God somehow again become a living problem. Western thinkers are continuously thinking about the mystery of sex – what it is.

Uma appeared before Indra and Indra asked Uma, "Who was this force? Who was this spirit? Who was this presence which has disappeared before me?" This is what mind asks the sex force: "What is life? What is God? What is *brahman*?" Asking the sex center is Tantra. Tantra means the Yoga of sex. This can be said as a prophecy – that for the coming, future generations, only Tantra can be helpful because only Tantra knows the secrets of how to ask Uma, how to ask the sex center, sex energy, about the ultimate source of energy.

> *And Uma answered: "That Yaksha was brahman," said she. Uma answered that that presence was brahman.*

Two things that sex can answer: for a man, a woman is the answer and for a woman, the man is the answer. If you can rightly ask, sex can become for you the deepest answer possible. But there are dangers. If you cannot ask rightly, then sex will prove to be a misery for you. Then sex will become for you the greatest fall. If you can rightly question, then sex can become for you the deepest secret to be known. But if you wrongly question, then sex will become the greatest fall possible. This is bound to be so because sex has a height. If you travel toward that height wrongly, you will fall.

Christianity understands sex to be just a fall, and Tantra thinks sex to be the right answer. Christianity and Tantra are just opposed to each other. Not only Christianity: Jainism and many other religions are also opposed to sex. They are opposed for a reason. The reason is the fifty percent possibility of falling down. It is dangerous.

So try to travel in some other way where this fifty percent fall is not a possibility. And it is mathematically fifty percent. Actually it is ninety-nine percent, because sex is such an attraction and sex is such an unconscious force that it is difficult to remain alert, meditative. While experimenting in it, you will become unconscious. And if you become unconscious in orgasm it leads you nowhere.

The possibility is ninety-nine percent is that you will fall through sex. There is only a one percent possibility that you may rise. But Tantra says that that percentage of fall can be reduced through right techniques and a man or a woman can be trained. Then making love becomes an art – the greatest art. And if you know the art, then you approach very cautiously, very delicately. And then it is not just a temporary release, a relief. It becomes a sacred worship.

So Tantra trains people first to be nonsexual. Tantra teaches first to come to a point where sex is not a madness for you. Tantra first teaches you to be totally unattached, without desire. A nude woman, a beautiful woman will be sitting before a tantric seeker, a *sadhak,* and he has to contemplate on her, on her beauty, but as a divine force. And he has to go on watching inside that no lust arises. If lust arises the point is lost.

This is the most difficult thing. For months together the seeker is to practice going beyond lust. And when a beautiful woman appears to be just like a beautiful flower and the seeker has no lust in the mind, only then will the master allow the seeker to approach this beautiful woman without lust, to enter this woman without lust. Then it becomes a meditation, and the orgasm becomes cosmic. Then individuals are not there because individuals exist through desire, lust, and passion. Then love happens and this love is prayer. And through each other they have entered the greater depth that encompasses all.

Sex can give you the answer and if you have become too intellectual then *only* sex can give you the answer. Any intellectual age will have to ask through sex. If you have moved too much in the head you will have to fall back to the other extreme. Only then do your two opposites within meet and you become a unity.

Uma said: "*That Yaksha was brahman*"... Through deep sex experience, meditative sex experience, you will come to know that this sex energy is nothing but divine energy. Then sex becomes *samadhi.*

Uma said,

> *"It was through the victory of brahman, indeed, that you achieved this glory." It was from that that Indra understood that the Yaksha was brahman.*

The mind cannot understand directly. Sex becomes the mediator: Uma becomes the medium. And through that medium Indra could understand who that spirit was, who that presence was. Mind needs a mediator because mind is abstract and reality is not abstract. Only through a mediator, a transformer, can mind come in contact with reality.

Greek philosophy lost its path only because of this – because they depended totally on mind and reason and they thought nothing else was needed: go on thinking and through thinking the truth will be achieved. It has not been achieved yet. Greek philosophy goes on. It has changed its land, it has changed its abode. It has traveled through the whole Western history of thought.

The river that was born in Athens has traveled through Berlin, through Paris, through London, through New York. It has been going on and on, but it simply gives more words. It gives Hegel and Kant, it gives Berkeley and Hume, it gives Russell and Wittgenstein – words and words and words. It cannot produce a Buddha, it cannot produce a Jesus – it cannot produce experience. And now the West is becoming interested in Tantra. That may be the turning-point. The head comes back to the roots.

Through Uma, Indra could understand that the Yaksha was *brahman*, that this presence which had disappeared, which was now not visible – and instead of it Uma was visible, a beautiful woman, a sex symbol was visible – was *brahman*. Sex can give you the answer to what the reality of life is because sex is the most alive thing in you. Mind is the most dead thing in you and sex is the most alive thing in you. That is why mind is always against sex, and mind is always for suppressing it. They are enemies. Mind is a dead thing and sex is the life force; they go on fighting. And whenever you move into sex, the mind feels frustrated and the mind says, "This is wrong. Don't move into it again."

The mind becomes the moralizer, the mind becomes the puritan, the mind becomes the priest. The mind goes on condemning. All that is alive the mind goes on condemning and all that is dead the mind goes on worshipping. And sex is the most alive thing in you because life comes through it: you are born through it, you can give birth through it. Wherever there is life, aliveness, sex is the source. Not only in man: these trees are also sexual. Flowers are nothing but maturing seeds; they are sexual. The animals are sexual.

Now scientists feel that sex even penetrates matter because there is a polarity of the feminine and the masculine in matter. Even in the deepest atom there exists a force as positive and there exists a force as negative. And those two forces create all that is there. The constant fight between the two forces and the constant meeting – the fight and meeting, the attraction and repulsion – creates energy. The whole existence is a creation between two opposing forces. So whenever you are nearest to life, you are nearest to sex. Or vice versa: whenever you are nearest to sex, you are nearest to life. You are young when sex energy is young; you are old when sex energy is old.

Now, scientists say, biologists say, that if we can replace the sex glands, only then can old age be stopped – because if the sex glands are young, then the whole body will be young. If the sex glands are old, then you cannot do anything to make the body young.

There has been a constant effort: all the medical researchers all over the world have been trying to make man live longer, stay younger longer, and now the right point has been touched. The sex glands become old first and then your whole body follows. Your sex glands become youthful first and then your whole body follows. So really it is not a question of the whole body, it is only a question of the sex center. If the center is young you are nearer to life; if the center is old you are nearer to death.

Some day or other – it is possible now – we will be able to replace the sex glands. Once we are able to replace the sex glands, man can live younger forever. The body will follow. The body is just an expression. You may not have thought about it, but the sex center is the center of your whole body. The whole body is just a circle around it. Biologists say the whole body exists for the sex center to survive. The body is just a situation in which sex hormones can live and survive. The sex glands are not for the body: the body is for the sex glands.

Once the sex energy has traveled and given birth, the body goes on becoming old. Once the sex energy is exhausted, the body has to be discarded. Now the abode is not worth living in. Now the energy will find another body to live in. Now the energy will find another more alive, younger body to live in so that the life force can continue on and on.

You see a fruit: deep in the fruit are the seeds. The fruit exists only to protect the seeds, to give life, energy, food, to the seeds. The seeds do not exist for the fruit. The fruit exists just to protect, so that the seeds can survive. And once the seeds are ready, the fruit is useless. The fruit will ripen, fall down, because the only need was just for the seeds. When the seeds are ready to sprout as a new life, the fruit will become ripe and fall down from the tree. Why does the fruit fall down from the tree? – because the seeds now want to move into the ground. Now they are ready. They want to move into the earth, into the womb.

When you feel sexual you think you can control it just by thinking. But you cannot because now the seeds are ready to move into a woman – and those seeds are struggling to move. So whatsoever you do, just by using your mind you cannot do anything because deep down the mind exists for the seeds, not the seeds for the mind. They will struggle and they will defeat you. They will move out of your body because your body has been just an abode – a fruit. Now the seeds are ready. They want to move out of your body. They will move anyhow. If you don't make love to a woman, they will move in your dreams. But now they want to move out. They are ready – ready to live in another body, ready to give life a further push.

Unless you understand this sex center and unless you do something deep within the center, you cannot attain *brahmacharya* – you cannot become a celibate. The so-called *brahmacharis* are just so-called. They may not be making love to women: that is not difficult. But the seeds of semen are going out; they cannot be contained. *Brahmacharis* are not honest, so they will not say anything. A person who is honest will say.

Mahatma Gandhi has said – and he was one of the most honest men – that even at the age of seventy he was having wet dreams. He said, "I have come away from sex as far as my conscious mind is concerned, but the moment I fall asleep I cannot do anything. In dreams, sexual imagery comes in and the semen moves out." He was honest.

Sex energy can be transformed only when sex becomes the door to the cosmic. And once you know the secret that sex can become the door to the cosmic, you have the key – and that key only can make you a *brahmacharin*. Why? – because now you can give birth to a higher sort of life. Now the sex energy can give birth to a higher sort of life. But it *must* give birth; if there is no higher movement, then it will move into a lower world. But it will move! Energy needs movement.

Tantra has discovered certain secrets by which a higher form of life is created through sex – not only bodies, but a higher form of energy. And once you know how to create that energy, sex disappears as sex. It starts moving in a higher dimension.

Tantra says – and Tantra has techniques which have been proved right for all those who have experimented with them – that when a woman and a man are in an orgasm, ordinarily the orgasm is a release: the man ejaculates and the orgasm ends. But tantric orgasms are without ejaculation. Simply, the two energies meet – not on the physical plane: the energies meet on a psychic plane. And when they move deeper they meet on a spiritual plane and that meeting becomes the door and energy starts moving. It becomes creative; it gives birth to you on a new plane. With every higher movement of sex energy, you are born on a higher level; you go on becoming superhuman. Sex can become the answer: that is the message of the parable.

Uma said that this Yaksha was *brahman* himself. *"It was through the victory of brahman, indeed, that you achieved this glory."*

So whatsoever man achieves, he achieves because of the life force. At the lowest that life force is known as sex energy; at the highest the life force is known as the *brahman*. And the mind can approach only the lowest. That is why Uma appeared. And only from that lowest, mind can move by and by to the highest. The lowest will become the medium.

> *It was from that – from the words of Uma – that Indra understood that the Yaksha was brahman.*

> *Therefore, verily, these gods – Agni, Vayu and Indra – excel all other gods, for they approached the Yaksha nearest; they were the first to know him as brahman.*

Three gods – Agni, Vayu, Indra. Agni is represented by your eyes in your body, Vayu is represented by your ears in your body, Indra is represented by your mind in your body. Your body is a miniature cosmos. Whatsoever is in the cosmos is in your body. You are a small representative of the whole cosmic existence, of the whole phenomenon.

So now let us decode these symbols. Agni, Vayu and Indra excel all other gods. Whatsoever you know about *brahman* is known either through the ears or through the eyes or through the mind. You have heard about him: it is through the ears – Vayu. All the scriptures are for the ears – the god Vayu. All the *smritis, shrutis* – all that has been known and recorded, is recorded for your ears.

Ears can give you a glimpse, the first glimpse, but if all the scriptures are destroyed and no one says anything to you about

God, still your eyes will feel. Your eyes will come to a glimpse of something unknown that is hidden everywhere. That is why we call our *rishis*, seers, *drashta* – because it is through the eyes that they have the first glimpse.

Hence, in this parable, Agni approaches *brahman* first. Agni approaches *brahman* first: that is, eyes give you the first glimpse. They cannot recognize, of course, but they touch the reality. They have a feeling that something is there, unrecognized. When eyes have known or felt or come to a contact, only then can whatsoever is heard become meaningful. So scriptures will not be of much help unless your own eyes have started to penetrate the reality around you. When you can see something, then scriptures become true. Only through your own seeing do scriptures become true.

So next Vayu approaches *brahman* – but even through the eyes or through the ears, you will not be able to recognize. Only then can your mind be of help. But when mind approaches it is abstract and the *brahman* disappears.

There have been philosophers who have believed only in the eyes: for example, Charvakas. They say *pratyaksha* – that which is before the eyes – is the only reality. They believe only in the eyes, so they say whatsoever is seen is real and because God is not seen, God is unreal.

There are philosophers, for example, *mimansakas,* who say that whatsoever is heard about him is true – the Vedas are true – and he cannot be known otherwise; the Vedas are the last authority. They believe in the God Vayu. And then there are the rationalists – those who say, "Only through mind can you know; there is no other way to know." Rationalists exist all over the world. They say that only through reason can you approach the reality.

These are the three doors: through the eyes, through the ears, through the mind. And then there is the fourth, Tantra, which says that the mind must approach through sex; only then will you know the reality.

This sutra says:

Therefore, verily, these gods – Agni, Vayu and Indra – excel all other gods, for they approached the Yaksha nearest; they were the first to know him as brahman.

And therefore, indeed, Indra excels all other gods, for he approached the Yaksha nearest; he was the first to know him as brahman.

So mind is the nearest, but only through a mediator. Alone, it moves in a circle, never reaching anywhere.

This is the teaching regarding that – brahman. It is like a flash of lightning; it is like a wink of the eye. This is with reference to its aspect as cosmic manifestation.

Now its description with reference to…its aspect as manifested in man: mind proceeds to brahman in all speed, as it were. By his mind also, this brahman is remembered and imagined as always near.

So the whole parable comes to a particular conclusion. You can try to approach the ultimate reality through the senses; you will touch it, but you will not be able to recognize it. You can approach the ultimate reality through mind: now you are capable of recognizing it, but it will disappear before you.

Your reason has to be tethered to the life force within you. Your reason must become total with your life force; it must not function as separate. Your head must not function as something separate from your life energy; it must be rooted in it. And you must move into the cosmos with your mind clear and with your life energy joined to it, together. Your life energy will become the mediator. Your mind will be on this side. In between your mind and the *brahman* will be the life energy. And only through that life energy, Uma, will you be able to know and recognize both.

The experience of the ultimate has to happen through you as a whole. You cannot approach it through parts. All parts will be failures. All your parts must become a whole when you approach the ultimate; only then will you be able to know it.

This is a key – the whole meaning of the parable. You must approach the ultimate as a total, a whole, with all your senses included, your reason included, your life force, sex included; nothing should be excluded. You should not approach in fragments. You should approach the ultimate as a unity – integrated, one.

Then there will be two phenomena. Like lightning the cosmic will appear before you – as if suddenly the darkness has disappeared and there has been lightning, and everything is seen in a flash. Whenever you are a unity, suddenly lightning happens. The very unity of your being becomes the situation in which the whole cosmos becomes lightning. All darkness disappears. In a single moment everything is revealed.

Remember well that the ultimate is not revealed in parts; hence, the use of lightning. If you move in a deep dark forest with a lamp, then that forest will be revealed in parts. Sometimes you will see some trees, and then you will move ahead, and then some other trees will be seen. But those trees which you had seen before will disappear. They will move into darkness. With a lamp, if you move in a dark forest, only in parts will the forest be revealed to you. The *brahman* is never revealed in parts, but as if you are standing in a dark forest and suddenly there is lightning in the clouds and the whole forest is revealed in a single flash.

So you cannot say, "I have known *brahman* five percent, ten percent, fifteen percent." Whenever you know, you know one hundred percent. Either you know one hundred percent, or you don't know. You cannot know the ultimate in parts. It is indivisible. Just like lightning, when you are ready the ultimate reality is revealed. And it is revealed in such a short time that it cannot be called a fragment of time.

So two things: as space *brahman* is revealed totally and as time it is revealed without a single moment. It is like a wink of the eye – as if you have winked: that much time. Really, no time – as a flash, as lightning, the whole space, the whole phenomenon of *brahman* is known, and without a single moment of time. It is not divided either as space or as time.

You are hearing me. I will say a sentence, then time will pass. Then I will say another sentence and time will pass. You cannot hear me totally; there is no possibility. Time will be there. You will hear me in fragments.

But *brahman* is heard without time; *brahman* is known without time. Hence, the Upanishads call him eternal, timeless, beyond time, *kalateet* – beyond time, beyond space. Time and space both disappear in a single moment of meeting. Everything is revealed. That is why the Upanishads say by knowing one, all is known. By knowing one, all is known! That one is the *brahman*. Enter into it as a total unity.

J. Krishnamurti goes on talking in abstract terms. The whole approach seems to be mental, as if only mind is to be used. The body need not be involved in it, emotions need not be involved in it: only the abstract mind, as if *brahman* is a mathematical problem. It is not, it is an organic problem.

Listening to Krishnamurti you are listening to the mind – the purest mind. You will feel good. Listening, you will feel that you are understanding. Listening, you will feel you are reaching somewhere. But you are learning only new words. You will learn *awareness* – the word, not awareness itself. You will learn *choicelessness* – the word, not choicelessness. And they will go on in the mind, and they will move in the mind, and you will become just a mind – a cerebral center. Your emotions are not touched; your body remains untouched. Only your mind is touched.

That is why Krishnamurti has been a failure. He is himself enlightened, but he has been a failure. His whole life he has been working with the mind and whatsoever he says is true, but it is not applicable because you are not only the mind: you are much more. And that "much more" has to be transformed with the mind.

You have to be transformed as a totality.

You must not only think about God: you must also dance about him. You must not only conceptualize: you must also have emotions about him. You must eat him, you must breathe him, you must walk him, you must dance him. You must come as a totality, as an organic whole. And when you come as an organic whole, undivided, the undivided is revealed to you. If you come divided, the undivided cannot be revealed to you. When you are undivided, you become a mirror for the undivided. You mirror it; it is reflected in you. When you are divided, then everything that you look at is divided.

It is just like a lake. There are waves on it and the full moon is in the sky. But the full moon cannot be reflected on the lake. The lake is disturbed, so the lake will know the full moon in fragments. It will be scattered all over the lake in parts. Then the lake becomes silent and the waves disappear. Not even ripples are there. Now the lake becomes a mirror – undivided, undisturbed. The full moon is reflected in it.

The only thing that is needed is to make you indivisible, without waves and ripples, without fragments – to make you one unity. Your body, your emotions, your thinking, all must become one – integrated. Then you will reflect the divine in a flash, like lightning, with no time lost. The whole will be revealed to you: Knowing one, all is known.

...

CHAPTER 15

NOW YOU CAN GO

The first question:

> **Osho,**
> **Do Hindu mythological gods, like Shiva, Uma and Indra have a real existence on some plane, or are they just symbols as you implied in your talks the last two mornings? And if they are really symbolic, why do people see visions of them in meditation and what do such visions of gods mean?**

Mythology deals with symbols. It is not history; it is not concerned with objective reality. But that does not mean that it is not concerned with reality itself. It is concerned with subjective reality. These gods, these mythological symbols, don't exist outside you, but they have a psychological existence and that psychological existence can be helpful, can be used. So the first thing to be understood is that they are not real persons in the world, but they are real symbols in the psyche of man.

Carl Gustav Jung came very near to discovering the secret of these symbols. He was working on mental patients, disturbed persons. He would tell his patients to go on painting things, whatsoever came to their minds. A person who is schizophrenic, divided, split, will paint certain things and the painting will show a particular pattern. All schizophrenic patients will paint certain things and the pattern will be the same. And when they get over their illness, their disease, they will start painting different things. That will happen to every patient; just by seeing their paintings you can say whether the patient is ill or not.

Then Jung became aware that whenever a person who has been suffering with a divided personality again becomes one, undivided, he starts painting something like a mandala – a circle. That circle, that mandala, shows somehow a deep relationship with his own inner circle that has been regained. Now, inside, he has become a circle, joined together; he has become one. Then in his paintings suddenly circles will erupt. So Jung came to conclude that your inner mind can express certain things in a certain state. If the state of mind changes, then your visions will change, your expressions will change.

Hindu mythological gods are certain visions of a certain state of mind. When you come into that state of mind, visions start happening to you. They will have a similarity. All the world over they will have a similarity. There will be minor differences because of culture, education, training, but deep down there will be a similarity.

For example, the mandala is one of the mythological symbols. It has been recurring all over the world. In old Christian paintings it is there. In old Tibetan paintings it is there. In Chinese, Japanese and Indian art the circle has a fascination. Somehow, when your sight becomes circular, when it becomes a current, joined together, undivided, you start seeing a circle in your vision, in your dreams. That circle represents your reality. In the same way, all symbols represent inner subjective realities. And if a society gives a particular shape to a deity, it becomes very helpful. It becomes very helpful for the seeker because now he can decode many inner visions.

Freud inaugurated a new era in the West by interpreting dreams. Before Freud, in the West, no one was really interested in dreams. No one thought that dreams could have some meaning, or that dreams could have some reality of their own, or that they could have some secret keys which could open the personality of men. But in India it has always been known. We have been interpreting dreams, and not only dreams, because dreams are ordinary: we have been interpreting visions. Visions are the dreams of those persons who are meditating and changing their consciousness. They are also dreams. In ordinary consciousness dreams happen and now Freudian psychology has come to conclude that a particular pattern of dreams shows a particular meaning.

For example, a person goes on seeing in his dream that he is flying in the sky, that he has become a bird. He goes on flying: over hills, mountains, rivers, oceans, cities, he goes on flying. Freud says this type of dream, a dream of flying, happens to the mind which is very ambitious. Ambition becomes flying in dreams. You want to be above everyone – above hills, above everyone. If you can fly, you will be above everyone. Ambition is an effort to fly above everyone. In dream, ambition becomes a pictorial image of flying.

Sexual dreams have a similar pattern all over the world. When boys become sexually mature they will start dreaming of holes, tunnels. Those holes, tunnels, are symbols of the feminine sex center, of the vagina. Girls will start seeing phallic-like symbols in their dreams – pillars or minarets. And this happens all over the world: all over the world there is no distinction; it is similar. Phallic symbols will come to girls and hole-like symbols will come to boys.

If in a particular sexual state particular dreams happen, they have a reality. That reality is subjective. It is just the same when you enter meditation: you are entering a different state of consciousness. Particular visions will start happening. They are also dreams, but we call them visions because they are not normal. Unless you achieve a certain state in meditation they will not happen. They show that something is happening within. They project your inner realities on the screen of the mind in a pictorial way.

Remember that your unconscious mind does not know any language. Your unconscious mind knows only the most primitive language, which is of pictures. Your conscious mind has learned language symbols, but the unconscious mind still remains pictorial just like the mind of small children. It converts everything into pictures.

So, for example, Shiva's *shivalinga* has many meanings. One I told you about this morning, that it is the very source of life energy – a sex symbol. But that is only one meaning. The *shivalinga* is egg-shaped – white and egg-shaped. It happens in a particular state of meditation that this appears before you: a white egg-shaped thing filled with light. Light is coming out of it, rays are coming out of it.

Whenever, deep down, you become cool, silent, and the whole being loses heat, this symbol appears. That is why the mythological story is that Shiva lives on the Himalayas, the coolest place in the world, where everything is cool. Just look at a *shivalinga* – a marble *shivalinga*. Just looking at it you will feel a certain coolness entering you. That is why above a *shivalinga* a pot is to be held continuously, and from that pot drops of water go on dropping on the shivalinga, just to make it cool. These are symbols just to give you a feeling of coolness.

In Kashmir there is one *shivalinga*, a natural *shivalinga*, which arises automatically when snow falls. It is a snow *shivalinga*. Just by the dropping of snow in a cave a *shivalinga* is formed. That *shivalinga* is the best one for meditation because it is so cool all around that it gives a glimpse of the inner happening – when the *shivalinga* appears within your consciousness, when it becomes a picture, a symbol, a vision.

These symbols have been found through centuries and centuries' work and effort. They indicate a certain state of mind. To me, all mythological gods are meaningful subjectively. Objectively they are nowhere to be found. And if you start trying to find them somewhere objectively, then you will become a victim of your own imagination – because you can find them; you can project them so strongly that you can find them.

Human imagination is such a forcible thing, it has such a tremendous force within it, that if you imagine something continuously you will start feeling it around you. Then you can see it, then you can realize it. It will become an objective thing. It is not objective, but you will feel it as existing outside you. So it is dangerous to play with imagination because then you can be hypnotized by your own imagination and you can come to see and feel things which are not. This is creating a private fantasy, a dreamworld; this is a sort of madness. You can see Krishna, you can see Christ, you can see Buddha, but this whole effort is wasted because you are moving in dreams and not in reality.

Hence, my insistence to always remember that these mythological figures are symbolic. They are meaningful, they are poetic, they are a certain language. They say something, they imply something, but they are not objective personalities. If you can remember this, then you can use them beautifully. They can be of much help. But if you think of them as objective they will be harmful, and by and by you will move into a dreamworld and you will lose contact with the reality. And to lose contact with the reality is to go mad. Be constantly in contact with reality. Still, don't allow the objective reality to kill the inner and the subjective. Be alive and alert in the inner world, but don't mix them.

This is happening: either we allow the objective reality to kill the inner and the subjective, or we allow the subjective to project a dream world on the objective, and then the objective disappears. These are two extreme viewpoints. Science goes on thinking in terms of the objective and goes on denying the subjective. Religion goes on talking about the subjective and denying the objective.

I am totally different from both. My emphasis is: objective is objective and let it remain objective, and subjective is subjective and let it remain subjective. Keep their purities and you will be saner for it. If you mix them, if you confuse them, you will become insane, you will lose balance.

The second question:

> **Osho,**
> **Yesterday you spoke of psychoanalysis and the phenomenon of patients falling in love with their analysts. Analysis calls this phenomenon transference and tries to make it happen on purpose. Through this total projection of one's feelings of love onto the analyst, a person grows and learns to love in a healthier way. Is not this concept the same as that of surrender in the Eastern tradition? Is it not possible that Freud discovered its value through some esoteric leak?**

Yes, transference can be helpful, but not with an analyst. It can be helpful with a master. It can be helpful only if the person you fall in love with has himself gone beyond lust, has himself solved all his love problems. If you fall in love with a master... By "master" I mean one who has gone beyond attachment, lust; who has gone beyond all problems of love.

Otherwise the transference is going to be double. The patient is transferring, projecting, his own love need onto the doctor and the doctor is projecting his own love need onto the patient. And a doctor who has his own love need cannot be of much help. Really, he himself is ill, and two ill persons cannot help each other to be healthier. This is again going to be a frustration, not a growth in love.

Love can grow only if the other person has grown beyond ordinary problems, the ordinary conflict of love. What is the problem of love? The first problem is that the moment you are in love with someone you are also in hate with the same person. This is the first problem because whomsoever you love, side by side you hate also.

Why do you hate a person you love? Love is a need, and just like love there is another need and that is of freedom. The moment you love a person you start feeling dependent; your freedom is lost. And the person who is killing your freedom is bound to be hated. And the person who is making you dependent will appear not only as an enemy but as the archenemy, because he is killing all your freedom, your liberty, your individuality. But love is a need, so you fulfill love at the cost of freedom. You love a person and you hate that person also.

Then the second problem arises: the moment you are in love with someone, you are not in your senses. You are mad. Really, you are a lunatic. You are not alert, you are not conscious. You are moving as if in sleep. And if the other person is also the same – and a doctor or a psychoanalyst is the same, there is no difference, he has no higher consciousness than you – then he is also moving in sleep. Two persons moving in sleep are bound to collide; they will be in conflict, struggle.

We in India have given another word for falling in love with a master, just to show the difference. We call it *shraddha* – we call it trust, a loving trust. If you fall in love with a master – and you will fall – then there is a difference. You are in sleep, but the master is not in sleep. You will try in every way to create a conflict, violence, aggression, but he can laugh at it – at you. He can be kind and he can arrange things so there is no collision. He can arrange things so there is no violence and no hate. But with a psychoanalyst, you are meeting a person of the same state of mind. The quality of the mind is similar; you will both create problems for each other.

In love, lovers create problems for each other. They go on throwing their problems on the other. And if both are throwing their problems on each other, then it cannot be a growth, it cannot come to a healthy maturity. Impossible! Again it will be an experience in failure. And the more you fail, the more you become experienced in failure. Then you know more how to fail. And with every love experience and relationship, if misery is created, by and by you will come to feel that love is a sort of disease.

Oscar Wilde has said somewhere that love is a fever, a feverish state. It is not health, because whenever you are in love you are in a fever. You cannot sleep properly when you are in love, you cannot be at ease. You are uneasy, a turmoil goes on, a fever grips you.

The third problem is that whenever you are in love you try to possess the other, you try to become the master of the other – the possessor. And the same is being done by the other: he or she is trying to possess you. And what does this possession mean? What is possession? Possession means to transform the person into a thing so that you can manipulate him. Then the person has no freedom. And each lover is making an effort to kill the other as a person.

Only with a master will this not happen. With the master the disciple will try in every way to possess, but you cannot possess a master. That is impossible, because you can possess a person only if he deeply cooperates with you. He may be insisting that he wants to remain independent, but there also is a deep need to be possessed. A master cannot be possessed, so your effort toward possession will fail. And he will not try to possess you. Rather, on the contrary, he is trying to make you more of a person – more alive, more free, more conscious, more alert. His whole effort is to make you more a person than a thing. But lovers are trying to make each other a thing. A psychoanalyst is an ordinary person with some expertise, but with no change of consciousness.

There are some psychoanalysts like Wilhelm Reich and his followers who say that this transference, this falling of the patient into a love relationship with the doctor, is good. But I have been reading the memoirs of Wilhelm Reich's wife and she says that he was making love to each woman patient, but he would not allow his wife even to talk with another man.

His wife was away at some resort for two months. When she came back, he inquired in detail about what she had been doing there – who she was meeting, whether she fell in love with someone… And his wife says that he was making love with a new woman every day, yet he was jealous of his wife and possessive. How can this man be helpful? What type of help can come from this man? He is himself in trouble with his own love problems. It is possible that he is just giving a philosophy. He is a maniac, a pervert, and he is philosophizing the whole thing, he is rationalizing the whole thing.

I don't say that love cannot be helpful. Love can be helpful. But it can be helpful only when you are in love with a person who is higher than you; otherwise it cannot be helpful. And we call that love *shraddha* – a loving trust.

If you are in love with a master, with a buddha – and of course you will be if you are near a buddha – then in the beginning your love towards the buddha will have a certain sexuality about it; it is bound to be so. That's why it happens that around Buddha, around Mahavira… It is known about Mahavira that he had forty thousand disciples – monks and nuns. Of forty thousand monks and nuns, thirty thousand were women, only ten thousand were men. The proportion was three women to one man. Of four followers, three were women and one was a man.

These thirty thousand women must have had a deep love and in the beginning a sexual attraction. It is bound to be so, it is natural. But by and by, the presence of Mahavira will change that sexual part. By and by, living near him, the sexuality will drop and the love will become purer; it will become more spiritual.

In the beginning it will be possessive. Even I feel that it becomes possessive. Around me there are many women and they start being possessive, unknowingly. And nothing is wrong in it; it is natural. But if I am also of the same state of mind, then I cannot help them. Then, rather than me bringing them to a higher state of mind, they will bring me down to their level. And there is a constant struggle for equality. Remember, just as water seeks its own level, whenever you meet a person you both struggle to create a level. Either he should come down or you should go up, but sooner or later you must settle on the same level; otherwise it will be difficult, you won't be able to remain related.

Just like water seeks a level, a relationship seeks a level. If you fall in love with me, then there will be a struggle. Long or short, it depends on what type of a person you are, there will be a struggle. You will try to bring me down so that equality is established. Nature likes equality. But if you can bring me down, then I cannot help you. So while you are trying to bring me down, I must try to bring you up to a higher state. And remember, to go to a lower state is very easy; to bring someone to a higher state is very difficult. It is a long struggle.

When the doctor and the patient are of similar consciousness, only their knowledge differs – not their being. One man has studied psychology, psychoanalysis, psychiatry: he is an expert. The other has not studied it; that is the only difference. Their memories differ, their information differs. They are, as far as their minds are concerned, different; but as far as their consciousness is concerned they are similar.

So I don't think that this phenomenon called transference, projection of love, can be of any help; it cannot be. It can be only if the psychoanalyst is also a master, is also a guru. Then it can be of help; otherwise it cannot be of any help. The person with whom you fall in love must be of such integrity that you cannot bring him down whatsoever you do. And you will make every effort, you will make a desperate effort, to bring him down. This is natural because you feel uneasy with a person who is higher than you. Either you must go higher, which is difficult, or he must come down – and it looks easier for you to bring him down.

If he can come down, or if he is already down and simply pretends that he is not down, then he cannot be of much help. But if he remains higher than you, then your love can really become a growth.

Disciples and masters are in constant struggle, remember this – in constant struggle because the disciples are trying to bring the master down and the master is trying to bring the disciples up. It is a very penetrating struggle and the disciples will not leave anything undone. Not that they know; they don't know what they are doing: they are unconscious, and they can be forgiven. The master cannot be forgiven because he must be aware, he must be alert, he must be conscious of what is happening around him.

A psychoanalyst is not a master; that is why I say that, in the West, the relationship between psychoanalysts and patients has become a sexual license – nothing else. It is helping neither.

And the second part of the same question is: "Is not this concept the same as that of surrender in Eastern tradition? Isn't possible that Freud discovered its value through some esoteric leak?" No. Surrender is different from love. In love you remain yourself. Love is a relationship between two persons who remain two. It is a relationship, it is a bridge. Surrender is not a relationship. You simply disappear, you are no more. When you surrender to a master, you say, "I am not now, so do whatsoever you like; I am not." It is not a relationship. Surrender is not a relationship, because one disappears through it and a relationship needs two. Only the master remains.

Really, when you surrender the master is working in you – you are not there. Then it becomes very easy to work because the struggle that the disciple puts up, the resistance that he usually gives, is no longer there. He is simply in a let-go. When the master says come to the left, he comes to the left. Or if he says come to the right, he comes to the right. Whatsoever the master says he simply follows. He doesn't allow his ego to assert itself; it is not a relationship.

Love is a relationship. Both the lovers are trying to remain themselves; hence, the struggle. Both are trying to be related and yet to remain independent. This is contradictory because the very relationship will change you and you will have to compromise and adjust with the other. And you will not be the same again.

A person who is unmarried will not be the same person when he is married. He cannot be. It is impossible to remain the same person because now a new compromise has entered. Now a new person has entered and a relationship is created. This relationship will change both. Remember, in love both change; in surrender, only the surrendered changes – not the master. He is not related. He remains aloof, he remains faraway, he remains distant. You surrender and you change. In love it is always a condition. You give something to take something. This is a give and take. In surrender, you simply give; there is no condition to it.

Surrender is a very different phenomenon. Really, the West is absolutely unacquainted with it. The master-disciple relationship is absolutely an Eastern happening. In the West there are teachers and the taught, not masters and disciples. That is why Krishnamurti's teachings have been so influential in the West, because he says there is no master and no disciple.

The East has come to evolve a new type of relationship – if you can call it a relationship – in which one exists and the other dissolves, in which the surrendered changes but the master makes no compromise. It is one-way.

Love is two-way, so both do something; both give and take. It is an exchange. Surrender is one-way. The disciple simply offers himself. The master remains untouched. Only then can he work. If he is changed by you, he cannot change you. So many times masters look very hard: they look very unkind, they look very cruel because you go on weeping and crying and they remain untouched. Or even if they show that they are touched, you can see that they are pretending, that they are play-acting.

Surrender is one-way, totally one-way. That is why it is so difficult. If you feel that the other is also bending, it becomes easier. Then it is a contract, then it is a marriage. Marriage is a contract. Surrender is not a marriage; there is no contract. You simply dissolve yourself on your own and the master will not even thank you. You are dissolving yourself totally, surrendering, and he will not even say a single thank you to you. He may not even look at you.

It is said that Bayazid, a Sufi mystic, came to his master and the master said, "Are you ready to surrender? Otherwise, go and move in the world to have some experience of the world, some experience of the failures of the ego, so that you don't resist."

But Bayazid said, "I am ready."

The master said to Bayazid, "Now remain silent. Unless I say something to you, you need not say anything."

It is said Bayazid remained silent for twelve years. He would come every day, sit by the side of the master, and wait. And it is said that just by waiting he achieved.

One day, after twelve years, the master looked at him for the first time, and that was the moment, Bayazid remembers, when he was absolutely in waiting. Not a single thought was there. It was then that the master looked at him, and this was the recognition: "Now you are accepted."

Then another three years passed, and one day the master took Bayazid's hand in his own. Bayazid remembers that that was the day when even the waiting had disappeared. Even that was a subtle thought: "Waiting, waiting, waiting – someday something is going to happen." Even that had disappeared when the master took his hand in his own.

Then three more years passed and one day the master called him near, took him near his heart, embraced him and said, "Now you can go." These were the first words uttered: "Now you can go."

This is surrender.

And Bayazid remembers: "That was the moment when I was so totally one with existence, with the present moment, that the master had disappeared. I was sitting by his side; he was no longer there – no one was there. Simply, existence was there. That was the moment the master called me near, embraced me, and said, 'Now you can go.'" This is surrender – one-way.

But when disciples come to a master, in the beginning they fall in love, not in surrender. And they call that love surrender. That creates problems because love is not surrender. Surrender is a higher state – totally, qualitatively different: undemanding, nonpossessive, not asking for anything, unconditional. But it is natural that surrender is not known to you, while love is a natural phenomenon. First love stirs you. And if the other person is not in a love need, only then can he bring your love toward surrender.

It will depend on how much you resist. You can resist your whole life: then it will not happen. And no master can do anything unless you are cooperating, no master can do anything unless you allow, because no master can be aggressive. If you are open, he can enter; if you are nonresistant, he can change and transform you.

Surrender is the easiest way to be transformed. All other ways are difficult, take a long time. If you can put yourself aside, then the master can immediately enter in you and can change your total being. But no master can be aggressive. Against your will nothing can be done. Surrender means that you are cooperative – totally! Whatsoever is done, you will cooperate. In the West it has never existed; even Jesus' followers, the twelve apostles, were not really surrendered.

On the last night, when Jesus was going to be caught by the enemies, and the rumor was that he was going to be crucified, killed, murdered, Peter said, "I will follow you wherever you go."

Jesus laughed and said, "Before the sun rises in the morning you will have denied me three times."

And it happened so. Jesus was caught. It was dark and the people who had caught him, the enemies, started taking him away somewhere. Peter followed. Someone saw his face. They had lit torches so someone saw his face. Peter looked like a stranger because those in the group were known to each other, so someone said, "Who are you? Are you a follower of Jesus?"

He said, "No, I don't know him at all."

And Jesus looked back and said, "You have denied me already."

On the last night, when he was departing, the disciples asked him, "We know that soon we will enter the kingdom of God. You will sit at God's right hand because you are his only begotten son, but it will be good if you can tell us where we twelve will be sitting. What will be our positions?"

This is not surrender. This is not surrender at all. They are ambitious, they have egos, and they are thinking in terms of greed and contract. Jesus could not get surrendered disciples. Because of that, Christianity went against him. It carries the name of Christ, but it does not belong to Christ at all. It is absolutely against him because only surrendered disciples can carry the real message, the authentic message. Those who are not surrendered will distort it. So it can be said now the pope is the *most* anti-Christ person in the world. The concept of surrender is Eastern.

Someone said to Buddha one day, "You have ten thousand monks around you. How many of them have become buddhas – enlightened?" Buddha said, "So many."

So the person asked, "If so many have become enlightened among these ten thousand monks, then why don't they shine like you? Why are they not known like you? Why are they not worshipped and adored like you? Why have they not become godmen?"

So Buddha said, "They are just waiting for my permission – just waiting. If I tell them to, they will disclose themselves. They are surrendered disciples. If I say, they will disclose themselves – they are just waiting for me. If I don't say anything, they will dissolve into the cosmos without uttering a single word."

This is something absolutely different which has not existed anywhere else. The East has come to create surrender, the phenomenon of surrender, out of the elements of love. But it is a new synthesis, it is a new phenomenon. It is not natural. Love is natural: surrender is supernatural. It is something new which doesn't come out of evolution itself. It has been created by superconscious beings. It is a new phenomenon, it is a creation.

The last question:

> **Osho,**
> **I am deeply under the impression that unknown forces control my every thought and action. I feel like a puppet being manipulated by unseen strings. It is as if I am being tested from moment to moment. Still, I am unaware of this and don't know whether I am making things up. Even this question seems arranged by another force beyond my doing and control. Please explain what this means.**

This is so clear, there is no need for any explanation. This is not a question – just a statement of fact. And this is good. If you really feel that you are a puppet, you don't need to do anything else. If you really feel that you are in the hands of some greater force, you are no more. And this is what is needed – to be no more.

But I think when you say that you feel like a puppet there is a little condemnation in it. You don't feel good about feeling like a puppet. But still you are. Who is feeling like a puppet? If you are *really* a puppet, then who is it that is feeling like a puppet? Who can feel, who is there to feel? You will be a puppet and there ends everything.

So do one thing: drop this idea that you are a puppet. Simply be aware of the cosmic forces around you. You are nothing – not even a puppet – just a crossing point of so many forces, just a crossroads of so many forces passing. And because so many forces pass, a point arises. Just at the crossing, a point arises. If you draw many lines crossing each other, a point will arise. That point becomes your ego and you feel that you are.

You are not. Only the cosmos is. You are not even like a puppet: that too is carrying the ego in a new form. And because the ego is being carried, it feels a little condemnation about the whole situation.

Be ecstatic that you are not, because with the disappearance of *you* all misery disappears. With the disappearance of the ego there is no hell. You are freed – freed from yourself. Then there are only cosmic forces working eternally. You don't exist anywhere, not even like a puppet. If this can go deep in you, you have arrived. You have come to the real thing all religions want you to come to. You have touched the core – the very ground.

But it is difficult. You may be imagining it; you may be making it up really. It is very difficult. You can think it, but thinking will not help unless you feel it, unless it becomes a realization. It can happen only through deep meditation; otherwise it cannot happen. Only in meditation can you come to a point where you feel, "Everything is happening and I am not the doer." And not even that you are not the doer: you are simply not there; things are happening in a space. You have become a space and things are happening there – and you are not there.

This can happen only when all your thoughts cease and your being becomes unclouded – unclouded by thoughts. You exist only in that pure existence; you can feel this. But if you feel that this is happening, it is a good sign. Move ahead and drop that puppet also; don't carry it. When you are no more, why carry a puppet? Drop that puppet also. Be free totally from the ego.

This is why I am here – to make you completely free of the ego. That is why I say to jump, to dance, to sing, to be ecstatic, like a madman – because if you can do this the ego cannot exist, because the ego always exists as a controller. If you don't control anything, it disappears. It is a function of control.

When you start dancing, the ego says, "What are you doing? You will look foolish. Such an intelligent man like you, dancing like a primitive?" The ego will say, "Don't do it. Control yourself!" If you control, the ego remains. Be uncontrolled; don't listen to this controlling force. Just allow yourself for the first time to be simply alive without any control and immediately you will feel that the ego is not there. Existence is there, forces are there, but the ego is not there.

To me, to exist uncontrolled is the only discipline. If you can exist uncontrolled, you have attained to the highest discipline possible. If you don't control yourself and there is order, then this order doesn't belong to you. This order comes from the higher sources. If you discipline yourself, then you are the only source of your life. Then you are cut off from the cosmic source. Drop yourself completely.

I will tell you one anecdote, and then we will try this dropping.

One day, a king came to Buddha with a very precious diamond in one hand and a lotus flower in the other. He thought that Buddha might not like the diamond because he had renounced all riches, so he brought the lotus flower in order not to take a chance. He would have liked to present the diamond. It was rare; it belonged only to him. That was the point really; Buddha was not the point. He was going to present Buddha with a diamond that no one else could present. And then it would be known all over the world that this king had presented Buddha with such a precious thing.

That was the point; Buddha was just an excuse. But Buddha might not like the diamond, he might not accept, so he brought a lotus flower. That too was rare because this was not the season for it. It was unseasonal.

He came before Buddha with his diamond in his right hand. Buddha, just seeing him, said, "Drop it!"

The man understood that he didn't like it, so he dropped the diamond on the ground. Then he brought the lotus flower in his left hand and Buddha said, "Drop that also!" So he dropped it.

Then he brought his empty folded hands. Buddha, for a third time, said, "Drop that also."

Now he had nothing to drop, so he looked puzzled, confused. Buddha said, "Don't think – drop that also."

Then suddenly he understood that Buddha was not saying to drop the diamond or the flower, but the ego which brought the diamond and the flower.

He fell down at Buddha's feet, and Buddha said to the

assembly, "This man is a man of understanding."

When he arose, when he stood back, he was a different man – altogether different. The old had simply disappeared. The man who had fallen at Buddha's feet was no more; a new man had come up. What had changed? The ego.

Now get ready, and drop it!

...

CHAPTER 16

THE GREAT DANCE OF SUCHNESS

Brahman is well known by the name Tatvanam – that – so it is to be meditated upon as Tatvanam – that. All beings love him who know brahman as such.

"Sir, teach me the Upanishad."

"The Upanishad has been imparted to you. We have, verily, imparted to you the Upanishad relating to brahman."

Of the Upanishad, tapas – austerities; daman – self-restraint; and karma – dedicated work; form the support. The Vedas are its limbs, and truth its abode.

One who realizes it – knowledge of brahman – thus destroys sin and is well established in brahman, the infinite, the blissful and the highest.

The word *God* is not God, because the ultimate cannot have a name. It is nameless – because names are given by others. A child is born. The child is born nameless, then a name is given. That name doesn't come from the inner source of the child's consciousness. It comes from without. It is a label – useful, utilitarian, but artificial. The child will become a victim. He will identify himself with this name which is given, which really doesn't belong to him.

But who will give a name to the *brahman*? There are no parents, no society, no "other." And what is the use when the *brahman* alone is? A name is needed because you are not alone. You need to be categorized, named, defined, so that others can call you, remember you. If you are alone on the earth, you will not need a name. And *brahman* is alone – who will give him a name? There is no other and there is also no use in it.

So that is the first thing to be understood and very basic to the Upanishad – because all the religions have given certain names. Hindus have given thousands of names. They have a book, *Vishnu Sahastranam* – God's one thousand names. The whole book consists only of names. Christians, Mohammedans, Hindus, have all given certain names to God to make prayer possible. The name remains false, but how are you going to call the divine? How are you going to invoke it? How are you going to relate yourself to him? You need a name for the divine, but the Upanishads are not ready to give a name.

The Upanishads are the purest teaching possible; they don't make any compromise. They don't make any compromise for you. They are rigorous, very hard and they try to remain totally pure. So what do the Upanishads call *brahman*? They simply call it *Tat* – *that*. They don't give it any name. *That* is not a name; *that* is an indication. And there is a great difference. When you don't have a name, then you indicate and say "That." It is a finger pointing towards the unknown. *That* is a finger pointing towards the unknown, so the Upanishads call it *Tat*.

You may have heard one of the most famous sentences of the Upanishads: *Tat-tvam-asi* – That art thou. That art thou – you are also *brahman*. The Upanishads go on calling him *that*. Even to say "calling him" is not good because the moment we use he, him, the ultimate becomes a person. The Upanishads don't say that he is a person – just a force, energy, life, but not a person. So they insist on calling him *Tat* – *that*. *That* is the only name given by the Upanishads to the ultimate.

Many things are implied, of course. One: if there is no name – or if *Tat*, *that*, is the only name – prayer becomes impossible. You can meditate on *that*, but you cannot pray. The Upanishads really don't believe in prayer; they believe in meditation. Prayer is something addressed to a person. Meditation is simply sinking, drowning, within yourself. Your "person" is somewhere outside you, but *that*, the *brahman*, the ultimate force, is within you. You need not relate to it as the other; you can simply drown yourself inwardly. You can simply sink within yourself and you will find *that* – because "That art thou."

To take *brahman* as the other is false for the Upanishads. Not that the other is not *brahman*: everything is *brahman*; the other also, the outer also, is *brahman*. But the Upanishads say if you cannot feel him within, it is impossible for you to feel him without – because the nearest source is within; the without is faraway. And if the nearest has not been known, how can you know the faraway, the distant? If you cannot feel him in yourself, how can you feel him in others? It is impossible.

The first step must be taken within. From there the *brahman*, *that*, is nearest. You are *that*. To say nearest is false; there is not even that much distance – because even when someone is near, there is distance. Nearness shows a certain distance; nearness is a sort of distance. He is not even near you – because you *are that*. So why go wandering without? He is in the home. You are looking for the guest and he is the host. You are waiting for the guest to come and he is already the host. He is you.

So the first implication is: for the Upanishads there is no prayer; there is meditation. Prayer is a relationship between two, just like love. Meditation is not a relationship between two. It is just like surrender. Meditation is going withinwards, surrendering yourself unto yourself – not clinging to the periphery; sinking deep to the center. And when you are at your center you are in *that* – *Tat*, *brahman*.

The second implication: when the Upanishads call him *that*, it means he is not the creator; rather, he is the created – because the moment we say, "God is the creator," we have made him a person. And not only have we made him a person: we have divided existence into two – the creator and the created. Duality has entered. The Upanishads say he is the creation. Or, to be more accurate, he is creativity – the very force of creation.

I always like to illustrate this point by the phenomenon of dance. A painter paints, but the moment he has painted his picture, the painter is separate from the picture. Now the painter can die and the picture will remain. Or you can destroy the picture, but by doing that the painter will not be destroyed – they are separate. Now the picture can exist for centuries without the painter. The painter is not needed. Once painted, it is finished; the relationship is broken.

Look at the dancer. He dances, but the dance is not separate; it cannot be separated. If the dancer is dead, then the dance is dead. Dance is not separate from the dancer; the dance cannot exist without the dancer. And the dancer cannot exist without the dance either because the moment there is no dance, the person may be there, but he is not a dancer.

God's relation to the world, for the Upanishads, is that of dance and the dancer. Hence, we have pictured Shiva as Nataraj, the dancer. A very deep meaning is there – that this world is not something secondary that God has created, then forgotten about and become separate from. The world is not of a secondary order. It is as much of the first order as the divine himself because this world is just a dance, a *leela*, a play. It cannot be separated.

Calling *brahman that*, says all that is, is *brahman*, all that is, is he – the manifested and the unmanifested, the creation and the creator. He is both.

The word *that* – *Tat* – also has a very subtle meaning. Buddha has used that meaning very much and Buddhists have a separate school of teaching just based on this word. Buddha has called *that* suchness, he has called it *tathata*; hence Buddha's name, Tathagata

– the man who has achieved suchness, who has achieved *that*.

This word *suchness* is very beautiful. What does it mean? If you are born, Buddha will say, "Such is the case that you are born." No other comment. If you die he will say, "Such is the case – you die." No other comment, no reaction to it; things are such. Then everything becomes acceptable. If you say, "Things are such that now I have become old, ill; things are such that I am defeated; things are such that I am victorious; things are such…" then you don't claim anything, and you don't feel frustrated because you don't expect anything. Such is the nature of things. Then one who is born will die, one who is healthy will become ill, one who is young will become old, one who is beautiful will become ugly. Such is the nature of things.

Unnecessarily you get worried about it; this suchness is not going to change because of your worry. Unnecessarily you get involved in it; your involvement is not going to change anything. Things will go on moving in their own way. The suchness, the river of suchness, will go on moving in spite of you. Whatsoever you do makes no difference; whatsoever you think makes no difference. You cannot make any difference in the nature of things.

Once this feeling settles within your heart, then life has no frustration for you. Then life cannot frustrate you, then life cannot disappoint you. And with this feeling of suchness a subtle joy arises in your being. Then you can enjoy everything – *you* are no more, really. With the feeling that "Such is the nature, such is existence, such is the course of things," your ego disappears.

How can your ego exist? It exists only when you think that you can make certain changes in the nature of things. It exists only when you think that you are a creator – you can change the course, you can manipulate nature. The very moment when you think that you can manipulate nature, ego enters, you become egoistic. You start functioning and thinking as if you are separate.

Someone asked Rinzai, "What is your *sadhana* – what is your meditation?"

So he said, "No meditation. When I feel hungry, I feel hungry and I go begging. When I feel sleepy, I fall asleep. When sleep is gone and I feel awake, I am awake. I have no other *sadhana* – no other meditation, no other practice. I move with things as they are. When it is hot, I move into the shadow of a tree; the very nature moves towards shadow. When it becomes cold under the shadow of a tree, I move under the sun – but I am not doing anything. Such is the nature of things."

Look at the beauty: he says, "Such is the nature of things. When feeling hungry, I go begging – not that *I* go begging; such is the nature of things. The hunger goes begging, not that I move from the hot sun towards the shadow of a tree – such is the nature of things. The body moves and I allow it all to happen, and I am happy because I allow everything to happen. Nothing can make me miserable."

Misery enters into you because you start interfering, you become resistant. You don't allow the suchness to move: you start creating blocks for it. You want to change the course of things, then misery enters.

Someone gives you respect, honors you – you feel elated. You think something very great is within you and now it is being appreciated. It was always there – that was your feeling – but now people have become recognizant, now people have become more understanding so they can recognize the greatness of your being. But then dishonor follows... And such is the nature of things, that dishonor follows honor, it is the shadow of it. It is just the other part, the other aspect of the same coin. And when it follows you feel dejected, you feel depressed, you feel like committing suicide. The whole world has gone wrong around you, the whole world has become inimical to you.

The person who understands the nature of things will enjoy both. He will say, "Such is the nature of things, that people honor me. And such is the nature of things, that dishonor follows honor, defeat follows victory, happiness is followed by unhappiness, health is followed by disease – such is the nature of things. Youth is followed by old age and birth is followed by death – such is the nature of things."

So whatsoever is the case, if you can feel it is so and nothing else was possible, then that which is possible happens. It is always happening – that which is possible. And that which is impossible is never happening. And if you start asking for the impossible, you are trying to move against the nature of things. The philosophy of suchness or *that*, *thatness*, is simply this statement: "Don't try for the impossible; move with the possible and you will never be unhappy." Bliss happens to those who can move with a feeling of suchness.

Buddha became old and his followers thought, "Buddha should not become old. A buddha becoming old?" The followers could not conceive of this because followers have their own fantasies. They think Buddha is not part of the nature of things. They think he must not die, that he must always remain young. So Ananda said to Buddha, "It is very depressing that now old age is settling upon you. We never imagined that you, one who has become awakened, one who has realized the ultimate, should become old."

Buddha said, "Such is the nature of things. For everyone, whether a buddha or nonbuddha, enlightened or ignorant, the nature of things is the same – equal. I will become old and I will die, because whosoever is born will die. Such is the nature of things." Ananda is unhappy; Buddha is not. Ananda is unhappy because he is expecting something impossible, against the nature of things.

When Sri Aurobindo died, the whole ashram of Sri Aurobindo was not ready to accept the fact that Aurobindo could die. They couldn't believe it. The followers all over the world were surprised that Shri Aurobindo could die. For a few months this was the rumor – that he will resurrect again. And for a few days they tried to preserve the body. This was the rumor around the circle of his followers – that he is in deep *samadhi*, in deep meditation, and he has not died. But after three days, the body started deteriorating and a bad smell started coming out of it. He was really dead. Such is the nature of things.

Nature is a great equalizer; it makes no distinctions. And it is good that it doesn't make any distinctions. It is not partial. If you are awakened, the only change will be this – that you will accept this suchness. If you are ignorant, the only difference will be this – that you will go on resisting, fighting with suchness. This is the only difference – the only, I say. And this difference is great, the greatest, because the moment you realize that things move in their own way – nature has its own law, its own order – you are freed from it. Not that it will change its laws for you, but *you* have changed, your attitude has changed. You will say, "Such is the nature of things."

Brahman is the ultimate nature of things, the very suchness. With this comes total acceptance. In total acceptance, suffering disappears. Suffering is your resistance, suffering is your nonacceptance. You create your own suffering. Bliss is always available, but because of your attitudes you are not available to it. Now we will enter the sutra.

> *Brahman is well known by the name that – so it is to be meditated upon as that. All beings love him who know the brahman as such.*

Brahman is well known by the name that – *Tat – so it is to be meditated upon as Tat – as* that. Don't meditate upon him as a person. Then your imagination will have entered; there is no person there. Don't meditate upon him as *sagun* – as with attributes. That is not the teaching of the Upanishads. Don't conceive of him in some form. Just remember him as *that*.

But this is very difficult. How do you remember him as *that*? You can remember him as Krishna, as Rama, as Christ, as Buddha, but how can you remember him as *that*? The very concept of "that" shatters your mind. It will stop. If you remember him as *that*, as the suchness of things, as this great cosmos – and all is implied in it – your mind will stop through shock. You cannot think about *that* – or can you? You can think about Krishna because you can picture, you can imagine, that he is playing on his flute or he is dancing and his girlfriends, *gopis*, are dancing around him – or can you picture him making love to Radha?

You can picture him, but how to picture *that*? There is no flute, there are no girlfriends, there is no dance. There is nothing to be pictured. How can you imagine *that*? Imagination stops. If you really try to conceive of *that*, through that very effort mind will stop and you will enter meditation. This that is just like a Zen koan. That which cannot be conceived – if you try to conceive of it your mind will stop and stopping of the mind is meditation.

The very effort to meditate on *that* is absurd. You cannot meditate upon *that*: there is nothing to meditate upon; there is no object. *That* is not an object. But if you try hard, in the very effort – because you cannot meditate upon it... Not that you will succeed in meditating upon *that* – in the very effort, in the very failure that you cannot think about it, thinking will stop. Because thinking has no goal it cannot move with *that*, and when thinking stops you are in meditation.

It is not that *Tat*, the *brahman*, will appear before you; it is not that you will come to know and realize the truth in front of you – no. The moment your thinking has stopped you have become *that*, you have fallen into it. The wave has disappeared into the ocean. And this disappearing always happens within because you fall from there. The wave disappears in the ocean. You are *that*. Meditating upon *that*, you will become *that*.

The Upanishads go on saying that one who knows the *brahman* becomes the *brahman*; one who meditates upon him becomes him: he becomes *that*.

Brahman is well known by the name that, so it is to be meditated upon as that. All beings love him who know brahman as such. All beings naturally fall in love with the person who comes to know *brahman* as *that*, as the suchness of existence.

Why does this happen? You suddenly feel love arising within your heart and flowing toward the person who has come to attain suchness. Why does it happen? It is not that it is necessarily so; you can even hate such a person because hate is a form of love. But you cannot be indifferent to such a person, that is the point. If such a person is there, either you can love him or hate him, but you cannot be indifferent. Hate is possible because hate is the opposite form, the reverse, of love. It is just love doing *shirshasan* – standing on its head. But you cannot be indifferent.

Why does love happen? Why does hate happen? And why is indifference not possible? Because the very being of such a person touches your heart deeply. It goes on playing on your heart; your heart becomes a musical instrument. Just the presence of such a person stirs something within you. The very presence of such a person makes your own *that* alive. It becomes a magnetic force and your own sleeping *brahman* feels its sleep disturbed. Your own sleeping *brahman* opens his eyes and looks at this awakened *brahman* and a love or hate happens.

If you are receptive, surrendering, trusting, then love will happen. If you are doubtful, skeptical, nonsurrendering, egoistic, then hate will happen. But indifference is impossible. You cannot conceive of Buddha moving in a town and someone being indifferent. Either love or hate is bound to happen. But both are relationships; you will start being related.

Love says, "I am ready to move with you." Hate says, "Don't pull me. I am not ready to surrender; I will resist." Love says, "I am ready to follow you and fall with you." Hate says, "I cannot surrender my ego. And just because I cannot surrender my ego I will hate you, because the moment I love, the surrender will happen." And sometimes it happens that when you are in love with a person you may not be so deeply related as when you hate him.

There is one anecdote I have heard...

A *rishi* got angry with someone. He was so angry that he

cursed the man. The curse was very terrible and this man would have to be born again and again and suffer. The man fell down at the feet of that *rishi* and asked forgiveness. But a curse cannot be reversed. The *rishi* said, "Now nothing can be done to reverse the curse. You will have to pass through it. Only one thing can be done. If you remember God's name, then the curse will not have such a terrific effect upon you. You will remain detached; you will not suffer so much. But you will have to pass through suffering."

So the man asked, "Tell me the secret of remembering the name so that I may not forget it."

Then the *rishi* said, "Then hate God. Don't love – because love can forget, but hate cannot. Hate God, and go on cursing and cursing him, swearing against him. Just by cursing him you will remember him."

Love may forget; hate cannot forget. Love can forget because love, by and by, becomes one with the object of love. Hate is a constant vigilance; you have to protect yourself. The pull is there – a buddha is pulling you – you have to struggle. If you lose for a single moment, if you are forgetful for a single moment, you will be in the current. So you have to be constantly alert. Hate is just a love relationship in the reverse order.

A person who happens to be enlightened will attract you – either your love or your hate. But one thing is certain: you cannot be indifferent to him, because he has gone so deep that his depth will resonate within you, will resound, reflect. His depth will call your depth. He will become an invocation. It is not that he will do something: just his being, just his very being, will do something – no effort on his part.

Just looking at a flower, you say, "Beautiful." Something has happened within you. It is not that the flower has done anything; the flower is completely unaware that you are passing. But you say, "Beautiful." When your heart says that something is beautiful, something has happened within your heart; the flower has touched you deep down. You see the full moon in the night and suddenly you become silent. The depth, the beauty, the grace, has touched you.

Similar is the case here: when a person who has achieved *brahman*, who is enlightened, touches you, it is deeper than any flower can touch. It is deeper than any full moon can touch, it is deeper than anything in the world can touch you because the feeling of *brahman* is the deepest, the ultimate core, the very ground. Just by being near such a person you are changed.

Hence so much insistence in India just to be near the master – just to be *near* the master! The very nearness goes on changing you because the depth calls your depth, the inner silence calls your inner silence, the bliss invokes your bliss. The very presence of a master is seductive. He goes on changing you, transforming you.

> *"Sir, teach me the Upanishad."*

Now speaks the disciple. Up to now the master was speaking, and now the disciple asks the first and the last question – the only question. This is beautiful because he was simply waiting. You must not have even been aware that there was a disciple. Only the master was speaking, as if the disciple was not. He must have been just ears and eyes; he has not interrupted at all. Now, in the last moment, he asks for something: *"Sir, teach me the Upanishad."*

The word *upanishad* means the esoteric teaching, the hidden teaching, the secret teaching. *Upanishad* means the secret path, the secret key – the esoteric, the hidden, the unknown. *Upanishad* means the mystery. Asks the disciple: *"Sir, teach me the Upanishad."*

And the master says:

> *"The Upanishad has been imparted to you. We have, verily, imparted to you the Upanishad relating to brahman."*

Here there is a very subtle and delicate point to be understood. The master has been teaching, talking, and the disciple must have been intensely, intellectually alert, aware, to understand whatsoever was said. And all that can be said has been said. All the knowledge relating to *brahman* has been imparted. All that can be verbalized, all that can be spoken has been spoken.

And the student asks, the disciple asks, "Now teach me the Upanishad, the secret of secrets. What is the meaning of it?"

And the master says, "The Upanishad has already been imparted to you." The master is talking – this is on one level – and while the disciple is engaged in listening, on another level the secret is being imparted.

That is why the disciple is not aware: he is intellectually engaged. His attention is on the words, but deep down something else is being transferred. And that transfer is the secret: that is the real Upanishad. But that cannot be said. It is a transfer without words, a communication without language.

Bodhidharma, one of the greatest masters India has ever produced, went to China. It is said about him that he came to China with a scripture that didn't exist – with a scripture that didn't exist! He transferred the scripture without transferring anything at all. He must have been a past master in communicating things, silently, without words.

He used to sit looking at the wall; he would never look at his audience. Just his back would be toward you. He would never look at you; he would just look at the wall. And many people would ask Bodhidharma, "What type of way is this? What type of manners? What type of man are you? We have never seen anyone looking at the wall and we have come to listen to you."

Bodhidharma used to say, "When the right man comes I will turn toward him. And the right man is one who can understand me in silence. I am not interested in you at all."

And then one day a right man came and that right man said to Bodhidharma, "Turn toward me; otherwise I will cut off my head."

So Bodhidharma turned immediately and said, "So you have come? Now sit in silence and I will impart."

Not a single word was uttered in imparting and the other was made a master. And Bodhidharma disappeared. He had said, "I was waiting for this man for nine years." And the other became a master, but not a single word was used.

There are layers in your being. The uppermost layer, the most superficial, understands language, and the deepest understands silence. And masters have to create devices. These teachings, verbal teachings, are just devices. I have just been talking to you...

One young man came to me just the other day and he said, "You are very contradictory. You go on saying nothing can be said and you go on talking every day continuously for three hours in the morning and in the evening. You are very contradictory. You say nothing can be said about *that* and yet you go on speaking."

He is right, I am contradictory. Nothing can be said about *that*, and still I go on saying something. This something is just to catch your attention on one level so that on another level something can penetrate in silence.

The master says, "The Upanishad has already been imparted to you, and you are saying, 'Teach me, sir, the Upanishad.' And what have I been doing all the time?" But the disciple was engaged intellectually. He is not yet aware what has happened to him. The news has not yet reached to his intellect. It will take time.

So it happens. While you are here you may not have understood me, but that doesn't make any difference. If there has been a contact in silence, it will take time for you to realize that something has happened within. The news will take time because the intellect is very far away from the deepest center of you. If something happens there, you will not become aware. Rather, I will become aware first. So I go on looking at you while you are meditating, just to feel what is happening – because you are not yet able to feel what is happening. It will take time. The message will come one day; it will travel; it will pass through all the centers and layers. And then it will come to your mind and then you will recognize – but it may take years.

Someone very near to me was saying just the other day, "You have not done anything for me and I have been with you for two years." The news has not yet reached. It will take time.

The master says:

> *"The Upanishad has been imparted to you. We have verily imparted to you the Upanishad relating to brahman."*
>
> *Of the Upanishad, tapas – austerities; daman – self-restraint; and karma – dedicated work; form the support. The Vedas are its limbs and truth its abode.*

In short, the master defines what the Upanishad calls *tapas. Tapas* means effort – intense effort. When you bring your total energy to any effort it becomes *tapas* – any effort! If your total energy is brought to it, it becomes *tapas.*

While doing meditation, if you withhold yourself it is not *tapas*. You are just making an effort which is so-so, on the surface. You are not deeply in it, not moving in it totally. When you move in it totally it creates heat; hence the name *tapas*. *Tapas* means heat. When you move totally in any effort it creates heat within you. Exactly that: it creates heat, and that heat changes many things chemically. You become a different being. You become a different person through *tapas* because that heat changes you chemically. It makes a different type of personality for you.

Gurdjieff used methods of *tapas* very much in this age. He would give some method to you and he would say, "Bring your total effort to it. Not a single fragment should be left behind to watch it. Bring yourself totally in it, become the effort." And you may be surprised that any effort…

Gurdjieff would say to someone, "Go into the garden and dig a hole and bring total effort into digging. Forget the digger completely; become the digging." And the man would go and he would dig and he would dig. The whole day he would be digging and then Gurdjieff would come and throw all the mud back and would say, "This was useless. Start again tomorrow morning."

And the man would start again the next morning and this would go on for days and days. And Gurdjieff would come every evening and throw the mud back, and he would say, "Start again."

When the digger becomes the digging, when there is no one left behind, when the whole being has moved into effort, it becomes *tapas*; it becomes a subtle heat.

The master says *tapas* and *daman. Daman* is self-restraint, not suppression. This word *daman* has been very wrongly used. It is not suppression; it is self-restraint. And there is a deep difference.

While doing meditation, while standing in silence, you may feel a sneeze coming. You can suppress it, you can start fighting with it, then it is suppression. But if you simply remain indifferent, if you don't do anything about it, if you don't suppress and you don't express, if you don't do anything about it and you simply remain indifferent, this is self-restraint. You remain in yourself. You don't move towards the sneeze to do anything.

If you move to express it, you have come out of yourself. If you move to suppress it, again you have come out of yourself. You simply remain in yourself as if the sneeze is happening to someone else – you are not concerned. You don't suppress it, you don't fight with it. You simply remain indifferent, a witness. That is self-restraint.

Suppression is easy because you are allowed to do something. Self-restraint is very difficult because you are not allowed to do anything. You are to remain passive, a nondoer, nonactive, simply watching.

...Tapas, daman and karma – dedicated work; form the support. These three things form the support of the secret teaching, of the Upanishad. Dedicated work – all karma, all action, is not karma. When karma is dedicated; when karma is egoless; when karma becomes a sort of prayer, a meditation; when

karma is only outwardly karma and inwardly something else is reaching toward the divine; then it is really karma – then it is dedicated work.

For example, you are serving an old man or an ill man. If you can make it a meditation, if you can make it a prayer; if you can see the divine, *that*, in that old, ill man; if you serve not to achieve anything, you serve to be in deep meditation – in this moment your service becomes meditation. Then it becomes karma. If you want to achieve anything out of it, it will create a chain of cause and effect.

If you want this old man to have property, a bank balance, if your eyes are on the bank balance then it is not karma, even if he is your father. But the bank balance can be there in many shapes: you may be serving this old man to achieve heaven; that again is a bank balance. You may be serving this old man because you have been taught that service leads to God; then again it is a sort of bank balance. You are not here. Your mind is somewhere else.

When karma is totally here and now, when your mind is not moving anywhere else into the future, then it doesn't create any chain. In this very moment it becomes a meditation.

These three: *...tapas – austerities; daman – self-restraint; and karma – dedicated work; form the support. The Vedas are its limbs...*

Veda is a beautiful word: it simply means knowledge. Whatsoever has been known about the *brahman*, wherever, it is all *Vedas*. So I call the Bible a Veda and I call the Koran a Veda; to me there are thousands and thousands of Vedas. And whenever a person becomes enlightened, whatsoever he says is a Veda. So the Vedas are not only four. The word *veda* comes from *vid*; *vid* means to know. And wherever this knowing is accumulated, wherever this knowing is symbolized, it becomes a Veda.

...Vedas are its limbs and truth its abode.

These three things have to be remembered: make intense

effort so an inner heat is born and changes you chemically; be in a self-restraint so you become more self-centered, unmoving, unwavering, centered, rooted; and make your work a karma – a dedicated prayer, a meditation. Try to know all that has been known before. Not that through it you will come to truth, but all that will become a help. It can also become a barrier if you become too much attached to it. Otherwise, it will be a help, an indicator.

Ultimately truth is the abode – and truth means *that*. And *that* comes to you when you live a life of suchness.

One who realizes it thus destroys sin and is well established in brahman, the infinite, the blissful and the highest.

...

CHAPTER 17

MAKE EVERY MOMENT A CELEBRATION

The first question:

> **Osho,**
> **In the morning you said that one who realizes the brahman thus destroys sin and is well established in brahman. In this reference, explain the difference between the concept of sin in the Upanishads and in the Bible. And please also explain the implications in human life.**

There is a very basic difference. To the biblical religions – to Jews, Christians, and even Mohammedans – the concept of sin is totally different than it is to the Hindus and Buddhists. The concept of sin in Christianity, in the Bible, is related to your acts – to what you do. What you do can be a sin, or it may not be a sin; it can be a virtue, but it is related to your doing. To the Upanishads, it is not related to the doing at all. What you do is irrelevant; what you *are* is the point. It is not the doing, but the being itself that is significant.

So what does it mean to call a man a sinner? It means that he is ignorant, unaware of his own self. Because of this ignorance, his acts become sins. The act can become a sin only because the doer is ignorant, unaware, unconscious, is living in a state of sleep.

Ignorance is sin and awareness is virtue. Your acts are irrelevant because they are not central; in the center is your consciousness. If something is wrong with the consciousness, your acts will go wrong. If the consciousness is set right, your acts will follow.

So just to go on changing your acts will not lead you anywhere. You can commit a sin, you can repent a sin, you can replace a sin by a virtue, by a virtuous act – but it will not be of any meaning for the Upanishads if you remain the same. Unless you change, your consciousness changes, unless you attain a new plane of being, a new plenitude, just a change of your acts is useless.

The Upanishads don't think in terms of acts; they think in terms of your being. Alert, aware, conscious, you are virtuous. Why? – because the more you are alert and conscious and aware, the less is the possibility of committing a sin. The basic requirement for committing a sin is to be unconscious.

For example, you can be angry only if you forget yourself. If you are self-remembering, aware, anger is impossible. It cannot exist with awareness. No coexistence is possible. So, when you are aware, it is not that you control your anger, restrain your anger, suppress your anger – no. It simply cannot be there. In a fully aware person anger cannot exist, just as in a fully lighted room darkness cannot exist. The coexistence is impossible.

The moment you bring a lamp into the dark room, the darkness is no longer there. With the light the darkness cannot exist. And the Upanishads say it is futile and foolish to fight with darkness because you cannot fight with darkness. If you fight you will be defeated. Howsoever strong you may be, you cannot fight darkness because darkness is only the absence of light. Bring the light and darkness disappears.

The Upanishads say sin is darkness. Bring the light of consciousness and sin disappears. Don't fight with the sin; don't be concerned directly with sin. Don't think in terms of sin, otherwise you will feel guilty and it will not be a spiritual growth; rather, it will be a fall.

Christianity has made people very guilty because whatsoever

you do is a sin and you have to fight with it. And nothing comes out of it. The more you fight with a sin, the deeper its roots go in you. The more you fight, the stronger it becomes. The more you fight, the more you are a victim of it. Why? – because the fight is with darkness. You cannot win; there is no possibility of victory. And when you get defeated again and again, you become guilty, inferior.

This whole effort of fighting with sins, with wrongdoings, makes you feel guilty and inferior. You start feeling that you are absolutely unworthy, that you cannot do anything. Your spirit is not integrated through this fight; rather, it becomes ill with an inferiority complex, a guilt complex.

The Upanishads say sins are not important. What you do is immaterial, what you are is the point. If you are committing sins it shows only one thing: that you are fast asleep, unaware. So don't fight with the sins; rather, on the contrary, move within and become more and more alert. As alertness grows within, sins disappear without. A moment comes when you are simply a flame of light within, alert to whatsoever you do, alert to whatsoever moves in the mind, alert to whatsoever happens in you. There is no sin then.

And this is possible; this victory is just within your hands. Then you will never have the feeling of being guilty and inferior; you will never feel that you are unworthy. The more you make an effort to be conscious, the more and more you will feel accepted, worthy, welcome – the more you will feel that existence has some destiny to fulfill in you.

I call this approach more scientific, more religious, because it gives man dignity. If you are concerned with sin as an act, it gives you guiltiness and guiltiness cannot make you religious. And through guilt you cannot feel the divine because your own guilt becomes a barrier. If you are deeply in guilt, you cannot feel in any way grateful to the divine. Gratitude cannot exist there.

When you are accepted, when you feel worthy, when you feel the abode of the divine, when you feel that a center in you exists which is beyond all acts, when you come nearer and nearer to this inner flame, you become more and more grateful. Gratitude is the perfume that happens to a religious mind. Guilt is just bad odor, just a bad smell. If you feel guilty, around you there is a bad odor, a bad smell.

To me, the Upanishads are more penetrating because they reach to the very being, to the very core of the problem. Christian or Jewish attitudes are more superficial because they touch on the periphery. They touch the act, not the being. And they think that by changing the acts the being will be changed. It is not possible. You can go on changing the acts, but the being cannot be changed because the periphery cannot change the center, the outer cannot change the inner, the superficial cannot change the basic. But if you change the center, the periphery changes automatically; if you change the inner, the outer follows it.

If I change you, your shadow will be changed. But if I try to paint your shadow and change it, you will not be changed by it. And my whole effort will be futile because a shadow cannot even be painted. If you move, the shadow will move with you and my paint will remain on the earth and your shadow will remain untouched. Working with acts is like working with the shadow. What you do is just superficial. What you are, what your being is, is the central thing.

The Upanishads touch the being, so they call *agyan* – ignorance, unawareness – the only sin. So the sutra says that one who realizes thus, destroys sin. Just by realizing the *brahman* sins are destroyed – all your past sins. You may have committed many wrong acts through lives and lives; they are accumulated there. And they are also destroyed just by reaching and touching the innermost core of your being.

How are they destroyed? Our calculating minds will think, "I will have to repay each sin. For each sin I will have to do something virtuous to cancel it." But the Upanishads say that just by realizing it, just by realizing the suchness, all sins are destroyed.

How are they destroyed? – because you are not doing anything to destroy them. The phenomenon is very subtle. It is just like this: you dream in the night that you are committing adultery, you are committing murder, you have burned a whole city – that you have committed many sins. In the morning you are awake. The dream lingers a little, you remember it, but you don't feel any guilt about it – or do you? If you still feel some guilt about it, that means you are not yet awake. You are still sleepy and the dream still has a little hangover around you; it is still with you. When you are really alert and awake, you can laugh about the whole thing because it was a dream. Really, you never committed anything.

The Upanishads say that what happens is, when a person is awakened into *brahman*, all the lives that he has lived and all that he has done simply disappear like a long dream. With a new awareness, all that is past appears to be illusory, as if it never happened, or as if it happened in a story – a dream-drama.

That is why Upanishads call this world *maya* – illusory. Not that it is not, not that it is unreal, but because of this happening: when a person awakens into deep meditation, the whole world that he has been living in up to now appears dreamlike; it has no substance to it.

Hence, this sutra: this sutra says when one realizes *that*, the suchness of existence, the *brahman*, all sins are destroyed. Nothing is to be done about them. They simply are no longer with you, you have passed them, you have gone beyond them. Now they only belong to a past memory with no substance in it. You can relate to them as if they were dreams.

The Upanishads say that human consciousness has four states. One: while you are awake, the waking consciousness; second: while you are dreaming, the dreaming consciousness; third: while you are so fast asleep that there is no dream, the sleeping consciousness. And beyond these three is the fourth. The Upanishads have not given it a name. They simply call it the fourth – *turiya*. *Turiya* means the fourth. That fourth is the state where you realize *brahman*. All of the first three states are illusory if you enter the fourth. Think of it in this way, because that fourth is not yet your experience. But you have experienced these three; thinking about the three, something can be inferred about the fourth.

While you are awake, while you are in the waking consciousness during the day, what happens? The dreaming consciousness has disappeared, it is no more. The sleeping consciousness has disappeared, it is no more. Then the night will fall and you will fall asleep again; dreams will start. When the dreams start you change the consciousness. The gear of consciousness is changed; now all that was in your waking consciousness simply disappears.

You were awake in Mount Abu, but you can dream you are in London or New York or Kolkata. Mount Abu simply disappears; it is no longer present to the dreaming consciousness. For the dreaming consciousness London is more real, and you cannot even remember that you were in Mount Abu while awake. It disappears so completely that there is not even a trace left. And you cannot feel any contradiction and you cannot raise any question: "How did it happen? I was in Mount Abu and now I am in London." No, not even a doubt arises because the one has so totally disappeared that you cannot bring it in to compare.

In the waking state you were living with your wife in the house. In the dream the wife has disappeared, the house has disappeared. You are living with another woman; you have again married. And there is not even any guilt that you have not divorced your wife – because you cannot compare. The first has disappeared so completely that there is no contradiction, no inconsistency about it.

And then you enter the third state, deep sleep, where dreams disappear. Now the waking state, the wife, the house, have already disappeared. *Now*, the dreaming state, the wife you have just now married and the new house have disappeared. Now both states have disappeared. You are so fast asleep that you don't remember anything.

And then in the morning you are entering waking consciousness again. Now the dream has disappeared, the sleep has disappeared. The same wife, the same house, again start – the same world. Now again you are in Mount Abu. The Upanishads say these three states show that whenever one of these states gets a grip on you, the other two disappear.

There is a fourth state. We are making all the effort for that fourth – to be beyond these three. That fourth state is called *turiya* – total awareness. In that total awareness all three disappear and all that belongs to these three disappears. That fourth cannot be transcended. There is no fifth state of consciousness. The fourth is the last. Buddhas live in it, Christs live in it, Krishnas live in it. It cannot be transcended. Because it cannot be transcended, it cannot be canceled by anything. Hence, the Upanishads say this is the ultimate reality. All else was just relatively real. That which cannot be canceled by anything is the final, the ultimate, the absolutely real.

The sins, all that you have done, simply disappear because you come to realize your being which is not a doer at all. It has not done anything; it is just a witnessing self. And all that was done, was done by nature – the natural laws.

It is very difficult for the society to understand it. That is why no society exists in the world which has Upanishadic teaching as its basis. No society can exist with it, it is so dangerous a teaching. Hindus go on reading the Upanishads, but even they never try to construct a society, to create a society around this teaching, because it is such a high standpoint for looking at things. It says that if a murderer is committing a murder this is how things are – how nature is functioning within him, how nature has become murderous through him. One day, when this man will achieve the final consciousness, he will laugh. He will say, "I never committed this. Just a situation, natural forces, did the whole work."

But if this is taught right now, it will create a confusion in the mind and a fear: "If this is taught then everyone will commit murder and will say, 'What can I do? It is how nature is functioning in me.'" This fear is also false because those who commit murder will commit it no matter what you say. We have been punishing as much as possible – imprisonment, life sentence, even death – but nothing has changed. Murders go on being committed; rather, they go on increasing.

We have never tried the other alternative. As far as I feel, as far as I know, if we base the society on the Upanishadic teaching, not a single extra murder will be there. Things will remain as they are, but there will be more possibility for man to be transformed.

This is difficult because the whole of humanity has been conditioned to believe that man is a sinner and he must be prevented; otherwise he will go on committing sins. He must be imprisoned, punished. He must be tortured so that he is prevented from committing sins. But we have not prevented anyone – not a single man have we been able to prevent.

I have heard that in England in the old days, just two hundred years ago, whenever a thief was caught he was to be flogged naked before the whole town at the crossroads. He would be tied up there and flogged, just to teach the whole town what happens if you steal. But then it had to be stopped because the whole village would gather to see the thief being flogged, and the pickpockets would practice their art just there on the crowd. And people were so attentive in looking at this torture that they would forget their pockets. So then it became obvious that this was nonsense; no one was learning anything. Exactly there on the spot people were stealing, they were doing the exact same thing.

To me, this phenomenon seems to be very symbolic. All our imprisonments, sentences, death sentences, our tortures, have been futile; they have not changed a single man. They cannot because a man is a configuration of so many natural forces. Just by punishing, you cannot change that configuration. A man is such a deep-rooted phenomenon that just by beating him you cannot change his consciousness.

And really, this has been a very long game, very futile because the person who is beating is of the same type. Policemen and thieves belong to the same category. Murderers and judges belong to the same category. They are just standing on opposite poles, but their quality of consciousness is similar. One is committing a sin against the society; another is committing a sin for the society.

If you murder someone you will be murdered by the society and a murder by the society is not a sin. How can you change murder by murder? How can you change violence by violence? You increase it; you double it. You can take revenge, but you cannot change anything.

The Upanishads say that when you come to the innermost core of being and become alert, totally alert about what has happened, then you know it was *prakriti* – nature – which was doing all. You have always been a witness – the *purusha*.

The deepest philosophy in India has been *samkhya*, and *samkhya* says all activity belongs to nature; only consciousness belongs to you. All activity, virtuous or sinful – all activity – belongs to nature. To you belongs only consciousness. Attain consciousness, become one with *that*, and all sins will be destroyed and you will be established in *brahman*.

The second question:

> **Osho,**
> **In many traditions the total transmission was passed from a master to only one disciple, such as from Buddha to Mahakashyapa, from Bodhidharma to Hui-Ke, down to Hui Neng, whom you mentioned this morning. Do you have such a one right disciple to whom you plan to transfer total knowledge among your disciples? Is there a possibility that you will do this with a number of persons rather than only one? Why is it that the ultimate secret is usually transmitted to only one in many traditions?**

It is not transmitted to only one. It is transmitted to many, but only one is authorized to transmit it further. Buddha transmitted his knowing to thousands, but he gave his authority to Mahakashyapa because he was the most capable of being a master. It is not so difficult to become enlightened, but to become a master is very difficult. There are many enlightened persons, but not all enlightened persons are masters.

When you become enlightened it is your own thing, but to be a master you need some art to convey it to others. And it is the most difficult art because something has to be conveyed which cannot be conveyed, and something has to be transmitted which is not transmittable; something has to be said which cannot be said in language. So a very highly qualified artist must be appointed to transmit it.

It happened that Buddha came one day with a flower in his hand and he sat under the tree. He was going to talk to the disciples, but he remained silent and the disciples became uneasy. It had never happened before. He would come and he would start talking, so why was he silent on this day? And he went on looking at the flower as if he had forgotten completely that ten thousand disciples were gathered there to listen to him.

Minutes passed and they looked very long at him, but no one had the courage to say, "What are you doing? Have you forgotten us? Have you forgotten what you have called us for and what you wanted to say?"

He had called them particularly and they had come with great expectations. He had become very old, so they thought that before he left the body he was going to say something secret, esoteric, something very essential that he had not said before. And then he remained silent and he continued looking at the flower. The silence became heavy, it became a burden. Everyone was uncomfortable. And then Mahakashyapa, one of the disciples, laughed. And this Mahakashyapa is rare because his name had never been mentioned before this. He was an unknown disciple as far as the world is concerned, but not to Buddha. Buddha must have known him.

There were many famous disciples. Sariputtra, who was a great teacher in his own right, was there. Moggalayan was there: he was also a great teacher in his own right; he had thousands of disciples of his own. Ananda was there, the closest one, who was constantly with Buddha like a shadow. And there were many – very well known, famous in some way or other. This Mahakashyapa was never mentioned in Buddhist scriptures before this episode.

He laughed. Buddha looked at him. Buddha smiled and asked Mahakashyapa to come near. Mahakashyapa reached near. Buddha gave the flower to him without saying a single word. And then he said to the assembly, "All that which could be said through language I have said to you and that which cannot be said through language I have given to Mahakashyapa."

This is called the great transmission. Mahakashyapa could understand the language of silence and one who can understand the language of silence can teach and convey things through silence. Mahakashyapa is not the only one to whom Buddha had given his secret key; the secret key had been given to many. But the secretmost key can be conveyed only in silence and Mahakashyapa understood that language. Then he was appointed to go on conveying this silent teaching.

Bodhidharma is the sixth in that tradition. Mahakashyapa was the first who got the teaching from Buddha; Bodhidharma is the sixth. And Bodhidharma went around India to find a person who could understand that language of silence. He couldn't find him here; that is why he had to go to China. There he met Hui-Ke, after sitting for nine years in front of a wall.

Buddha had given his enlightenment, the taste of it, to many, but they were not all masters. They attained it for themselves and then they dissolved into infinity.

To be a master is a very difficult and delicate thing. You have attained the infinity, and still somehow you remain here on this shore to teach others. It is very difficult. In a sense, it happens so rarely that it seems exceptional because one who has known the infinity would like to dissolve into it. Why bother teaching you? Why bother saying something to those who cannot understand or to those who can only misunderstand? Why go on teaching them? Why bother? One would like to move into silence, into bliss, into the infinite, and forget the world.

A master means someone to whom the call of bliss is less urgent than the call of compassion. He says, "Wait." The infinite can wait; there is no hurry about it. The bliss can wait, the ultimate dissolution can wait a little; there is no hurry about it.

A master means a being who lingers on a little more on this shore. It is very difficult because he will have to devise things which will allow him to linger here a little more. And this is going to be very arduous because now the body wants to rest, to go back to nature. Once you become enlightened, the body wants to rest. Now there is no need to carry it. The body would like to dissolve back into nature because the destiny is fulfilled. Now the house is not needed; now the bird of the soul can fly to the infinite. This abode is useless. Why carry it on? But a master has to carry on. He has to create devices through which he can go on carrying the body in order to help others.

The body is not the only problem. The very effort seems so futile because you talk to ten thousand people and maybe only a single one will understand. And the remaining nine thousand nine hundred and ninety-nine will create such problems for you – they will create problems and troubles for you in every way.

This is natural because they cannot understand you and whatsoever you say and do becomes dangerous for them because their established values are challenged. Their established life is challenged, their way of living is challenged – everything. You go on giving shocks to them, so they will take revenge. They will do whatsoever they can do to stop you – to stop you from helping them. Thus, it is easy for an enlightened person to simply dissolve.

So Buddha says that there are two types of enlightened persons. One he calls an arhat; by arhat he means one who has attained his self and who is not bothered by anything else, he simply dissolves like a drop into the ocean. The other he calls bodhisattva. By bodhisattva he means one who has become an arhat, but who resists the ultimate desire – the ultimate desire to dissolve; who resists the ultimate desire and lingers on this shore, on this bank, to help others. And Buddha says that the bodhisattva is making a great sacrifice.

Arhats can never become masters; only bodhisattvas can become masters. And not all bodhisattvas can become masters because mastery needs a particular training – a particular training to convey, a particular training to help, a particular training to advise and counsel, a particular training to create new devices – because with every individual something different is needed and with every age something different is needed.

That is why all old techniques become meaningless. They were devised for particular minds and those minds are no longer in the world. And we go on practicing those techniques. They cannot help many; they can help only very few. New devices are needed. You can become a master only when you are able to create new devices and be inventive and creative.

It is not that enlightenment and the secret keys of its knowledge are delivered to only one. They are delivered to many, but to only one as a master who will be capable of delivering the key on further.

Now, because this will be the last meeting, I would like to say something to you before you leave the campus. Firstly, this has been my observation – that ninety percent of you, and this is a very great number, have been doing meditation very intensely. This is very hopeful, but the intensity was more or less dependent on the group. It may be difficult for you to be so intense back at home.

So do one thing: when you do the meditation at home, close your eyes first, feel me present just before you as I am here. Visualize me, visualize the group around you and then start the meditation as you have been doing with the group. That will be very helpful. If you have a tape-recording, then put it on so that the whole atmosphere is created and you are not alone. It is very difficult to do it so intensely individually. Here, the group soul possesses you.

Back home you will even wonder, that for three times every day you were making such strenuous effort. You may not be able even to imagine how you could do that. The group soul grips you. Then you are just in a current; then you are just moving in a flood; then the whole group pushes you on.

Many people come to me and say, "In the camp it is wonderful, but when we go back it is lost." Even back home remember the group, visualize the group, feel the group, and the group will be there. At least I will be there.

If you are a sannyasin, then just take the locket in your hand and exhale deeply three times. Don't inhale. Exhale deeply and allow the body to inhale: don't inhale. Just exhale three times, remember me, and start – and I will be there. Space and time don't really matter. If your intensity is such that you can feel me, I will be there. The space disappears, time disappears, and ninety percent of you will be capable of doing the same as you are doing here. And it is good to do it alone. It is good to start in a group, but it is not good to become dependent on the group forever.

But don't leave a gap. The day you are back home start immediately. Don't say, "Let me rest for a week and then I will start." Then you will never start; that is a trick of the mind. Immediately you are home, start it. It will be happening to you there. And once it can happen to you individually, you have become independent. Meditation can be started in a group, but it must end in independence. You must become independent of the group.

The second thing: many of you will feel afraid of your neighbors, of your family. They will think you have gone mad. Here it is no problem because everyone is madder than you, so you are not afraid. No one here is going to say that you are mad. The whole atmosphere, the milieu, is different. It is cooperative here. But back home the whole atmosphere will be against you. That creates a barrier. So it will be good to tell your family, "I am experimenting with this method and this is a mad method." Go around to your neighbors and tell them, "In the morning for one hour I will be doing this method – and this is absolutely mad, but don't get disturbed."

Tell them this rather than hiding because if you hide you cannot do it rightly; you will always go on suppressing something. Just go around and tell them by yourself. And only for a few days, three or four days, will people be interested in you. Then they will forget because no one has the time to go on thinking about you, that you have become mad. After three or four days they get adjusted and they know that you are doing something.

If you continue it for three months, they will start asking you what you are doing because now something will be happening to you – so apparently, so obviously. It will be coming on your face, in your eyes, in your movements. The way you will behave, everything, will change. You will take on a new grace. A new silence will follow you and a subtle joy not caused by anything. Just because you are alive, a subtle joy will be there with you and everyone will be able to feel the difference. Then they will start asking you. Then they will never think you mad.

So if you can persist in this madness, no one will think you a madman. But persistence is needed – and in the beginning, a little courage. If you are a coward, then of course you cannot continue it. Don't try to rationalize it; don't say others will be disturbed. No one is disturbed. You can even invite your whole family to look at you. They will enjoy it. No one will be disturbed; it will be a free entertainment for them.

Invite the neighbors. Tell them that you have come from a meditation camp where you have learned a technique and you want to show it to them. In the beginning they will laugh, but they cannot laugh for long. They will get serious about it. But your change will prove its effect; nothing else can prove it. You cannot argue about it.

The third thing: don't try to convince anybody about it; don't argue. It is useless; you simply waste your energy. There is only one argument which can prove anything and that is you. If you change, you become a very vital argument. If you don't change, just arguing is useless; you cannot convince anybody. Just reasoning never convinces; only your being convinces. So don't be argumentative about it.

This has been my feeling: when you learn something new, you become argumentative; you go on talking about it. And it is not that you are doing harm to anybody – you may be simply thinking to help them. When something is so fresh to you and you have experienced something new, you want to share it. This is natural. It may be natural, but it is not wise because the other is absolutely unacquainted with what you are talking about.

And *my* methods particularly are so mad that you cannot convince anybody. Don't try it, because if you cannot convince anyone, it may have a harmful effect on you because your failure will make you less confident. Then you will become hesitant within. You cannot convince anybody and others can convince you that you have gone mad – that you are wrong. They can convince you because you have had a subtle experience which is inexpressible. How can you convey it? Unless someone is very welcoming and receptive, you cannot convey it. To say no to anything is very easy; to negate is very easy. To be positive, to say yes, is very difficult.

Chekhov has written a story:

One man in a village was so idiotic, so stupid, that the whole village knew about it, that he was stupid. And he himself became so convinced that he was stupid that he became afraid even to talk, to utter a single word, because the moment he said anything someone would say, "What a stupid thing you are saying. What a silly thing."

He was so depressed, he went to a sage and asked him, "What to do? I am such a proven idiot that I cannot even utter a single word. Before I utter anything, they say, 'Be silent. Don't speak!'"

The sage said, "Do one thing: never say yes to anything from now on. Whatsoever you see, condemn it."

The idiot said, "But they will not listen to me."

The sage said, "Don't bother. If they say, 'This is a beautiful painting,' say, 'This painting beautiful? Such an ugly thing I have not seen before!' If they say, 'This novel is very original,' say, 'This is just a repetition. Thousands of times the same story has been written.' Don't bother to prove it. Simply say no to everything; make it your basic philosophy. If someone says that the night is beautiful, the moon is beautiful, say, 'You call this beauty?' And they cannot prove otherwise, remember. They cannot prove."

The man went back to his village. He started saying no to everything. Within a week there was a rumor around the village: "We were wrong. That man is not an idiot. He is a great critic; he is a genius."

To say no needs no wisdom. If you want to become a great genius, say no, be a critic. Never bother to say yes to anything. Whatsoever anybody says, deny it flatly. And no one can prove it because to prove anything is very difficult. No is the simplest trick.

When you are talking of higher experiences, anybody can say no to you. Any stupid man can say no and you cannot prove otherwise. So be alert. Don't talk about it unless you feel a very sympathetic heart is there to listen, to receive. And don't argue. If something has happened to you, your being will become the argument. Don't waste any energy convincing anyone. Use all the energy that you have in transforming yourself. Your transformation will help many; your argument can help no one.

Once you are transformed, people will start falling in love with you. They will become receptive, inviting; they will become hosts. And whatsoever you say to them will be received as a seed; they will carry it in their hearts. But don't try to convince anyone; don't argue; don't be intellectual and rational about it. The whole phenomenon is so absurd, it is so paradoxical.

It is paradoxical because through being consciously mad you

go beyond all madness. A person meditating with this technique cannot go mad. It is impossible because he is throwing out all madness, not accumulating it. And unless you accumulate, you cannot be mad.

You are cleansing yourself daily; you are passing through a catharsis daily. You are changing – transforming your madness into meditation. Doing this method, apparently so mad, you will create the possibility where real sanity will happen to you. This is paradoxical; this is why I call it absurd.

Laugh, sing, dance, but don't argue. Your dance can become infectious, your singing can become infectious. Your laughter, coming deep from your heart, can penetrate others' hearts. Be more joyful, blissful, ecstatic, as if every moment is a blessing and every moment is a gratitude. And make every moment a celebration.

These are my last words for this camp: Make every moment a celebration; then you will not need to search for God. God will try to search for you wherever you are.

…

ABOUT THE AUTHOR

Osho defies categorization. His thousands of talks cover everything from the individual quest for meaning to the most urgent social and political issues facing society today. Osho's books are not written but are transcribed from audio and video recordings of his extemporaneous talks to international audiences. As he puts it, "So remember: whatever I am saying is not just for you... I am talking also for the future generations."

Osho has been described by *The Sunday Times* in London as one of the "1000 Makers of the 20th Century" and by American author Tom Robbins as "the most dangerous man since Jesus Christ." *Sunday Mid-Day* (India) has selected Osho as one of ten people – along with Gandhi, Nehru and Buddha – who have changed the destiny of India.

About his own work Osho has said that he is helping to create the conditions for the birth of a new kind of human being. He often characterizes this new human being as "Zorba the Buddha" – capable both of enjoying the earthy pleasures of a Zorba the Greek and the silent serenity of a Gautama the Buddha.

Running like a thread through all aspects of Osho's talks and meditations is a vision that encompasses both the timeless wisdom of all ages past and the highest potential of today's (and tomorrow's) science and technology.

Osho is known for his revolutionary contribution to the science of inner transformation, with an approach to meditation that acknowledges the accelerated pace of contemporary life. His unique OSHO Active Meditations are designed to first release the accumulated stresses of body and mind, so that it is then easier to take an experience of stillness and thought-free relaxation into daily life.

Two autobiographical works by the author are available:
Autobiography of a Spiritually Incorrect Mystic,
St Martins Press, USA
Glimpses of a Golden Childhood,
OSHO Media International, Pune, India
www.biography.osho.com

OSHO INTERNATIONAL MEDITATION RESORT

Location

Located 100 miles southeast of Mumbai in the thriving modern city of Pune, India, the OSHO International Meditation Resort is a holiday destination with a difference. The Meditation Resort is spread over 28 acres of spectacular gardens in a beautiful tree-lined residential area.

Uniqueness

Each year the Meditation Resort welcomes thousands of people from more than 100 countries. The unique campus provides an opportunity for a direct personal experience of a new way of living – with more awareness, relaxation, celebration and creativity. A great variety of around-the-clock and around-the-year program options are available. Doing nothing and just relaxing is one of them!

All programs are based on the OSHO vision of "Zorba the Buddha" – a qualitatively new kind of human being who is able both to participate creatively in everyday life and to relax into silence and meditation.

THE DETAILS

Meditations

A full daily schedule of meditations for every type of person includes methods that are active and passive, traditional and revolutionary, and in particular the OSHO Active Meditations™. The meditations take place in what must be the world's largest meditation hall, the Osho Auditorium.

Multiversity

Individual sessions, courses and workshops cover everything from creative arts to holistic health, personal transformation, relationship and life transition, work-as-meditation, esoteric sciences, and the "Zen" approach to sports and recreation. The secret of the Multiversity's success lies in the fact that all its programs are combined with meditation, supporting the understanding that as human beings we are far more than the sum of our parts.

Basho Spa

The luxurious Basho Spa provides for leisurely open-air swimming surrounded by trees and tropical green. The uniquely styled, spacious Jacuzzi, the saunas, gym, tennis courts ... all these are enhanced by their stunningly beautiful setting.

Cuisine

A variety of different eating areas serve delicious Western, Asian and Indian vegetarian food – most of it organically grown especially for the Meditation Resort. Breads and cakes are baked in the resort's own bakery.

Night life

There are many evening events to choose from – dancing being at the top of the list! Other activities include full-moon meditations beneath the stars, variety shows, music performances and meditations for daily life.

Or you can just enjoy meeting people at the Plaza Café, or walking in the nighttime serenity of the gardens of this fairytale environment.

Facilities

You can buy all your basic necessities and toiletries in the Galleria. The Multimedia Gallery sells a large range of OSHO media products. There is also a bank, a travel agency and a Cyber Café on-campus. For those who enjoy shopping, Pune provides all the options, ranging from traditional and ethnic Indian products to all of the global brand-name stores.

Accommodation
You can choose to stay in the elegant rooms of the Osho Guesthouse, or for longer stays opt for one of the Living-In program packages. Additionally there is a plentiful variety of nearby hotels and serviced apartments.

www.osho.com/meditationresort
www.osho.com/guesthouse
www.osho.com/livingin

BOOKS BY OSHO IN ENGLISH LANGUAGE

Early Discourses and Writings
A Cup of Tea
Dimensions Beyond The Known
From Sex to Super consciousness
The Great Challenge
Hidden Mysteries
I Am The Gate
The Inner Journey
Psychology of the Esoteric
Seeds of Wisdom

Meditation
The Voice of Silence
And Now and Here (Vol 1 & 2)
In Search of the Miraculous (Vol 1 &.2)
Meditation: The Art of Ecstasy
Meditation: The First and Last Freedom
The Path of Meditation
The Perfect Way
Yaa-Hoo! The Mystic Rose

Baul Mystics
The Beloved (Vol 1 & 2)

Buddha and Buddhist Masters
The Book of Wisdom
The Dhammapada: The Way of the Buddha (Vol 1-12)
The Diamond Sutra
The Heart Sutra
The Discipline of Transcendence (Vol 1-4)

Indian Mystics
Enlightenment: The Only Revolution (Ashtavakra)
Showering Without Clouds (Sahajo)
The Last Morning Star (Daya)
The Song of Ecstasy (Adi Shankara)

Kabir
The Divine Melody
Ecstasy: The Forgotten Language
The Fish in the Sea is Not Thirsty
The Great Secret
The Guest

The Path of Love
The Revolution

Jesus and Christian Mystics

Come Follow to You (Vol 1-4)
I Say Unto You (Vol 1 & 2)
The Mustard Seed
Theologia Mystica

Western Mystics

Guida Spirituale (Desiderata)
The Hidden Harmony (Heraclitus)
The Messiah (Vol 1 & 2) (Commentaries on Khalil Gibran's The Prophet)
The New Alchemy: To Turn You On (Commentaries on Mabel Collins' Light on the Path)
Philosophia Perennis (Vol 1 & 2) (The Golden Verses of Pythagoras)
Zarathustra: A God That Can Dance
Zarathustra: The Laughing Prophet (Commentaries on Nietzsche's Thus Spake Zarathustra)

Jewish Mystics

The Art of Dying
The True Sage

Sufism

Just Like That
Journey to the Heart
The Perfect Master (Vol 1 & 2)
The Secret
Sufis: The People of the Path (Vol 1 & 2)
Unio Mystica (Vol 1 & 2)
The Wisdom of the Sands (Vol 1 & 2)

Tantra

Tantra: The Supreme Understanding
The Tantra Experience
The Royal Song of Saraha (same as Tantra Vision, Vol 1)
The Tantric Transformation
The Royal Song of Saraha (same as Tantra Vision, Vol 2)
The Book of Secrets: Vigyan Bhairav Tantra

The Upanishads

Behind a Thousand Names (Nirvana Upanishad)
Heartbeat of the Absolute (Ishavasya Upanishad)
I Am That (Isa Upanishad)
The Message Beyond Words (Kathopanishad)
Philosophia Ultima (Mandukya Upanishad)
The Supreme Doctrine (Kenopanishad)
Finger Pointing to the Moon (Adhyatma Upanishad)
That Art Thou (Sarvasar Upanishad, Kaivalya Upanishad, Adhyatma Upanishad)
Vedanta: Seven Steps to Samadhi (Akshaya Upanishad)

The Ultimate Alchemy, Vol 1&2 (Atma Pooja Upanishad Vol 1 & 2)
Flight of the Alone to the Alone (Kaivalya Upanishad)

Tao

The Empty Boat
The Secret of Secrets
Tao:The Golden Gate (Vol 1&2)
Tao:The Pathless Path (Vol 1&2)
Tao: The Three Treasures (Vol 1-4)
When the Shoe Fits

Yoga

The Path of Yoga (previously Yoga: The Alpha and the Omega, Vol 1)
Yoga: The Alpha and the Omega (Vol 2-10)

Zen and Zen Masters

Ah, This!
Ancient Music in the Pines
And the Flowers Showered
A Bird on the Wing
Bodhidharma: The Greatest Zen Master
Communism and Zen Fire, Zen Wind
Dang Dang Doko Dang
The First Principle
God is Dead: Now Zen is the Only Living Truth
The Grass Grows By Itself
The Great Zen Master Ta Hui
Kyozan: A True Man of Zen
Hsin Hsin Ming: The Book of Nothing
I Celebrate Myself: God is No Where, Life is Now Here
Nirvana: The Last Nightmare
No Mind: The Flowers of Eternity
No Water, No Moon
One Seed Makes the Whole Earth Green
Returning to the Source
The Search: Talks on the 10 Bulls of Zen
A Sudden Clash of Thunder
The Sun Rises in the Evening
Take it Easy (Vol 1 & 2)
This Very Body the Buddha
Walking in Zen, Sitting in Zen
The White Lotus
Yakusan: Straight to the Point of Enlightenment
Zen Manifesto : Freedom From Oneself
Zen: The Mystery and the Poetry of the Beyond
Zen: The Path of Paradox (Vol 1, 2 & 3)
Zen: The Special Transmission
Zen Boxed Sets
The World of Zen (5 vol.)
Live Zen
This. This. A Thousand Times This
Zen: The Diamond Thunderbolt
Zen: The Quantum Leap from Mind to No-Mind
Zen: The Solitary Bird, Cuckoo of the Forest

Zen: All The Colors Of The Rainbow (5 vol.)
The Buddha: The Emptiness of the Heart
The Language of Existence
The Miracle
The Original Man
Turning In

Osho: On the Ancient Masters of Zen (7 volumes)*
Dogen: The Zen Master
Joshu: The Lion's Roar
Hyakujo: The Everest of Zen – With Basho's haikus
Isan: No Footprints in the Blue Sky
Ma Tzu: The Empty Mirror
Nansen: The Point Of Departure
Rinzai: Master of the Irrational

**Each volume is also available individually.*

Responses to Questions
Be Still and Know
Come, Come, Yet Again Come
The Goose is Out
The Great Pilgrimage: From Here to Here
Invitation
My Way: The Way of the White Clouds
Nowhere to Go But In
The Razor's Edge
Walk Without Feet, Fly Without Wings and Think Without Mind
The Wild Geese and the Water
Zen: Zest, Zip, Zap and Zing
From Bondage To Freedom
From Darkness to Light
From Death To Deathlessness
From the False to the Truth
From Unconsciousness to Consciousness
The Rajneesh Bible (Vol 2-4)
Beyond Enlightenment (Talks in Bombay)
Beyond Psychology (Talks in Uruguay)
Light on the Path (Talks in the Himalayas)
The Path of the Mystic (Talks in Uruguay)
Sermons in Stones (Talks in Bombay)
Socrates Poisoned Again After 25 Centuries (Talks in Greece)
The Sword and the Lotus (Talks in the Himalayas)
The Transmission of the Lamp (Talks in Uruguay)

Osho's Vision for the World
The Golden Future
The Hidden Splendor
The New Dawn
The Rebel
The Rebellious Spirit

The Mantra Series
Hari Om Tat Sat
Om Mani Padme Hum
Om Shantih Shantih Shantih
Sat-Chit-Anand
Satyam-Shivam-Sundram

Personal Glimpses
Books I Have Loved
Glimpses of a Golden Childhood
Notes of a Madman

Interviews with the World Press
The Man of Truth: A Majority of One

For any information about OSHO Books, please contact:
OSHO Media International
17 Koregaon Park, Pune – 411001, MS, India
Phone: +91-20-66019999 Fax: +91-20-66019990
E-mail: distribution@osho.net
Website: http://www.osho.com

FOR MORE INFORMATION

It wasn't long ago when websites were the sole source of all information and social networking sites were considered vehicles for teens and college kids to interact with each other and share personal interests. Times have changed and so have we—
You can now find more OSHO unique content in multiple languages and formats at the following websites online:
Official website of @ www.OSHO.com

You can search the open access OSHO library for your favorite topic @ www.OSHO.com/Library

A complete presentation of all the OSHO meditations and related music can be found at
@ www.OSHO.com/Meditation

To plan a visit to OSHO International Mediation Resort you can visit @ www.OSHO.com/MeditationResort

Latest updates about events, festivals, media releases and quotes are updated daily @ www.facebook.com/OSHO.International

All latest happenings, including information about the Multiversity courses, are updated daily
@ www.facebook.com/OSHO.International.Meditation.Resort

You can wake up to a daily OSHO quote on
www.twitter.com/OSHOtimes

Your instant access to OSHO video channel can be found
@ www.youtube.com/OSHO International

To make OSHO available in your local language you can register and transcribe or translate OSHO talks @ www.OSHOtalks.info

Please take a moment to ***register and browse*** these sites as they provide much more information about OSHO.

You may also discover many fun and exciting ways to **get** involved in making OSHO available around the world.

JAICO PUBLISHING HOUSE

Elevate Your Life. Transform Your World.

ESTABLISHED IN 1946, Jaico Publishing House is home to world-transforming authors such as Sri Sri Paramahansa Yogananda, Osho, the Dalai Lama, Sri Sri Ravi Shankar, Sadhguru, Robin Sharma, Deepak Chopra, Jack Canfield, Eknath Easwaran, Devdutt Pattanaik, Khushwant Singh, John Maxwell, Brian Tracy, and Stephen Hawking.

Our late founder Mr. Jaman Shah first established Jaico as a book distribution company. Sensing that independence was around the corner, he aptly named his company Jaico ('Jai' means victory in Hindi). In order to service the significant demand for affordable books in a developing nation, Mr. Shah initiated Jaico's own publications. Jaico was India's first publisher of paperback books in the English language.

While self-help, religion and philosophy, mind/body/spirit, and business titles form the cornerstone of our non-fiction list, we publish an exciting range of travel, current affairs, biography, and popular science books as well. Our renewed focus on popular fiction is evident in our new titles by a host of fresh young talent from India and abroad. Jaico's recently established translations division translates selected English content into nine regional languages.

Jaico distributes its own titles. With its headquarters in Mumbai, Jaico has branches in Ahmedabad, Bangalore, Chennai, Delhi, Hyderabad, and Kolkata.

SINCE 1946

